CHEMICALLY DEPENDENT ANONYMOUS

Copyright © 1990 by
C.D.A. COMMUNICATIONS, INC. GENERAL SERVICE OFFICE
All rights reserved.

The Twelve Steps and Twelve Traditions
are reprinted and adapted with permission of
Alcoholics Anonymous World Services, Inc.

Permission to reprint and adapt the Twelve Steps and Twelve Traditions does not mean that A.A. has reviewed or approved the contents of this publication nor that A.A. agrees with the views expressed herein. A.A. is a program of recovery from Alcoholism. Use of the Twelve Steps and Twelve Traditions in connection with programs and activities which are patterned after A.A. but which address other problems does not imply otherwise.

C.D.A. FOR THE NEWCOMER is copyrighted © by
CDA Communications

Adaptations of the last paragraph of the Introduction, the first ten questions, the final paragraph of our Chapter 11, and C.D.A.'s Twelve Steps and Twelve Traditions are reprinted here with permission.

Library of Congress Catalog Card Number 90-81598

ISBN 0-9626438-0-7

PRINTED IN THE UNITED STATES OF AMERICA

CHEMICALLY DEPENDENT ANONYMOUS

C.D.A. COMMUNICATIONS, INC.
GENERAL SERVICE OFFICE
P.O. Box 423
Severna Park MD 21146-0423

1990

CONTENTS

Chapter | Page

FOREWORD | vii

PART I: CHEMICALLY DEPENDENT ANONYMOUS

1. THE FELLOWSHIP — 1
2. WHY C.D.A.? — 3
3. LET'S REDEFINE "ADDICT" AND "ADDICTION" — 11
4. THE ESSENTIAL ELEMENTS — 19
5. ACKNOWLEDGMENTS — 23
6. C.D.A. ROOTS — 31
7. THE PROGRAM: C.D.A.'S TWELVE STEPS — 35
8. C.D.A.'S TWELVE TRADITIONS — 41
9. H.O.W. — 59
10. LOW SELF-ESTEEM — 65
11. QUESTIONS: C.D.A. FOR THE NEWCOMER — 67
12. A C.D.A. JOURNAL — 73
13. FUN IN RECOVERY — 87
14. EPILOGUE: THE FUTURE — 91

PART II: PERSONAL HISTORIES

15. I FINALLY FOUND MY NICHE — 95
16. THY WILL BE DONE — 101
17. OUT OF THE CRACK HOUSE — 107
18. THINGS I MUST EARN — 121
19. RECOVERED, NOT CURED — 125
20. DREAMS COME TRUE — 133
21. RITES OF PASSAGE — 141
22. DARKNESS DISPELLED — 147
23. GOING TO ANY LENGTH! — 157
24. GOD DOESN'T MAKE JUNK — 161
25. I AM — 171
26. MY LOVE FOR C.D.A. — 175
27. IN GOD'S OWN GOOD TIME — 189

28	LOVE SET ME FREE	205
29	MISERABLE MIKE	215
30	A SIXTIES IDEALIST	227
31	EVENING THE ODDS	239
32	HAPPINESS, TOO, IS INEVITABLE	255
33	I COULDN'T KNOCK THE LOVE	269
34	A MEDICAL MIRACLE	283
35	NO MORE EXCUSES	297
36	KEEP AN OPEN MIND: SOMETHING MAY FALL IN	309
37	A LOVE STORY	325

APPENDICES

A	THE TWELVE STEPS OF ALCOHOLICS ANONYMOUS	341
B	THE TWELVE TRADITIONS OF ALCOHOLICS ANONYMOUS	343

FOREWORD

This is the fellowship of Chemically Dependent Anonymous's first attempt to share its history, its philosophical underpinnings, and its program with others in our own book. In so doing, we in C.D.A. have based our program on one proven successful by Alcoholics Anonymous, for over half a century, in helping alcoholics find a road to recovery and a new way of life. We have adapted A.A.'s Twelve Steps and Twelve Traditions, changing them only so they refer to chemical dependency, as a whole, rather than alcohol abuse, alone, as the focus of our program. We are grateful to A.A. for pointing the way for us, as it has for many other anonymous groups.

The C.D.A. First Edition Committee, consisting of four members of the fellowship, first met in May, 1986, at Thanksgiving Farm in Harwood, Maryland, to discuss the possibility of publishing a book for C.D.A. We delegated various committees, such as the Steps Committee, the Traditions Committee, and the H.O.W. Committee, to begin work on enlarging upon fundamental principles of our program. We found a lawyer to advise us on the legalities connected with our literary endeavor.

We then made several announcements to the general membership, over a period of three years, requesting personal story contributions to the book. We found editors to compile all our material and prepare it for publication. We incorporated our publishing division, C.D.A. COMMUNICATIONS, INC., General Service Office, in October, 1989. At long last, our dreams have come to fruition, as we present *Chemically Dependent Anonymous* to the world.

The First Edition Committee wishes to thank all the individuals and committees who generously contributed their time and ideas, or who gathered or submitted material for this volume. But special thanks go to the twenty-three courageous recovering men and women who have been willing to share their personal stories about their addictions, their attempts at recovery, and their success in combating many varieties of substance abuse. Their stories have been kept as nearly as possible in their exact words. Only those who have been there can so eloquently explain how they have been able to rebuild their lives. These C.D.A. members want to give hope to others that they, too, may find freedom from their addictions through C.D.A.'s own time-tested program of recovery.

We, the C.D.A. First Edition Committee, dedicate this book to you, the reader, with our sincere wish that what you find herein will help you, or those you are helping, discover the new life of health, sanity, and sobriety that C.D.A. has to offer. May God (as you understand Him) guide you on your way.

PART I

CHEMICALLY DEPENDENT ANONYMOUS

Chapter 1

THE FELLOWSHIP

Chemically Dependent Anonymous deals with the disease of addiction. We of C.D.A. do not make distinctions in the recovery process based on any particular substance, believing that the addictive-compulsive usage of chemicals is the core of our disease and the use of any mood-changing chemical will result in relapse.

C.D.A. is not affiliated with any political, religious, or commercial organizations or institutions.

The primary purpose of C.D.A. as a whole is to remain clean and to help others like us to gain recovery. By sharing our experience, strength, and hope with each other, we solve our common problem and help others to recover from chemical dependence which has made their lives unmanageable.

C.D.A. remains grateful to the co-founders and fellowship of Alcoholics Anonymous for the Twelve Steps and Twelve Traditions which are the basis of our program.

Chapter 2
WHY C.D.A.?

There is nothing more powerful than an idea whose time has come. That has been amply demonstrated by the program and the fellowship of Chemically Dependent Anonymous in its very brief, yet dynamic, existence. The idea behind C.D.A. is not original, by any means, as its co-founders and members will readily admit. What is that idea? It is one based on the principle of simplicity that Alcoholics Anonymous has so strongly advocated in a time-proven format designed to give direction to those suffering from addiction to alcohol.

The program of Alcoholics Anonymous has been the core of hundreds of other self-help groups that thrive throughout the world today. These fellowships give group support and guidance to people afflicted with maladies, ranging from social-behavior problems to terminal illnesses, that have baffled professionals trained to heal them. These disorders had previously been considered hopeless situations, beyond all possible remedy. The essential ingredients, or universals, that all these groups share are the Twelve Steps of A.A. (usually altered only in order to identify the groups' purposes or to define requirements for membership) and the basic concept of anonymity, found in the Twelve Traditions of A.A. From these two cornerstones, along with the willingness of the groups' members to change their lives and their development, or expansion, of a recognition of the spiritual factors surrounding the recovery process, comes the miracle of what is commonly known as the self-help movement.

Ask a member of Overeaters Anonymous, for instance, how that program works for him, and he will probably answer, "Just fine, thank you," or "One day at a time." The answer usually defies logic or reason. And unless the inquirer shares the particular dilemma of the responder and wants help with it, too, he will probably not comprehend fully, from the answer he receives, how that group actually operates.

But that's exactly where the "magic" takes place. Very simply, it is in the identifying of the mutual problem that the basis for understanding, which underlies the effectiveness of each of the separate groups, is to be found. Members share their individual experiences, their strengths, and their hope for recovery, not cure. That is what makes miracles happen.

That's a big word, "miracle." But take the example of a person who has been gambling obsessively for, perhaps, thirty years; who has gone through fortunes and families in his helpless, compulsive binges of reckless, insane wagering; who has even been institutionalized as a direct result of his actions. If then, remarkably, he makes a return to the mainstream of life with no apparent, overwhelming problems, can we call it a coincidence? Hardly. In this anonymous gambler's case, it is the ultimate result of his diligent effort at "working his program." This is only one of the many examples of what occurs, all the time, in the programs based on A.A., with increasing numbers of success stories as time goes by.

Simplicity is a major key in helping to solve complicated problems. It eliminates confusion and allows growth to occur where destruction would be otherwise inevitable. After all, the human mind is a complex network of thoughts and beliefs, emotions and mentality. We are each as different as one snowflake crystal is from another. Add in a pattern of obsessive behavior, or self-destructive habits that seem to progress, and behold: confusion, despair, and hopelessness dominate. If the problem is ignored, or if a person is isolated from others with the same disorder, there will rarely be a happy outcome. Furthermore, the people nearest the troubled one will be grossly affected, also, although they seldom realize the source of their problems.

If the one who has the initiating illness seeks, and finds, support from others of his kind, and his co-victims then find their corresponding programs, it is not at all unusual for so-called impossible situations to turn into amazing, wonderful developments of new-found hope and direction. Most recipients of such help will agree that the gratitude they feel and express for their metamorphic miracles is the fuel that perpetuates ongoing recovery. They have discovered that the simplicity inherent in their self-help programs works.

But why C.D.A.? Why start a new organization when A.A. and Narcotics Anonymous already exist, the former for the drunks and the latter for the junkies? It could be said, "If it works, don't fix it." If these groups are working well, it seems reasonable that there is no need to change things. Yet that is true only if society and man remain consistent and static. And both society and man have proven to be nothing of the kind.

Society recognizes, as do all the self-help movements, that it is now dealing with a new species of addict, one who shows no real preference for any single drug of choice. It is true that there will always be those who adhere to only one chemical preference for their escape. But most younger people who are seeking help at this time have been through the wringer with anything that is available. Economic factors seem the sole determinants of the quality, or types, of the chemicals that they have chosen to use.

Society makes only a distinction between their legality or illegality in deciding upon the availability of the many drugs it allows and the way in which it will dispense them. And it is cranking out multiple-addiction cases by the truckload. Alcohol is only one of the drugs we use. Ours is a culture with a high percentage of drug-dependent people, many of whom are at various stages of near-disastrous usage patterns. And most often, because of the denial factor preceding treatment, the problem continues to go unrecognized, and is accepted as normal, until it is too late.

Alcoholics Anonymous has been lovingly tolerant of these new drug dependents, so long as they express the desire to stop using alcohol. But, flexible as the A.A. program is, it can only bend so far before it begins to pose a threat to its own traditional structure. It may even alienate those of its members who cannot, or will not, relate to their fellow alcoholics who have drug dependencies other than alcohol, or to those whose problems include the use of combinations of substances.

There is an ever-increasing number of those recovering from multiple addictions who have found A.A. useful, however. That program was the beginning of new lives for them. It has helped them to free themselves from dependencies on the entire gamut of the drug market's wares, in addition to booze. But all of these recovering users agree that their problem was not so much the substance of choice as it was the addiction itself, their dependency pattern, which had crippled them mentally, physically, and spiritually before they turned to A.A.

And that leads back to simplicity, again. If the drunk, junkie, acid head, speed or Valium freak, coke snorter and/or shooter, pill head, glue nose, needle nut, Sterno Joe, or one who is all or a combination of any of the above, is willing to accept that the substance just does not matter that much, but that it is the recovery process that is applicable to all and is the most important part of any self-help program, then he understands the basis for Chemically Dependent Anonymous and is ready to accept what it can give him. We are concerned about *substance* abuse, in this program, and what to do about it. We keep it simple. What is more, the concept works. Of course, C.D.A. does rule out the gambler, the sex offender, the overeater, and most other strictly behavioral-problem types. But it acts in, and simplifies, the lives of chemical abusers who are honestly looking for help through our fellowship.

C.D.A. also deals, immediately, with the possibility that an addict will transfer his chemical dependency from one substance to another. It is rigorously honest in its approach and does not allow for half measures, or for the "exceptions" that the more exclusive self-help groups, who do not want to deal with them directly, permit for prescription-drug abuse or "recreational" pot smoking. It saves lives. If the topic of total abstinence had been freely discussed in the meetings they were attending, such seemingly harmless drug use might not have caused some members of other anonymous fellowships, as has happened, to continue in their addiction patterns to the point of fatal usage. These hapless victims believed, right up to the end, that they were recovering addicts because they were strictly following their programs. They misunderstood what it took to succeed.

The co-founders of C.D.A. had only N.A. and A.A. as choices for help when they were first seeking it. The willingness they all shared, and the understanding that was provided for them by the existing members of those fellowships, allowed enough time to pass in the healing process for the basic concepts to take hold. How fortunate they were! Most of the multi-addicts that these groups tried to persuade to "keep an open mind" did not stick with the program long enough for that process to occur in their lives.

Wise A.A. and N.A. members do know, very well, that to use anything that changes the mood or alters the mind is wrong. But not everyone is so wise, especially not the newcomers. And where is that "anything" specifically written down, or named as such? Only in C.D.A. It is very important to understand that persons seeking help usually know little, if anything, about how these groups work when they first come in. Whether other types of addicts may apply, also, really doesn't seem to matter, on first sight. But the first contact made will usually be based on how a fellowship is titled.

Perhaps, by now, this all seems like an awfully complex path towards simplification. But there is one final example that must be stressed because it best illustrates the importance of their names to self-help groups. It is found right in their pledges of responsibility: "It is a primary goal of *?.A.* to carry the message to the still suffering *?* if he/she reaches out for help." Don't look now, but those question marks are reaching out from institutions, unhappy homes, halfway houses, the streets, and everywhere you look, only to find that those they need to relate to, in most of the fellowships, won't call themselves by name, won't let these poor people talk about their complete histories. And so they

8

are going back out to die, or, even worse, to continue to exist in their private hells.

"Well, it could be that they are not ready, yet," you say? Maybe. "They are just constitutionally incapable." Perhaps. Or could it be that they haven't been dealt with honestly? They are chemically dependent. They are addicts without a name. But now there is hope. These people are reaching out, and Chemically Dependent Anonymous is there and ready to work for them.

New faces are showing up at every meeting. Many who were, at first, skeptical have kept coming around and are now able to celebrate anniversaries of several years of being clean and sober. C.D.A. is gradually becoming known, throughout our nation, by those working in the chemical dependency field. It has been greeted in these quarters with much praise and many sighs of relief. Chemically Dependent Anonymous is, indeed, an idea whose time has come.

Chapter 3
LET'S REDEFINE "ADDICT" AND "ADDICTION"

Communication, especially in the English language, gets scrambled, all too often, because of what is known as semantics. That is, the word or phrase involved in conversation, or the written word, will mean something different to each person receiving the message. Each one of us brings his own mental images and understanding to words as they are presented to him. Even a solid dictionary definition of a concept does not cover all that the word conjures up in the brain because of the differing backgrounds and experiences of those hearing or seeing that word, and the ways in which they therefore relate to it.

A word may bear a stigma, due to its many possible meanings, that takes it so far from its original meaning that it can never recover its original intent. It is often necessary to reevaluate, or to redefine, such words for the purpose of regaining their commonly accepted meanings, in order to eliminate confusion in communicating. Words such as "addiction," or "addict," are cases in point. Although there are dictionary definitions for these nouns, few care to take the time to try to understand their meanings objectively by detaching themselves from the connotations of these words to arrive at their literal definitions. *Webster's New World Dictionary of the American Language*, Second College Edition, defines "addiction" as: "the condition of being addicted (*to* a habit); specif., the habitual use of narcotic drugs." It defines an "addict" as: "a person addicted to some habit, esp. to the use of a narcotic drug."

These words will have different meanings for those who have had some experiences, however indirect, with them: for those who work in the fields designed to deal with the addicted; for those who have had only direct, negative experiences with addiction; and for those who are actually addicted at this time. Despite the literal descriptions of these people and their problem, we each hold different pictures of the drug addict in our minds and have different feelings about addiction. But in order to understand the concept behind Chemically Dependent Anonymous, it is necessary to drop all those images of what these words mean to us, including *Webster's* version, in order to consider the drug addict's own definition of a drug addict and of his addiction.

Who has a greater right to redefine these words than the people who have been defined? Surely those who have truly looked into the meaning of the words "addict" and "addiction" from a very personal standpoint, who have done so in a positive manner so as to improve themselves through an honest attempt to reach a deeper understanding of what they really are, what their problem actually is, have won that right. Sorry, *Webster's*. And no stigmas are acceptable here, either.

The most common conception of a drug addict is that of the desperate, emaciated pincushion junkie in a dark, dingy apartment with an eyedropper and a rusty syringe needle, nodding and puking between armed robberies and drugstore holdups. It cannot be denied that this picture does apply in some cases. But most addicts who once fit this bill and are now recovering useful lifestyles will quickly assert that their addictions began long before their world got that ugly. In fact, the self-proclaimed drug addicts who are finding recovery in the self-help movements, and who stopped before they reached the above-described stage, readily agree that their addiction patterns were present long before they arrived at whatever junctures turned them onto the path to recovery.

However, those who fit this latter definition of an addict know that, if they begin to use again, they will probably end up qualifying for the worst-case description, even though they had never reached that point previously. In some cases, they had never become as truly addicted, physically, as the dictionary definition would seem to imply, before they came for help. Sorry again, *Webster's*.

Further, C.D.A. members, although they may drink coffee or smoke cigarettes, will tell you that these are also addictions. These people have simply not chosen to become free of those substances, yet. That's right. The notion of the addict most commonly accepted by another addict (if he is an honest one) is that the use of any chemical, compulsively or obsessively, to any degree, qualifies a person to be counted among those who need to seek help for their addictions.

And alcoholism is simply one form of addiction, an addiction to alcohol, as C.D.A. sees it. Effective professionals who work with addicts agree with this viewpoint, as well. Many other people acknowledge this fact, too, but are also quick to make at least an unspoken distinction between the alcohol addict and the dope fiend, as even the dictionary seems to do by omitting a specific reference to alcohol as an addictive substance in its definition. C.D.A. refuses to make such a distinction, however, particularly as far as the important aspects of the recovery process are concerned.

The young person who commits repetitive acts of problem behavior while using any type of chemical, including alcohol, is not just a problem child to the addict who has run this course. To him, that youngster is already an addict, even if only in the early stages. We are not certain whether preventive measures, if forced on such a person, will work or not. All we know about prevention is that it did not work for us, and we find it to be futile for the ones who have reached such a point. It is too much like the story of the boy trying to plug the dike with his finger unless the one in question is willing to do some preventing on his own. He can only avert a further progression of his disease by totally abstaining from all drugs.

However, we must acknowledge the existence of the social drugger who never seems to have problems with using chemicals. Hats off to him! We cannot understand that phenomenon, nor can the professionals in the field of addiction. And we lose some members when they begin to believe that they are in that fortunate category. Their thinking gets twisted, and they forget where they have come from. Somehow, they think that recreational drugging will be all right for them. That happens most often when addicts drift away from the meetings and the support groups that had been saving their lives. The terrible problem with addiction is that it is a disease that can convince the victim that he does not have the disease, should the addict drop his defenses at any time. It can happen to any one of us, and does, all too often.

Our redefinition is not complete unless we include our fellows who have been on the pharmacy circuit for all too long a time with the aid of often well-meaning, undereducated physicians who take them on as patients. Traveling from one doctor to another, filling "script" after "script," day after day, in order to stay within the "legal" limits of their drugs of choice, these drug users, many times protected from reaching their "bottoms" by their families, doctors, and society at large, frequently die without ever having had the occasion to wear the label of "addict," or to be called chemically dependent. That identification might have given them the opportunity to be pointed toward recovery. Instead, they are allowed to remain hidden behind the enabling walls of their homes and communities, and those of society. Stigmas can kill.

It used to be that way for the alcohol addict before Alcoholics Anonymous came along and suggested to society that it ought to reconsider its original definition of the drunk. That organization proved that an alcoholic *can* recover: Take Uncle Bill out of the attic, and get him into A.A., and miracles may happen. He can be changed into a responsible member of his community, a loving, giving, spiritually oriented human being. "Of course, it's a good thing he wasn't a *drug* addict," people might say. "Or he wouldn't have had a chance." Get the point?

We are seeing a change in the medical profession's viewpoint about drugs and addiction, however. It is slowly taking place as the truly dedicated people in the field are beginning to understand that there is such a thing as unnecessary medication. Medical and psychological workers are now detecting the disease pattern of addiction much earlier, and probable addicts are usually directed to the self-help groups much sooner as statistics have begun to indicate that the most effective medicine that addicts can ever receive is to be found there.

Remember that we are using the term, "unnecessary

medicines" here, seeing only those as the possibly abusive elements. C.D.A. cannot honestly denounce the use of painkilling drugs, or even sedatives, if they are truly needed. We have members who have had to undergo surgery, painful dentistry, and other such treatments which necessitated the induction of addictive substances into their bodies. These members have proved that the C.D.A. program is effective by withstanding periods of use of *necessary* chemicals without reinstituting self-destructive patterns of usage or increasing dosages without physicians' orders.

How? They clung to the program like epoxy. Their fellow members showed them love and support throughout the duration. They returned, afterwards, clean and free as if they had never broken the pattern of abstinence. Their desire to *live* the program was stronger than the chemicals that had formerly enslaved them. They represent one more example of the effectiveness of a program that prefers not to limit its understanding of addiction to any one substance. Addiction is addiction is addiction.

Obvious social and, sometimes, moral issues arise when such a diverse group of addicted people as we are gathers in the C.D.A. setting. The Valium-eating homemaker has existed in a much different world from that of the motorcycle-riding junkie or the paranoid speed freak. And if we were to emphasize these differences in this setting, endless possibilities for confusion and dissension might arise.

But even as our diversity makes us unique, our addiction makes us all one and the same. The emphasis, in C.D.A., is placed on this common ground. We each had different types and degrees of addiction, but we all want help in recovery. So let us work together to gain new understanding about the differing aspects of this disease of addiction that we and our fellow members have endured, seeing each as a piece of the much-larger puzzle to be solved. We can thereby learn to avoid mistakes in areas that we would never have thought of as problems without the help available to us through the past experiences, and the resulting valuable insights, of every person in our fellowship.

If you are reading this and think you may need help, try on our redefinition of addiction for size. It could lead you to the answers you have been looking for, by influencing you to seek them in C.D.A. If you don't believe that your identity fits the descriptions of the addict you have seen here, try to make use of this new understanding of our disease in your everyday living. It might save someone else's life, someday, if not your own.

Chapter 4
THE ESSENTIAL ELEMENTS

One question that comes up frequently, when outsiders show an interest in Chemically Dependent Anonymous, is: "What was the main thing that got you started toward recovery?" The answer is as varied as there are addicts: We each had a different "bottom." Sure, the stories are often similar, and sometimes run nearly parallel. But in C.D.A., the entire spectrum of addiction types is accepted. Therefore, a wide range of circumstances leading up to each member's entry into the program exists.

But no matter what the physical descriptions are (drug, place, age, duration of usage), the universal effects were deep, desperate fear and paralysis of the spirit. It seemed that there was nowhere left to turn for help. The drug of choice no longer worked as it had at first. Our friends and families had given up on us. We were isolated within shells of confusion and anxiety, along with guilt, self-pity, resentment, and the whole list of negative emotions.

For many, the worst of all of these was the tremendous self-loathing that we felt. We had become trapped within the enemy's walls. But the enemy was "self." We were living lives that only permitted enough room in the center of the universe for our own selves. Everything, everybody, everyplace circled around our feeble existences and our relentless needs to reinforce our right to use the drug of choice. That requirement was of the utmost priority. The final act, being left alone in the center of the universe with nothing but a habit that no longer worked for us, was a hell on earth, an extremely understated description of the state in which we finally found ourselves.

We were at the crossroads. The decision we had to make, as we stood on the tracks watching the oncoming freight train, was either to get off the track and stay off, or to let the damned train hit us. It sounds like an easy choice. Why is it, then, that so many choose to stay and take the full force of the impact? No one knows for sure.

It is true that many just do not believe it will happen to them. They feel that they are different. It is denial, to the bitter end. For others, it is because of plain old fear of the unknown. In their cases, the problem is obvious, even to themselves, but the rocky roadbed is at least a familiar one. Although it keeps getting worse, they believe that it is easier and safer than taking the risk of getting off the long, old track and trying a new way of life.

These explanations are mere speculation, however. Most of us were given opportunities for insights into our problems many times before we finally took the plunge and "got honest" with ourselves. It was not just a matter of a second chance. Sometimes it was the hundredth chance. An odds maker would be baffled at this news. We were extremely fortunate to live through all of these risks and to be able to make it into recovery.

But most of us who can now look back on our former lives from a relatively calm perspective do not think it was luck, at all. We believe that, for one reason or another, a Force of a positive nature, which we call a Higher Power, guided us here to C.D.A. That might sound mystical, or supernatural, or even religious, we know. It seems even stranger to us.

After all, weren't we, each and every one of us, our own centers of the universe at one time? Weren't we the ones who cursed God when we thought there was the remotest possibility that such a Being might exist out there, somewhere? We even cursed our own existences, because "that God" was just out there to make our lives miserable. Most of us really did believe that. And now, there is this change of tune about a Higher Power? It doesn't make sense!

Our new track records show that, although it may not make sense or even seem reasonable, this adjustment in our spiritual attitudes is one of the characteristics, or essentials, of "getting" the program. If you are reading this book with the idea of getting help from C.D.A., however, rest assured that we are not a religious movement or a fanatical group. Should you be turned off by the very thought of joining such a fellowship, you have nothing to fear. The essentials for belonging are simply these, as encompassed in the Twelve Steps and the Twelve Traditions: reaching our own "bottoms" and the eventual grasping of a spiritual understanding that fits our individual needs.

It must be added that conscious spiritual recognition was, in most cases, absent, or at best very cloudy, at the time when those of us who are already members first came to seek help. It was not until later that most of us could look back over our recoveries and realize how our Higher Power had led us into the program, from the very beginning, and has guided us ever since. As He did it for us, your Higher Power will work for you. He has brought you this far. Just give us a chance, and leave the rest up to Him.

Chapter 5
ACKNOWLEDGMENTS

We are grateful to those in the mental health professions, to members of other anonymous organizations, to business people, to the clergy, and to the public in general for their support and their recognition of our efforts to continue carrying our message of hope for recovery to others:

SLIGO CREEK PSYCHOLOGICAL SERVICES
1420 Woodman Avenue
Silver Spring, Maryland
20902

Dear C.D.A. Members,

I am very pleased that the Chemically Dependent Anonymous (C.D.A.) meetings are now available to younger teen-age clients and other young-adult residents of Montgomery County, Maryland, and that they are encouraged, confronted, and supported in their efforts to become chemical free by others of this peer group. I know that the therapists of this and other private practices, as well as public services for adolescent day treatment, family therapy, and adult addic-

tions have been deeply inspired by the supportive work of the C.D.A. meetings. The attendance of voluntary and mandatory clients and the high volume of participation at these meetings speak very well for the dedication and sincerity of involvement by their leaders. The resulting changes in attitude, lifestyle, and school grades of C.D.A. adolescents and young adults have been very encouraging.

Thank you for your continued efforts in the collaborative support of private and public programs here in Montgomery County. I wish continued success to your fellowship in its endeavors to provide a program for those who seek recovery from drug and alcohol dependence. I strongly endorse your Twelve-Step method as a viable process for achieving recovery from substance abuse.

Sincerely,

Thomas W. Summers, Ph.D.
Psychologist, Clinical Director

To Whom It May Concern:

Years ago, my life was utterly hopeless because of a drinking problem. Then I got "trapped" into attending Alcoholics Anonymous meetings and gradually started working the program. That saved my life and showed me a way to personal freedom. Indeed, I have seen the miracle of A.A. work for countless others in our country and around the world.

Along with A.A.'s success has come a profound change in the public's attitude. People now recognize alcoholism, once thought to be a moral deficiency, as a health problem. This conversion is having a beneficial effect on the prospects for still-suffering alcoholics.

Alcoholics can help other alcoholics because they understand each other and are unified by their common problem. This wholeness, however, has suffered in recent years because of changes in society and the way drugs are used today. Many newcomers to A.A. now have other drug problems along with their alcoholism, and a small number are not alcoholics at all.

This inconsistency has been lessened, in our area of the country, because of the influence of Chemically Dependent Anonymous, an organization that began in Annapolis, Maryland, in 1980. C.D.A. is open to anyone who is dependent on mind-altering chemicals of any sort. Although not allied with A.A., C.D.A. closely follows the model provided by Alcoholics Anonymous. Having both programs available, newcomers can decide whether they properly belong in C.D.A., A.A., or both. And, as a result, both fellowships have become healthier and more complete.

I was initially attracted to C.D.A. because a family member had recovered from cocaine addiction as a result of participation in that program. I started attending meetings, too, and I now consider myself eligible for membership because of my chemical dependency—on alcohol.

I believe that C.D.A. and A.A., working together, though still independently, will strengthen both fellowships and can offer greater hope and opportunity for recovery to those enslaved by drugs. Eventually the myths and hysteria about drug addiction will slip away, and the public will become more understanding and supportive. And I think that Chemically Dependent Anonymous will do for the drug addict, in the 21st century, what A.A. has done for the alcoholic in the 20th.

Bob R. (an active member of A.A. for over 30 years)

To Whom It May Concern:

In 1981, I had the good fortune of meeting a young man who was a member of C.D.A. After many conversations and interviews, and being fully aware of his background as a chemical dependent, I offered him a contract as a New York Life Sales Representative. To this day, I am very glad that I made the decision I did. This employee has become not only a strong force and a successful Sales Representative in my office, but one of the top Agents in the entire company.

In the years I have known him, I have had the opportunity to become acquainted with many others who are also part of the C.D.A. program. Some of these people we have hired, and some we rejected from a job application standpoint. However, I have been very impressed with the personal programs each one of these individuals has established. Although some of them were unable to become successful as Sales Representatives with New York Life, I think that every one who left us left with a better understanding of sales and went on to be successful in other fields.

Through C.D.A., these people have been able to establish new lives for themselves, with a commitment not often found in others. Until seven years ago, I had no idea of the impact C.D.A. had on its members, but I can assure you I am most impressed. Today, I do not hesitate to talk to any members of C.D.A. who have established programs of their own.

Sincerely,

James E. Adkins, CLU, ChFC
General Manager

My dear friends,

By the grace of God, and through His gift to me, the

blessed fellowship of Alcoholics Anonymous, I am a grateful recovering alcoholic. At this writing, I have been sober in Alcoholics Anonymous for thirteen-and-a-half years—since November 17, 1973. A miracle, believe me!

I am a religious brother, a member, for the past thirty-seven years, of a Roman Catholic order. Currently, I am the order's chief financial officer, its corporate treasurer.

On a daily basis, I am actively involved in Alcoholics Anonymous. I attend meetings, conduct Twelve Step-oriented retreats for members of Alcoholics Anonymous and Al-Anon, sponsor or serve as spiritual advisor to approximately forty men, do one-on-one counselling, and serve part time on the staff of an alcoholic treatment facility in this geographical area of Maryland.

I acknowledge, without reservation, that my sobriety is a gift which I received from God, as I understand Him, bestowed upon me through the program of Alcoholics Anonymous. I further acknowledge that my continued sobriety is contingent upon my fidelity to the principles of Alcoholics Anonymous's Twelve Step Program, to my continuing to practice these principles in all my affairs, and to my continued participation in A.A. meetings on a regular and frequent basis.

I have come to know that alcoholism and drug abuse are diseases—fatal diseases—and that compulsive addiction to the substance abused is the overriding characteristic of these illnesses. Truly, diseases of addiction!

My first encounter with the fellowship of Chemically Dependent Anonymous (C.D.A.) was in 1980, in Maryland—the Annapolis, Bowie, and Rockville areas. Chemically Dependent Anonymous publicly acknowledges, in its literature, its indebtedness and gratitude ". . . to the co-founders of Alcoholics Anonymous for the 'Twelve Steps' and 'Twelve Traditions' which are the basis of our program." Many Chemically Dependent Anonymous members who are alcoholics attend A.A. meetings. It was in this setting that I first met members of Chemically Dependent Anonymous.

I was immediately deeply impressed by individual recovering addicts I met, and agreed to share my experience, strength, and hope at a Chemically Dependent Anonymous meeting. Later, I agreed to lead discussions on the Twelve Steps, especially the Third and Eleventh Steps. I was privileged to conduct the first C.D.A.-oriented retreat. To demonstrate my support, my great esteem, and my deep affection for the members of Chemically Dependent Anonymous, I attend C.D.A. meetings where individuals are celebrating periods of being "clean and sober."

Chemically Dependent Anonymous deals with the disease of addiction, without any distinction as to the substance being abused. Chemically Dependent Anonymous calls for total abstinence from any mood-changing chemical.

In my judgment, based upon personal association and experience with C.D.A. members, that fellowship's program of recovery from the disease of addiction is viable. It works! "By their fruits you shall know them" (Luke 6, 44). Could it be otherwise? No! At least not when an individual unconditionally surrenders to the Twelve Step Program of C.D.A. The fellowship of Alcoholics Anonymous has fifty years of undeniable success of its members who have lived lives based upon that program's Twelve Steps. These approximately two hundred words of inspired wisdom, wisdom that transcends human wisdom, are the keys to sanity and sanctity, to wholeness and holiness. The Twelve Steps are what Father Al G. once described as: "A master plan for living—more accurately, the Master's plan for living."

Chemically Dependent Anonymous is rapidly devel-

oping its own undeniable record of success! Men and women are coming to this program in increasing numbers and are recovering—becoming, and remaining, clean and sober. They are happy people, living useful and productive lives, loving and serving God as each understands Him. They have learned to love and serve God in the person of His creatures, especially other suffering addicts, their "brothers" and "sisters." Each enthusiastically carries the message of hope and the conviction, based upon personal experience: "It can be done, with God's help!"

I have observed that the members of Chemically Dependent Anonymous are bonded together, merrily traveling the road to freedom. They do not limit their association with one another simply to "meeting time," but have expanded their times of togetherness to include many other dimensions of life, which enriches their fellowship and provides an even greater measure of support.

I am pleased, and feel honored, to humbly but enthusiastically endorse and recommend the goals of Chemically Dependent Anonymous, and the means that fellowship recommends to achieve those goals.

To the newcomer: "Sursum corda!"—"Lift up your hearts!" God wills your recovery. You do what you can: Study this book! Work the Twelve Steps! Go to meetings! Live the C.D.A. program as best you can! Then, God will do for you what you have not been able to do for yourself. Promise!

Friend, keep comin' back!

B.A.N.

Chapter 6

C.D.A. ROOTS

Chemically Dependent Anonymous is a fellowship that was created to fill a perceived need on the part of some younger members of Alcoholics Anonymous in the Annapolis, Maryland area in the last decade. We founders of C.D.A., in the 1976–1980 period, were people who had bottomed out on alcohol in our late twenties. Yet we also had extensive histories of using other drugs. We had used alcohol in the last stages of our active addictions, and so A.A. had seemed the logical place to come for recovery.

We began to see, in working with those who used drugs other than alcohol, or whose primary drug of choice was something other than alcohol or in addition to alcohol, that some of these newcomers were not getting the message, within A.A., that all mood-altering and mind-changing drugs were part of their problem of addiction. Alcohol was not the sole obstacle to recovery for them. Even more important was the fact that earlier A.A. members seemed to be uncomfortable when these incoming people shared their experiences about using drugs. Members new to the program felt alienated within the fellowship. Clearly, something had to be done to help them.

One of us, Rick R., attempted to start Narcotics Anonymous in the Annapolis area. It did not succeed there, however. And N.A. shared its parent organization's problem of *seeming* to disqualify those addicted to other substances for membership because of its very name. We wanted to found yet another group, one that, while it resolved that situation, was still based on the principles of A.A., whose structure, we recognized, was time-tested and God-given. Their program had been designed by a group of alcoholics in the 1930's. Through trial and error, they had managed to come up with the idea of a fellowship that has proven itself successful, for over fifty years, for people addicted to alcohol. We wanted to be a similarly anonymous organization based on the Twelve Steps and Twelve Traditions.

But we also wanted to choose a name that would contain no words that could lead a prospective member to believe that we would exclude any particular type of addict or addiction. Previously existing literature from the Hazelden Foundation, in Center City, Minnesota, gave us our name. There, we also found verification for the truths we had lived.

The first meeting of C.D.A., with twelve people in attendance, was held at the home of Rick and Elin R., in Annapolis, Maryland, on August 17, 1980. We decided, that night, upon our name and our purpose. For the next few months, meetings continued to be held at Rick and Elin's on Fridays, at 6:30 p.m. These Friday meetings were transferred to St. Anne's Church, in downtown Annapolis, as the membership steadily expanded. Within six months, there were three meetings a week, attended by about twenty-five regular members, and soon groups were meeting in church halls, basements, and schools all over the Annapolis area.

Today, C.D.A. has 450 members in Maryland, alone, in over fifty active groups. The fellowship now extends, locally, from the Eastern Shore of Maryland to Washington, D.C. and its vicinity. C.D.A. is also to be found in the Midwest, in Florida, in Connecticut, and in Portland, Oregon, where Rick and Elin R. moved in 1982 and have since started half-a-dozen groups. We are now active in Dublin, Ireland, as well. A typical group has from fifteen to forty members, ranging in age from mid-teens to mid-forties. Of the original twelve members who attended the first C.D.A. meeting ten years ago, eleven remain active in the fellowship today.

The only requirement for membership in C.D.A. is the desire to abstain from all chemicals, including all street-type drugs, alcohol, and unnecessary medication. There are no dues or fees for membership. We are self-supporting through our own voluntary contributions. All our meetings are open ones. We neither endorse nor oppose any causes, and we do not wish to engage in controversies of any type.

Our program was designed for the still-suffering, chemically dependent person who would otherwise have nowhere to turn. Because of the all-inclusive nature of our organization, we can open the door to recovery for anyone who has a sincere desire to be free from self-destructive chemical usage. We hope that our fellowship will continue to expand, to serve the needs of all tormented addicts. Their numbers are, today, at an epidemic level.

Using C.D.A. as an alternative to, or in conjunction with the other anonymous groups dedicated to helping chemically addicted people, members of all of these programs, as well as those millions of people who still suffer, have a better chance for recovery. C.D.A. does not attempt to replace A.A. for those of us who are also finding recovery there. Roughly 75 percent of our present members are active, too, in the program that was our source. Only 10 percent of us have drug addiction problems that do not include alcohol.

We can never forget the many beautiful A.A. role models who have been a support and an example of courage for us in starting the C.D.A. fellowship. Nor should we forget what their program has taught us about being responsible to the practicing addict who wants help. In order to keep what we have, we must give it away. We are confident that this book will aid in that cause.

Chapter 7
THE PROGRAM: C.D.A.'S TWELVE STEPS

If you want what we have and are willing to make the necessary effort, then you are ready to take certain steps. Here are the Steps that we took which have made recovery possible for us:

1. *We admitted we were powerless over mood-changing and mind-altering chemicals and that our lives had become unmanageable.*
2. *We came to believe that a Power greater than ourselves could restore us to sanity.*
3. *We made a decision to turn our wills and our lives over to the care of God as we understood Him.*
4. *We made a searching and fearless moral inventory of ourselves.*
5. *We admitted to God, to ourselves, and to another human being the exact nature of our wrongs.*
6. *We were entirely ready to have God remove all these defects of character.*
7. *We humbly asked Him to remove our shortcomings.*
8. *We made a list of all persons we had harmed and*

became willing to make amends to them all.
9. We made direct amends to such people wherever possible, except when to do so would injure them or others.
10. We continued to take personal inventory and when we were wrong promptly admitted it.
11. We sought through prayer and meditation to improve our conscious contact with God as we understood Him, praying only for knowledge of His will for us and the power to carry that out.
12. Having had a spiritual awakening as a result of these steps, we tried to carry this message to other chemically addicted persons and to practice these principles in all our affairs.*

There is one thing, more than anything else, that will defeat us in our recovery: an attitude of indifference or intolerance toward spiritual principles. Although there are no *musts* in Chemically Dependent Anonymous, there are three virtues that are indispensable. These are HONESTY, OPEN-MINDEDNESS, and WILLINGNESS to try. If we practice them, we are well on our way.

Many of us thought we had taken Step One long before we came to the program. Sure, we were powerless, but *who cared*? Sure, our lives were unmanageable, but we could get by. We have not truly taken this all-important Step, in a program sense, until we not only admit to our powerlessness over drugs and alcohol, but also have a desire and willingness to change. Only when we realize that the responsibility for our recovery lies with us and that we can't do it alone have we taken the First Step.

*Reprinted and adapted with permission of Alcoholics Anonymous World Services, Inc.

We come to the program beaten. Our disease has bankrupted us emotionally, spiritually, and physically. All efforts to stop using chemicals on our own have eventually failed. We feel hopeless. Still, we come, desperately hoping for relief.

In time, we see others staying away from drugs and alcohol, and, slowly, we begin to trust in Something that is doing for them, and for us, what we could not do for ourselves. A Power greater than we are is keeping us from doing something that our past shows is insane to do, and that is to take a drink or drug. Every time we do, something bad happens. That is not the act of a sane person. We are ready for the Second Step.

If we have honestly taken the first two Steps, and accepted them as reality, the Third Step is the only logical one to take, if we are going to have any chance to arrest our disease and begin the process of change in order to produce a better way of living. If we have really admitted our powerlessness, then we must turn it over to that Power greater than ourselves. We are many and varied, some with religious backgrounds, others with none. But we are not joining a sect or religion. Instead, ours is a spiritually based program. Our Higher Power, or God, or whatever you choose to call It, is one of your understanding, one that you can trust and have faith in.

In order to get on with the "process" of recovery, it is necessary to be honest with ourselves so we can break the chain of events that has always led us back to using. We must begin to rid ourselves of old habits and ideas. Therefore, we, to the best of our abilities, take a truthful look back over our lives. We make a list of our faults and the times we have been wrong. We cannot change ourselves until we know who we are. As we look back, if we are really honest, we will find the good things we have done, as well. We list those, too. The important thing, here in Step Four, is to be scrupulously honest and to begin getting in touch with the persons we really are.

C.D.A. is a *we* program. Alone, we are powerless. So we must learn to share ourselves with others. People cannot help us if they don't know who we are or what we are feeling. We must learn to trust. First, we learn to trust our God, then ourselves, and then another human being. We begin to open the doors to ourselves, to let the healing power in and to let the past go. By simply sharing honestly with another, we are able to lighten the load of the guilt, fear, and anger that burden us, in the Fifth Step.

In time, we come to realize that we are just as powerless over some of our faults and defects of character as we are over our addictions. We are able to acknowledge that these defects are as responsible for keeping us from having the kinds of lives we want to live as are the drugs and alcohol we have been using. After trying by all the means in our power to change, to little or no effect, we surrender. It is then that we are actually ready to turn our defects over to our Higher Power, in Step Six.

Step Seven means that we must give ourselves completely into God's care, if we are ever to be truly free. Don't ask if you don't believe He will do it for you.

Be as honest and thorough as you can when making the list called for in the Eighth Step. But most of all, be sure you have the willingness. That's all this Step asks of us, but it is vital if we hope to grow from this experience.

In Step Nine, as with all the Steps, it is wise to seek the advice of our sponsors. It is not always easy to determine to whom, and how, we should make amends. It is even more important to try to discover whether an attempt at making amends will cause more harm than good. But, again, it is most necessary that we are *willing* to make these amends. Sometimes, that is all that is necessary and is best for all concerned. In cases where we make apologies or attempt restoration for damages, we must be ready to accept the results and not fall into the trap of high expectations about the outcome. If we do, the sincerity of our amends is questionable, and self-gratification is more likely the motivation.

As we continue our journey along the road to recovery, we go through many changes. If we are going to continue to grow in self-knowledge and honesty, we must make it a habit to look inside ourselves and make sure we are not slipping back into our old ways. We are not saints, but if we are to keep maturing, in a spiritual sense, we must incorporate the practice of taking our inventories, and making amends whenever necessary, into our daily lives, as the Tenth Step states.

We rely on our Higher Power to provide us with whatever we need to remain clean and sober. In order to receive these necessities, we must find the time to be quiet and to listen for the answers to our prayers. Often, the problems of day-to-day living can become overwhelming, and we may lose sight of our "primary purpose" and forget where we have come from. The quiet time renews us spiritually and gives us the strength and faith to carry out God's will for us, in this next-to-last Eleventh Step.

Gratitude is a result, and gift, of living the principles of the program. Giving to others that which has been given to us is putting our gratitude into action. We are never cured of our disease. We must always be reminded of what it was like before we found the program and of how fragile our sobriety is. By carrying the message to others, in the Twelfth Step, we keep in touch with our own pasts and, at the same time, become tools for our Higher Power to use in order to pass on the miracle of recovery to those who need it.

Chapter 8
C.D.A.'S TWELVE TRADITIONS

1. *Our common welfare should come first; personal recovery depends upon C.D.A. unity.*
2. *For our group purpose there is but one ultimate authority—a loving God as He may express Himself in our group conscience. Our leaders are but trusted servants; they do not govern.*
3. *The only requirement for C.D.A. membership is a desire to abstain from all mood-changing and mind-altering chemicals, including all street-type drugs, alcohol, and unnecessary medication.*
4. *Each group should be autonomous except in matters affecting other groups or C.D.A. as a whole.*
5. *Each group has but one primary purpose—to carry its message to the chemically dependent person who still suffers.*
6. *A C.D.A. group ought never endorse, finance, or lend the C.D.A. name to any related facility or outside enterprise, lest problems of money, property, and prestige divert us from our primary purpose.*
7. *Every C.D.A. group ought to be fully self-supporting, declining outside contributions.*
8. *C.D.A. should remain forever nonprofessional, but*

our service centers may employ special workers.
9. C.D.A., as such, ought never be organized; but we may create service boards or committees directly responsible to those they serve.
10. C.D.A. has no opinion on outside issues; hence the C.D.A. name ought never be drawn into public controversy.
11. Our public relations policy is based on attraction rather than promotion; we need always maintain personal anonymity at the level of press, radio, and films.
12. Anonymity is the spiritual foundation of all our traditions, ever reminding us to place principles before personalities.*

FIRST TRADITION:

"Our common welfare should come first; personal recovery depends upon C.D.A. unity."

Unity is the most treasured quality that our fellowship possesses. Our lives, and the lives of those who come after us, depend on it. Without unity, there is absolutely no hope. Unless Chemically Dependent Anonymous continues to survive, most of us will die.

We believe the individual's service to the group is very important. In addition, individual recovery depends upon the group, and the presence of a God-consciousness in that group. However, we are not implying that the individual should be dominated by the group. There is not another society which is as willing to go to any length to help, love, and care for its fellow members as ours is. We are an organization which

---

*Reprinted and adapted with permission of Alcoholics Anonymous World Services, Inc.

allows its members to act, speak, and think as freely as they wish.

The primary problem facing any society is how to survive, and then to continue to grow and to prosper. We believe that, by placing our common welfare first, and by remaining unified, we are well on our way. Our lives depend upon obedience to spiritual principles shown to us in the Twelve Traditions.

SECOND TRADITION:

"For our group purpose there is but one ultimate authority—a loving God as He may express Himself in our group conscience. Our leaders are but trusted servants; they do not govern."

C.D.A. has no president or sole individual who governs us, nor do we have a so-called board of directors. No C.D.A. member can issue an order to any other member or try to force adherence to his or her own beliefs. In actuality, our fellowship is a democracy, with a loving God, as He may express Himself in our group conscience, as our Director. He is the only authority in C.D.A. We trust in His presence and guidance.

Each C.D.A. group has a set of elected officers. These individuals are trusted servants of the members. They carry out the groups' responsibilities. Most groups have a program chairman, whose duty it is to arrange meetings and, sometimes, to obtain speakers for the meeting. Most program chairmen make sure that the meetings open on time and that everything is in order at the end of the evening. There is also a treasurer, who deposits the money from the basket, pays rent and other bills, and gives a periodical report at the group-conscience meeting. The secretary of the group opens the meeting and makes sure the literature is put out.

Each group has an Inter-Group Representative, who attends the Inter-Group meeting and reports back to his group about what was discussed there. Each group also has a General Services Representative, who attends the Area Assembly meeting and reports back to his individual group on its proceedings. And last, but certainly not least, is the coffee maker, whose responsibility it is to make coffee for the meeting, to set up the tables and chairs beforehand, and to make sure everything is put away at the end of each meeting.

Elected officers cannot give any spiritual advice, issue any directives, or judge anyone's conduct. We, in C.D.A., believe that gratitude is an action word and that being a trusted servant is a positive way of expressing gratitude and passing on what has been so freely given to us.

THIRD TRADITION:

"The only requirement for C.D.A. membership is a desire to abstain from all mood-changing and mind-altering chemicals, including all street-type drugs, alcohol, and unnecessary medication."

You are a member of C.D.A. the moment you say you are. No matter what your past has been, or whatever other emotional problems you may have, we cannot deny you membership. We welcome you to C.D.A.

We will not deny anyone membership, so long as he or she has a desire to stop using. If someone comes to a meeting under the influence, no one has the right to tell him he is not welcome in our fellowship. The suggested method for handling an individual who is disruptive at a meeting is to take the person outside and talk to him, or her, alone.

To deny any chemically dependent person a chance would be to allow that individual to die or to force him to return to a life of endless torture. We are not judges. God is the only One who has a right to judge, for He alone knows the workings of our minds.

It has been our experience that our disease tries to deceive us when it comes to unnecessary medication. Therefore, rigorous honesty with yourself, and with your physician, is imperative concerning this matter. Consulting your sponsor may also be helpful in this regard.

FOURTH TRADITION:

"Each group should be autonomous except in matters affecting other groups or C.D.A. as a whole."

The Fourth Tradition suggests that each *group* should take an honest inventory of itself. C.D.A. groups should see the traditions as a tested guide toward the primary purpose of each group. And that is to carry the message to the chemically dependent.

The first part of this tradition states that "each group should be autonomous." Autonomy is described as self-government. In C.D.A., this is the process by which each group handles its own affairs, carefully following the Twelve Traditions as it does so.

Such freedom also requires responsibility. Each group is responsible for its own decisions and the way in which these decisions affect other groups, or C.D.A. as a whole. The self-governing process allows groups to be self-sufficient. Tradition Four gives each group the freedom of choice, as well as the responsibility that goes along with its choices.

Though groups may differ greatly, all members suffer from chemical dependency. Each group is a spiritual entity strictly reliant on its group conscience as a guide for direction. A group may be creative in shaping its own personality in order to help its members to recovery. However, it is suggested that it keep its creativity within the guidelines of the Traditions and always maintain the primary purpose of recovery as the main goal of the group.

The group should be responsible for electing its own officers, the trusted servants who carry out the duties and responsibilities of the group, as described in the Second Tradition. Participation in the service structure eliminates group isolation and program illiteracy. It is important to know what is affecting other groups, or C.D.A. as a whole, and participation in the service structure creates an awareness of such valuable information.

The Fourth Tradition is known, in the circle of anonymous recovery groups, as the addict's, or alcoholic's, loophole. It is sometimes mistaken for a right to do "what I want, how I want, when I want to do it." A group that reflects this attitude will exist in anarchy, where self-will becomes dominant. C.D.A. can profit by using the history of Alcoholics Anonymous as a learning tool and guide to proper self-government that allows us to continue to grow and prosper.

FIFTH TRADITION:

"Each group has but one primary purpose—to carry its message to the chemically dependent person who still suffers."

The very existence of our fellowship requires the preservation and practice of this Tradition. Our unity is the support enabling us to carry the message to others. In other areas of society, we may be able to help as individuals, but seldom as a group. The history of Alcoholics Anonymous, however, has shown how important group action is in helping addictive people to recover. C.D.A., as a society working in unity, has proven to be an effective source of recovery for an addict and/or alcoholic who desires to get clean and stay sober.

We believe that, in order to be able to keep the sobriety and the better way of life that we have found, it is necessary for us to pass on to the newcomer, and other chemically dependent persons, what has been so freely given to us. We, in C.D.A., believe that our recovery is a gift from God. And the primary purpose of that gift is to allow us to give it away to those who need it.

SIXTH TRADITION:

"A C.D.A. group ought never endorse, finance, or lend the C.D.A. name to any related facility or outside enterprise, lest problems of money, property, and prestige divert us from our primary purpose."

By related facilities, we mean any organization, group, or institution related to the field of addiction. A C.D.A. group should never support such facilities or enterprises. A C.D.A. group can cooperate with anyone, but never to the point of connecting itself to, or sanctioning, any of these facilities or enterprises in any manner.

In the area of property and finances, too many problems may arise where money is involved. Questions of prestige can become very detrimental to our anonymity, which is part of the spiritual foundation of our program. We have found it absolutely necessary to separate the material from the spiritual, allowing nothing to divert us from our spiritual goal. We have, above all else, found it to be in the best interests of C.D.A. to concentrate only on our primary purpose, that of carrying our message to those still suffering from chemical dependency.

SEVENTH TRADITION:

"Every C.D.A. group ought to be fully self-supporting, declining outside contributions."

As recovering individuals we learn, through the program, that we must not just stop using chemicals, but must also begin taking responsibility for ourselves, for our own lives and actions. Among the many pleasures of living a sober life is a growing awareness that we are capable of taking care of ourselves, which comes from doing the daily chores necessary for our survival. We learn, through the consistent practice of the program, that we can be the adult men and women we always yearned to be, but could never be while using chemicals.

A new sense of self-worth is born in us and, along with it, a sense of responsibility to those around us. We finally become a part of society, and we start giving back some of the care we have been given. We grow in knowledge, learning many other valuable lessons as we become self-supporting, responsible people; some of us become so for the first time in our lives. Similarly, we mirror the same attitude of responsibility that is necessary in our individual daily lives when we, within our groups, support the program with our money, time, and energy.

The lesson we are learning is the same for each of us: we have been incredibly dependent, heretofore, on drugs and alcohol, on other people, on social institutions. Now, in recovery, we must begin to take care of ourselves if we are to survive, sober, and to grow. The program provides us with the tools and the support necessary to enable us to become *real people*; it is up to us, as individuals, to pick up the tools and use them in the struggle to grow. If we continue to allow, or force, others to assume responsibility for us, then the changes we need will never occur.

Our groups, then, must be founded in the same mold, assuming responsibility for their operations and for the continuation of the program we are trying to live. If we allow outside contributions to support our groups, rather than pay our own way, we are simply continuing our old behavior. We have been given a second life through the program, and we are entitled to the opportunity to support it in return. Being fully self-supporting is necessary to our group well-being, and to the continued growth of each of us as individual members.

Like most of our other Traditions and Steps, there are several sides to being fully self-supporting in our groups. We have one primary purpose: to meet together, to share in recovery, and to spread the message to the still-suffering. Only a recovering chemically dependent person can understand the dramatic difference that the message of recovery makes to us. As recovering individuals we have all heard that message and have been given the opportunity to repair our lives. We know, through our own recoveries, that the spreading of hope and faith has been the single most important factor in turning our lives around. Our group experience tells us that supporting our groups to keep the message available is of paramount importance, not just to ourselves, but also to the dependent person who has yet to arrive at our door.

No gift, no matter how well-intended, is offered free from all commitments between the giver and the receiver. When we accept contributions from each other in our meetings, we are sharing in our collective commitment to keep the program alive and working in our lives, and the lives of others yet to come. If we accept contributions from outside our group, we are made vulnerable to commitments outside of our C.D.A. program and, perhaps, even outside of our primary purpose. We must, therefore, share the responsibility for the fellowship's continued well-being amongst ourselves, ensuring that C.D.A. will remain healthy and ready to receive the newcomer.

EIGHTH TRADITION:

"C.D.A. should remain forever nonprofessional, but our service centers may employ special workers."

This tradition contributes much to the stability of C.D.A. and helps clarify the relationships between individuals, as well as between individuals and their groups. It is in this Tradition that we define the differences between service to the still-suffering chemically dependent person, individual service to C.D.A. groups, and the role of people performing support services for C.D.A. as a whole.

We state clearly, here, that no one among us is a professional specializing in the treatment of chemically dependent persons. The privilege of helping these people is reserved, in our program, for individual recovering members who, through their Twelve-Step work, further their own sobriety and spiritual progress while helping others to recover. Because our experience has taught us so strongly that helping another dependent person is not just beneficial, but actually crucial, to our recovery, we state in this Tradition that C.D.A., as a whole, must never take credit for that act of reaching out. We will not become, nor hire, professionals in order to help recovering and still-suffering persons. We must always remain a group of equals helping equals to attain sobriety through the grace of their Higher Power.

This is not to deny the role of professionals in assisting us or in working with dependent people outside of C.D.A. We respect and admire the helping professionals, accepting them as powerful allies. We only state that we cannot, ourselves, become professionals because doing so would eliminate much of the unity and equality which has made our program effective.

Individual service to C.D.A. groups is properly considered to be beneficial to us, as recovering individuals, as well as necessary in facilitating the continuation of each group. Coffee always needs to be made and furniture has to be arranged. Doors must be opened. There is the pleasure of greeting newcomers, as well as other routine tasks involved with just the opening and closing of our meetings each week and administering our expenses. This group-level service is our responsibility as members, and we gladly share the work out of gratitude to the groups which keep us sober.

When we need service work done which will affect all of our groups, such as running a full-time area or national service office, we find that we simply cannot rely on volunteers to do the job, however. These offices, or service centers, are not actual C.D.A. groups. We do not meet there expressly to discuss sobriety. Rather, they perform essential administrative tasks relating to all our groups, such as clerical work and phone answering, or making printing arrangements for our literature. These centers can operate best, for C.D.A., if we allow them to perform their tasks in as businesslike a fashion as possible. So, as in any business, we allow our service centers to employ workers to perform these tasks for C.D.A. as a whole, recognizing that these people are doing jobs necessary to the welfare of us all.

We make a clear and sharp distinction between service workers doing essential tasks for all of C.D.A. and professionals reaching out to the still-suffering person. Service workers are responsible to the entire organization of C.D.A. when they work for its benefit. But allowing professionals to come inside of C.D.A. to accomplish its basic purpose would mean replacing individual Twelfth-Step work and would remove one of our greatest aids to recovery and individual growth: the benefit derived by one chemically dependent person when he helps another. While we need to employ service workers to grow as an organization, we members will always also need to do the work of the Twelfth Step, as individuals, to continue to grow in our personal recoveries. We remain nonprofessional in a spirit of gratitude, with full realization of where we have come from and acknowledgment of the Higher Power which has led us to freedom.

NINTH TRADITION:

"C.D.A., as such, ought never be organized; but we may create service boards or committees directly responsible to those they serve."

C.D.A. is an extraordinary organization in that there are no rules governing individual membership and no requirements imposed on groups by our area assemblies or Inter-Groups. No provisions are in place for the enforcing of such rules or regulations, if they did exist. In C.D.A., individuals are members "when they say they are," based only on a desire to stop using mood-altering chemicals. There are no requirements imposed by our groups on members, and our entire program is stated simply in the form of suggestions. Likewise, groups are free to structure their meetings when and how the members wish to hold them. No Inter-Group, or other assembly, can dictate to a group its format or membership, except in rare and exceptional cases where other groups, or C.D.A. as a whole, might somehow be affected by one group's decisions. Our Traditions, along with many other "traditional" aspects of our program, are also only suggested to our groups.

Such an unstructured approach might well spell disaster in other settings, but there is one unique feature of C.D.A. not to be overlooked here: C.D.A. deals entirely with the disease of chemical dependency, a devastating and all-too-frequently fatal problem for the dependent person. We keep ourselves free, in C.D.A., to have a program consisting of mere suggestions because our collective experience has been that to reject these recommendations is a most dreadful choice for the individual or group affected. Chemical dependency, itself, provides sufficient penalty, in our lives, for our failure to follow the spiritual principles that our program outlines.

Groups, as well as individuals, can deteriorate and die unless there is approximate conformity to C.D.A.'s Twelve Traditions. So we obey the spiritual principles of our program in both our personal and our group lives, at first because we must, but later because we have learned to live again in sobriety. We have all suffered much in active chemical dependency, but we have found great freedom in our program. Our experience has been that the program contains the roots of a greater discipline than any we might impose through formal organizational rules.

Clearly, such an unstructured organization ought never to have a governing body. Therefore, C.D.A. will have no area or national body centrally "organizing" our groups. This does not mean, however, that C.D.A. has no need of committees to do service work, or boards to assist in administering our collective affairs. There will always be a need for these boards or committees to assist us in the task of bringing sobriety within the grasp of all who seek it. Just as we elect informal service officers in our groups and Inter-Group associations for our areas, we can create special committees and boards to serve the larger organization for specific needs. It is in the spirit of service, responsive to the people we assist, that we work as individuals or that we invest special committees or boards with authority to aid us in our endeavors.

TENTH TRADITION:

"C.D.A. has no opinion on outside issues; hence the C.D.A. name ought never be drawn into public controversy."

C.D.A. should never take sides on any outside issues, nor voice any opinions on them, in such areas as drug and alcohol reform, religion, or politics, or on questions, such as abortion, which cross religious-political lines. No matter how worthy the cause may be, we do not become involved. It is especially important to remember that, when we speak on a public level, the opinion we express should be considered merely that of the individual, not the point of view of C.D.A.

History has dictated to us the importance of tradition in the survival of our fellowship. Many societies such as ours have been destroyed by engaging in such controversies. One example is that of a local group of alcoholics who had united together to help one another. They were successful for a period of time, but they soon became involved in outside issues and controversies which led to disharmony among the members and the eventual destruction of their organization.

C.D.A. takes only one stand. It is that we have been given, and are applying, Twelve Steps and Twelve Traditions in our lives, today, so that we may recover from chemical dependency. The only issue we concern ourselves with is the survival and growth of C.D.A., so that the individual member may recover and help others to do so. Concerning ourselves with any outside issues or controversies will only prove fatal to our fellowship and the individuals who depend upon it so much.

ELEVENTH TRADITION:

"Our public relations policy is based on attraction rather than promotion; we need always maintain personal anonymity at the level of press, radio, and films."

Most of us knew of the existence of Chemically Dependent Anonymous, or about one of the other Twelve-Step organizations, prior to becoming sober. C.D.A. is not a secret society, and we do not try to hide our existence from the public eye. In order for the "hand of help" to be grasped, those in need must be able to find our rooms and to locate sober people to show them the way back to the sanity and health which we have found. It is necessary, however, that those needing help reach us as we, ourselves, reached sobriety—by seeking it for ourselves, at the time our Higher Power had decided was best for us, rather than by being pushed or cajoled.

No amount of outside effort would have prevailed, with us, until we were ready to accept help. And we have found that no amount of advertising will lead those in need to the program any faster. Each of us serves as the program's best public relations person in our own daily lives, through the example set by our every action in living in sobriety.

People like us, afflicted with a disease characterized by inflated egos and flagrant behavior patterns, are particularly at risk of becoming caught up in any public relations policy which might call for more personal testimony. Furthermore, it would be far too easy for well-intentioned members, all for the good of C.D.A., to put forth their personal beliefs and experiences as typical, or as a model, for sobriety. That would do harm in two ways: in damaging C.D.A. by restricting sobriety to only one mold, and in doing the members a disservice by inflating their importance. Our program must be allowed to remain a broad and gentle one, with many diverse members and experiences, avoiding the self-seeking behavior which has driven us in our past lives. Anonymity is the best protection possible for C.D.A. and for our continued group and personal recovery.

We have found that this quiet public relations policy has brought great rewards. C.D.A., along with the other Twelve-Step organizations, is well-respected by the professional community which continues to forward many prospective members to our rooms. The public at large is generally aware of the existence of C.D.A. and similar groups and knows that we have achieved great success in dealing with the problem of addiction. And also, we, as individuals, remain chemical-free and able to serve as the best possible advertising—caring, sober people whose lives have been changed through the program.

TWELFTH TRADITION:

"Anonymity is the spiritual foundation of all our traditions, ever reminding us to place principles before personalities."

There are many reasons why we seek to disclaim personal importance in our program: because we have spent our previous non-sober lives in self-seeking behavior; because we stay sober through the continued survival of our groups, not as individuals; and because we know it is through the work of our Higher Power that we survive at all, and not by any effort of our own. For us, anonymity is acceptance of spiritual truth and an essential outgrowth of our sobriety. For us, anonymity means being living reflections of the humility that our sobriety demands of us.

We may disagree, as individual members, with a particular point of view. We may believe, strongly, that a particular approach to recovery is the best possible one. We may adhere to any of a thousand different ways of living our programs. But, in the tradition of anonymity, all of us are equal members of the group. The spiritual principle of anonymity renders all other distinctions meaningless.

There is an all-pervading spiritual quality in the lives of C.D.A. members who are working our program. Our experience teaches us that humility is an essential part of this spiritual quality. We lay aside the natural desire for personal distinction, as C.D.A. members, when we are with both C.D.A. groups and the public in general. Humility allows us to maintain this anonymity of ourselves and others. Anonymity, in turn, enhances humility and aids us in our spiritual growth toward that virtue because we are placing principles above personality.

Chapter 9
H.O.W.

We have found that the basic concepts of the C.D.A. program can be broken down into three major principles. Honesty, Open-Mindedness, and Willingness to Try are H.O.W. the program works. With these qualities, we are on our way to recovery.

HONESTY

Most of us in Chemically Dependent Anonymous can recall that, in the last stages of our drinking/drugging, we knew that something was wrong with us, and we pretty well knew that it had to do with our substance abuse. So, in spite of our denials, the truth was beginning to surface. We were starting to add two and two, and we were getting four, not the five or the three we had been accepting as correct answers in the past. Now, there could be no more shortcuts to truth.

After we had attended one or more meetings, we also had to face the fact that the only way we were going to recover was, first, by admitting that our lives had truly become unbalanced through addiction, and, then, by gradually understanding that we were going to have to live in total abstinence from all drugs and alcohol. At some point, I believe, we all got that revelation. I don't think that God says, "Well, I think these few people here are going to get honest." Rather, each one of us eventually gets a flash of the truth, and we all have to make decisions, in every area of our lives, whatever we're doing, whatever the issue of the day.

God gives people the freedom of choice. And we must choose, at some point, to say, "I have had enough of this pain," or we will perish. Making that right choice, to finally "get honest" with ourselves, may be our first true adult act. We realize that we have to grow up, to pull ourselves up by our own bootstraps, to become responsible for ourselves. We just can't suppress this kind of honesty, anymore.

After we enter the program, we come to understand that honesty is still the single most important ingredient in our recovery. We have to continue evaluating our motives and position on a daily basis, and the Twelve Steps are the tools that enable us to rise above our own egos so we can see the truth. The greatest element in the universe is truth. And we can reach it only through honesty. We all have these little places within us that refuse to grow up. But we have to become mature. We have to constantly work at staying straight with ourselves. We find a reliable aid in this struggle in the Serenity Prayer: "God grant me the serenity to accept the things I cannot change; the courage to change the things I can; and the wisdom to know the difference."

We become grownups in that prayer when we can sense what our true actions must be, even if that means just waiting, at the moment, to let other circumstances change. We will always know the truth, and be able to act on it, if we accept the guidance of that prayer. What will help us to get through most situations is to pause, to pray, to meditate about what the proper action might be, and then to do it. This is living honestly.

There is an old saying: "The shortest distance between two points is a straight line." For us, "straight" means not drinking and drugging, and staying true to our consciences—the straight life. We have, in the past, always tried to find the shortcuts. But there are none. The straight line, the straight life, *is* the right way. Alcoholics Anonymous has given us a clue about how to live the straight life successfully. They call it the H.O.W. of the program; that is, Honesty, Open-Mindedness, and Willingness to Try. The letters also stand for "Hang Onto Winners." In C.D.A., we employ the pure simplicity of such slogans to help us to stay on the straight line to success.

OPEN-MINDEDNESS

We of Chemically Dependent Anonymous cannot stress enough the importance of open-mindedness. This condition, completely foreign to us when we were practicing addicts, is essential to a healthy and clean recovery. We do not achieve such a virtue all at once, however, because years of using drugs have left us distrustful of others.

When we first decide that recovery is what we want for ourselves, that is the beginning of a change in our thinking. We put into action a positive direction in our lives, based on the results we see in others who are recovering. We have begun to trust what others say is possible, that we can stay away from drugs, as they have, for long periods of time.

We then become open to the realization that a new way of thinking is not only possible, but essential, and that many of our ideas were twisted as a result of our years of drug use. We become willing to listen, for the first time, to the experiences of others in recovering. And we begin to see more change in our lives.

The next step is to select a sponsor. This requires a new move toward open-mindedness because this person is going to be allowed by us to direct our lives on our way to sobriety. We have finally come to the point of honesty in our recovery where we know that we don't have all the answers and that we need help from one another. We begin to understand how insane our behavior was when we were using, and we start to realize that an examination of this behavior is now necessary. For the first time in our lives, we are willing to look at our pasts as honestly and thoroughly as we possibly can, and to share our experiences with another person. This is all new for us. We buried our pasts, for many years, because of the pain we suffered under the influence of drugs and alcohol.

This step of inventory can come only after we become receptive to the idea that not only do our fellow addicts care about our welfare and recovery, but also that they do truly love us. We have broken down a great barrier when we realize, gut-deep, that we have finally found people we can trust, and that their only motive is love. They want to help us, and we believe in them.

The only thing remaining, before we begin to delve into our former lives, is to open our minds and hearts to the concept of a Higher Power. This step is very difficult for some of us, at first. But after a while, we begin to see the miracles, not only in our lives, but also in the lives of others, and we do believe in God. With this new Force behind us, we can start to rid ourselves of the guilt that has bothered us for years. We share our pasts with another chemically dependent person, and it is over. We have dealt with the guilt caused by our addiction.

We are now ready to tackle staying straight. We have only come to this point in our recovery because we have broadened our understanding of trust, change, and love. We have accepted the Higher Power concept, and have begun to depend on this God to give us more love and the ability to continue to grow in open-mindedness.

WILLINGNESS TO TRY

Most of us can recall the first time we attempted to ride a bike. Even though we were full of apprehension, we got on and gave it our best shot. It wasn't that the fear of falling or the pain of injury had left us. Rather, the desire to learn how and to acquire the benefits that came from riding a bike became stronger. In a word, we became willing: to try something new, to try something risky that would improve our lives.

So it is in recovery. In order to take that all-important first step, we have to become willing to do something, to take responsibility for our own reclamation. It's not enough to just admit our dependency. Many admit, long before coming to the program, that they are powerless over chemicals. But it is not until they become willing to do something about it that recovery can begin. The more willing we are to accept the realities of our addiction, the more willing we are to take the actions necessary for change, the more likely our success in the recovery process.

There must be willingness to ask for, and to accept, the help of others. Chemically Dependent Anonymous is a "we" program. If recovery could be achieved by ourselves, on our terms, we would not need this program. In the beginning, we are asked to trust in the suggestion that there is a way to do together what we could not do for ourselves. Trust, an ability we lost because we couldn't even trust ourselves, much less another, is the first "risk" we take to improve our lives.

It remains a risk until we start to realize its benefits. As we come to believe that C.D.A. is working in our lives, we turn the risk into faith in others, the program, and ourselves.

It is said that if we stay the same persons, we will use again, so change and growth is what recovery is about. In order to assure ourselves of this continued growth, we should remain willing to look honestly at ourselves and to work at changing those *things* about ourselves that threaten our sobriety. Getting a sponsor and working the Steps will enable us to make these changes. As long as we remain willing, remain teachable, we will be able to accept this new way of living, and our growth and success will be limited only by our imaginations.

Chapter 10
LOW SELF-ESTEEM

There are very few of us who come to Chemically Dependent Anonymous feeling good about ourselves. The things that we did while under the influence of chemicals, or in the pursuit of them, usually involved hurting someone else—in most cases, someone we loved, or someone we knew loved *us*. Our broken promises, deceit, and, in many cases, immoral actions, left us feeling empty inside, with a sense of self-loathing. We felt like failures. We had abandoned all that was good in our lives, both people and principles, in order to fill a craving for something we could not control. The need to use had become more important to us than jobs, school, family, God, or our own health. The guilt and self-hatred had become so consuming that many of us lost hope entirely and tried to end it all, either through continued use of chemicals, or by more direct methods.

For those of us who have been fortunate enough to enter this program, many came in believing C.D.A. was like a prison sentence. We felt unforgivable, unlovable, and unworthy of any good in our lives. It was not until we became willing to follow the suggestions we heard in the meetings, and started to work on the

Steps, that we were able to begin the process of change necessary to relieve us of our guilt. We could then open our hearts to a different way.

Only when we start to sense that a Power greater than ourselves is doing for us what we cannot do for ourselves, and begin to feel grateful for the chance to rebuild our lives, can the process of forgiveness begin. When we wake up and realize that, without Him, we would not have been saved from a life of pain, fear, and guilt, that we would have had to live a life full of remorse, then we begin to get that glimmer of hope that our lives will get better. We must be able to make amends, where we can, and forgive ourselves. We have to be able to love and trust ourselves. If we can't, we will never be able to extend these benefits to others.

The God of our understanding loves and has forgiven us. He never stops loving us. All we have to do is reach out and accept, and believe that things will work out for the best. If He, Who is all-loving and all-powerful, has forgiven us, who are we to think we are so unique in our sinfulness that we are the only ones He cannot forgive? Our guilt trips, although genuinely painful, are nothing more than ego trips which allow us to wallow in self-pity, rather than do the difficult and painful work of change.

We are all children of the same God. He wants us to be happy. We are worthy of good things. If we ask for His help, and let His plan and time and will be ours, we can let go of our old ideas, and fear of the future will leave us.

Chapter 11

QUESTIONS: C.D.A. FOR THE NEWCOMER

Past experiences have shown that most newcomers, upon arriving at the fellowship of Chemically Dependent Anonymous, are unsure about many areas of the recovery process. Certain questions seem to arise most frequently. We hereby attempt to answer these questions to the best of our ability.

1) "What do these people want from me?"

We've been there—we know the pain and suffering caused by this disease. We have found a way out, a new freedom. We no longer feel the desperate "need" to use drugs. Our lives are more our own today than ever before.

In order to keep growing, we have come to understand and believe that we must give of that which we have received. We want nothing from you other than the chance to share with you our experience, strength, and hope.

2) "What is a 'bottom'?"

A "bottom" is the place we reach when, because of

the amount of pain caused by our use of chemicals, it becomes necessary for us to ask for help and get honest about our addiction.

You do not have to lose your house, driver's license, family, or years of your life in jails or institutions, although some or all of these things have happened to many of us. We have found, through our own experiences and those of others, that if we continue to use, these things will happen. It is up to you whether or not you become progressively better or continue the downhill slide.

3) "What is 'anonymity'?"

"Anonymity" means that what you hear or who you see at meetings is not discussed outside the meetings themselves. We respect each other's privacy. Whether or not you want someone outside these meetings to know about *your* presence here is a decision left up to you.

Anonymity is the spiritual foundation of our program. For the purpose of unity, we do not ever associate our names on the public level (i.e., newspapers, radio, film, etc.) with C.D.A.

4) "Do I have to stay 'straight' forever?"

Each one of us began by staying "straight" for just one day. We break "forever" down into "one day at a time." The choice of whether or not to use will always be there. We have found, after staying straight over several 24-hour periods, that we choose not to use rather than return to the misery which brought us here.

5) "What about prescription medicine?"

We realize that some conditions require the use of

prescribed medication; on the other hand, a great deal of medication is abused. Our disease tries hard to get us to use again, and often the use of prescribed drugs can provide the "excuse" we need to get high. Honesty with your physician, and yourself, about your chemical dependency is of the utmost importance.

6) "What is a 'compulsion'?"

When the only thing you can think about is the next fix, pill, or drink, you are suffering from a "compulsion." Compulsion is what ruled our lives while we were using, and what proved so overpowering whenever we tried to stop on our own. Willpower alone cannot overcome our compulsions. From our own experiences, we can assure you that the compulsion to use will lessen greatly, within C.D.A., over a period of time.

7) "How many meetings should I go to?"

In the beginning, we suggest that all newcomers aim at going to 90 meetings in 90 days. It's very difficult to stop using at first, and most of us have found that we needed all the help we could get. Most often, the compulsion to use is especially strong during our early stage of recovery. We have found that if we can just put off using until we get to a meeting, we can usually find the support we need to stay clean for one more day.

8) "What is a 'slippery place'?"

There is a saying you might hear, if you keep coming back, that goes: "If you hang around the barbershop long enough, eventually you'll get a haircut." This means that if you hang around people, places, or things associated with the use of chemicals, you are setting yourself up for a fall.

All too often, we have seen newcomers who could not say no when offered a drink or a drug in these "slippery" surroundings. We have found it wise and advisable, therefore, to question our motives for coming in contact with people who are using chemicals.

9) "What is a sponsor and why do I need one?"

A sponsor is someone who is willing to share his or her own experience, strength, and hope with you on a personal level. Having been clean and sober himself, for a while, a sponsor will help you to understand the program. From what we've learned so far, it seems best if men find male sponsors and women find female sponsors. In choosing a sponsor, it is important to look for someone to whom you can talk comfortably. We also believe, based upon experience, that it is best to find a suitable sponsor as soon as possible.

10) "What is a 'Higher Power'?"

When people talk about finding a "Higher Power," it means finding something greater than ourselves in which to believe. Some people use the group, some the God of their religion, and some use nature. Many people use the word "God" to describe their Higher Power. Many of us, as newcomers, were either turned off completely by, or had a great deal of difficulty with, this idea. We found it necessary to keep an open mind and, at least, to listen to the ideas of others.

In time, we came to understand, each in our own way, that a Higher Power is anything you choose it to be.

11) "What is a Home Group?"

A Home Group is the name of a member's favorite meeting, which he makes a commitment to attend every week. The member does everything in his power to make this the very best meeting in all of C.D.A., and he also usually celebrates his yearly anniversary at this meeting.

12) "What is an anniversary?"

A member's annual celebration of his sobriety is called his anniversary. On this day, he either leads the meeting or has someone he really respects lead it for him. The member also receives a birthday cake on his anniversary, with the candles indicating the number of years since his last drink or drug.

13) "What are 'chips'?"

"Chips" are tokens used as a symbol to remind a member how long he has been chemical-free. The C.D.A. member cherishes these chips and carries them in his pocket to remind him that staying free of chemicals is his Number One priority.

14) "How can I contact C.D.A.?"

The following are mailing addresses for C.D.A.:

C.D.A.
P.O. Box 4425
Annapolis MD 21403

C.D.A. Public Information Committee
P.O. Box 864
Arnold MD 21012

C.D.A. COMMUNICATIONS, INC.
General Service Office
P.O. Box 423
Severna Park MD 21146-0423

For the C.D.A. Hot Line, call:

In Annapolis, Maryland: 1-301-260-3009
In the Washington, D.C. Metro Area:
1-301-369-6556

15) "What should I read to help me learn how to grow in this program?"

Currently available C.D.A. literature, in addition to this volume, includes: *Where and When* directories, *Twenty Questions*, and the *C.D.A. for the Newcomer* pamphlet. We also recommend the reading and study of the Big Book of A.A., *Alcoholics Anonymous*.

It is unlikely that each and every issue and question that a newcomer might have could be fully answered or satisfied in this space. All we can say is that almost every question seems to answer itself in time. Just "Keep Coming Back!"

Chapter 12

A C.D.A. JOURNAL

PART I: A WEEK IN THE LIFE OF AN ADDICT

Sunday

I do not want to wake up. I'm so ashamed of what happened last night, I wish I were dead. When I got home (lucky I made it) I was so drunk, I do not remember getting into the apartment. I do remember trying to undress and then falling back on the bed, only to feel a violent spinning. I was completely *out* of control. I vomited all over the rug and table, and my hair stuck to my face. I thought it was finished and got into bed, and then it started again. This time, I began vomiting so hard, I started to choke.

I became hysterical, thinking that I would die that way, and crawled on my hands and knees to my neighbor's apartment. I saw a light on under the door and started pounding, and yelling, "Help me, please! I'm sick!" My neighbor was away for the weekend, and there was an out-of-town friend of hers staying there. He quickly dressed (he was in pajamas) and all but carried me back to my apartment. He was very alarmed, but he stayed with me for two hours, watching me cry, and scream, and vomit. He stayed until the attack was finished, and I fell out. Oh, I hope he doesn't tell H. about this. She'll never talk to me again.

But I am alive! I do want to stay alive. I'm stuck in this life, and I need to get out. I just don't know how.

Monday

Went to work on time today. That's a first, for a Monday. Still feeling regrets about Saturday night. I didn't drink yesterday, just smoked a little and took some pills so I could stop feeling so guilty. I don't want to think about Saturday—I hate that a stranger saw me so weak and pathetic. And now I have to avoid H., so I won't have to see her anger or accept her pity. I'm so sick of having to avoid people. The list steadily grows longer, and it's always due to something that happens when I'm high, when I lose control.

Work dragged on today. I'm always so bored and distracted. It's so hard to get high and enjoy it. There are too many perceptive people. Am supposed to go out tonight, but I think I'll cancel. Feel too depressed to be around anyone. I don't feel like pretending that I'm okay. Think I'll just get some wine and stay in and read. But I *can't* get drunk. Tomorrow, I have to take an exam in the afternoon.

Ate a little dinner. Wasn't too hungry. Stayed up until about 2 a.m.—and finished the wine.

Tuesday

Bad headache this morning. Took some speed and waited, but didn't feel anything. Took some more pills around noon (should have waited longer) and got crazy. Smoked cigarette after cigarette and cleaned my desk out fifty different ways. At lunchtime, K.

approached me and asked me what was wrong. I told her I had a headache. She said, "I'm not stupid. You look awful, and you're on something." We almost got into an argument, but P. walked by and distracted us for the next hour.

I feel so guilty lying to K., all the time, about the drugs and the drinking. She's my best friend, and I don't want to lose her. No matter what happens, she has always stuck by me and loved me, even at my worst. I hate hurting her with all the lies, but isn't the truth worse? Somehow, I feel acceptable when I'm with her because she's a normal human being who leads a fairly contented, regular life. As sick as I am, I've no idea what she can possibly see in me. K. is an angel; she only looks for the good in people and focuses on that.

Was so wired by 4 p.m. that I couldn't finish the exam. My mind went blank, and I forgot a lot of things that I knew. I don't know how I'm going to get out of this one. I'll have to come up with a good excuse.

Went out with K. after work, to her apartment. Sat around and talked and drank coffee—took some downers in the bathroom so I'd be able to sleep by the time I got home. Got home by 11—to bed by midnight.

Wednesday

Woke up in middle of night and couldn't sleep. Got up and took some pills and read for a while. Fell asleep with the light on and the book on my stomach. Got up around 7 a.m. I felt terribly depressed. Called work around 8 a.m., and said I was sick, and went back to sleep. Got up around one o'clock in the afternoon and felt a little better. Made some lunch and went back to bed. Pulled the plug on the phone. Don't want to talk to anyone, today. Back to sleep. Got up again around 6 p.m. It gets dark outside so early, now.

Got dressed and walked down to the grocery store. Saw a couple of people I know in the deli and had a cup of coffee. Went and bought some wine and walked home. The sky was so clear, tonight, and the stars were so bright, that I felt that there was some hope. Maybe things will be all right, one day, and I'll be able to live without this terrible shame and depression.

Have therapy tomorrow, after work. I dread going there, lately. Rehashing my past never seems to make me feel better, never seems to improve my present life. But I'm also too afraid not to go, not to work on feeling better.

Made plans with K. and some of the other girls at work to go out Friday night. I *will not* have more than two drinks. I'm just going to get a little buzz, and act right, and be like *them*.

Drank a little wine and took some pills. Read, and fell asleep by midnight.

Thursday

Back to work. Caught up on a lot of my paper work. I need to get more motivated, to start caring more about the things I do. Mother called this morning, and we had an argument. She claims that I was incoherent when she called on Tuesday night, and she talked about my needing to go into a hospital again. I flew into a rage and said awful things to her, to make her feel guilty, to force her to take responsibility for how terrible I've become. It seems that we can never talk without arguing and blaming. Something is really wrong, here! I can't stand living like this, fighting and hurting the people who love me, the people I want to love. I know, by now, she's called J. up. She always has to get the family to take sides against me.

Went to the shrink after work. Talked about my fight with my mother. And, for the millionth time, explored my childhood. Don't know why I go there, except that I can get some scripts from that doctor. He is so smug—probably thinking about his next vacation, the one I'm helping to pay for, while I'm talking. I'm so sarcastic, lately. Seems I don't trust anyone.

Came home and got very high. I just want to sleep and forget all of this. . .

Friday

Woke up in a pretty good mood. I'm so glad it's the weekend, and I can sleep late tomorrow. Really looking forward to going out tonight with the girls. Must be very careful not to drink too much and lose control.

Went shopping after work. It was too late to cook dinner when I got home. I'll eat something out, later. Have to hurry.

Saturday

Out of control, again, last night. It was horrible. I never intended to get like that. I only had about four drinks. But not eating all day, and taking all of those pills, made me so crazy.

All I can clearly recall is meeting K. and R. downtown, around 9 p.m. Don't know why, but I began to feel very anxious about being around people. Took some pills to relax, on the way down. Felt reassured by having my own car, so I could leave if I got too uncomfortable.

Vaguely remember making the rounds of the bars with K. and R. I remember, also, feeling irritated that they could drink one or two drinks, and get giggly, and have fun. I just sat there wondering how long it had been since my last drink, so I could order another without looking too greedy. I wished the girls would disappear, so I could drink as much as I wanted. I stayed until I couldn't stay a minute more. K. told me that I was in no shape to drive. That pissed me off, but what really angered me was that wounded look in her eyes, that look that let me know I had screwed up, again. At that moment, I hated myself, and hated her for arousing those feelings in me, so I left. I don't remember driving home, or getting home, but I must have fallen on the steps, because my back is bruised, today.

I don't know what it is about me, but I just can't enjoy being around people until I'm drunk or high. I'm so afraid to be *me* around them, whoever "me" is. There's no denying how sick I am, and have been, all these years. I've always believed that things would somehow get better one day; but nothing's going to change until *I* get better, and I don't know how. I really don't know how.

PART II: IN RECOVERY

Sunday

Woke up around 8 a.m. Got to hurry. I'm leaving at nine o'clock for a meeting at Reality. I wish I could rest more today, since it's Sunday, but I know that once I'm there, I'll be glad I went. Having institution commitments is a godsend, especially when I've been feeling a little down. It's so easy, sometimes, to forget the beginning, how hard it was, and how little hope I had of any recovery, then.

Meeting was great. S. always leads a good meeting at Reality. She explains the basics so well. She had everyone's attention. People really got honest in the meeting and shared a lot of the ugliness and pain they had gone through before treatment. One man there spoke of his guilt about the way he'd stolen from his mother and taken advantage of her. When I shared, I related to him my remorse, in my early recovery, regarding my mother. And I saw a little of the pain leave his eyes. It's so critical for me to remember the person I was and that using could change me back into that person, all over again.

Came home after the meeting and showered. Husband is out watching a football game with some friends. Someone I sponsor is coming over soon, for a visit. Will try to exercise before she comes. Oh, oh! J. is here, now, with her baby. I'll have to finish riding my bike later. Sometimes it's so overwhelming. Every minute of the day is accounted for. If you don't fit something in at exactly the right time, it doesn't get done. Being compulsive and rigid as I still am, I have a hard time shifting my schedule and accepting any changes in my routine.

J. and I talked for a long time, and we realized we were on H.A.L.T. (Am I: Hungry, Angry, Lonely, Tired?), absolutely famished. We had sandwiches and fresh strawberries with cream. How wonderful, just to share a simple meal and sit and talk with someone you care about! There has been so much growth in J.—physically, emotionally, and spiritually. There have been times when I have felt drained by her constant needs. But I have learned that, as a sponsor, I can be honest and ask for some space when that happens. Our relationship has been getting better, and J. is becoming a person I'm really proud of.

This is what the program is about—helping each other. My own personal growth can only go so far because of the time taken up by my work and other activities. But the real growth comes from the relationships that I'm involved in. Having such an enjoyable time with J. has really made the day for me.

J. left. Finished riding my bike, and it's almost

time for the meeting. Tonight, there's an anniversary meeting.

The meeting was very emotional and touching. Came home around 8:30. Will cook dinner for tomorrow night and refrigerate it. Then it's a bubble bath, some reading, and to bed. Tomorrow looks like a full, busy day, and I want to be rested.

Monday

Restless night. I was up frequently because of troubled dreams. This always seems to happen when I harbor a resentment. It is the last thought on my mind when I retire at night, and it enters my mind as soon as I wake up. Part of the problem is my lack of forgiveness toward people in my life. They tell me, in the program, that if I pray for the willingness to pardon others, God will provide it. Sometimes, I wonder if I'm praying the right way, because I still cannot arouse that sense of forgiveness within me. But I have to continue to believe that God will intervene with His assistance, because I am not able to do it alone. Just as I couldn't stop the drugs and alcohol without His help, I am unable to change my character without it.

Up and dressed and out to a beautiful hotel where a conference for work is being held. How easy it is, today, to greet people, look them in the eye, and make conversation. I couldn't do that before, without drugs. And, even then, drugs wouldn't have controlled my enormous anxiety. I am so grateful that most of the fear and shame is gone, and I no longer feel the need to hide.

Took a break for lunch. Found a book that I'd been looking for. The conference has been slow today—too much time to *think*!! Spent the afternoon writing some inventory, to explore my resentments. Seems that there's thirty-some years' worth of anger, stored up, that gets dumped on the people around me, at times. Many of the resentments result from repressed emotions that are reawakened in me, old wounds from the past.

Came home and went to work out. Warmed up dinner quickly. Got to the meeting a few minutes late, very unlike me. I'm usually an early bird.

Meeting was good. A lot of young people were there tonight. I really enjoy listening to them share. And I can relate, so well, to the confusion they feel about everything at that age. I sometimes wonder what my life would have been like if I'd gotten straight at 17 or 18 years of age. But I also believe that I came to on the exact day and moment that I was ready to surrender. Getting late, now. Time for sleep.

Tuesday

Up around seven. Slept straight through the night; no dreams that I can recall. Was asked, last night, to speak at an upcoming function. That created instant anxiety. I haven't confirmed, yet, that I'll do it. I wanted to pray about it tonight. At first, I wanted to decline, but then the "show-off" in me said, "Don't be so hasty. Hold off on saying no." Even though the thought of speaking before such a crowd is frightening, I know that I have to trust in God and confront my fears.

Had the conference again, but had company at it, today. Talked for a long time with someone I work with who is also in the program. It was like having our own little meeting, using the language we both understand so well. We found, through sharing, that although our backgrounds are so very different, we have many of the same personality traits, fears, and insecurities.

After work, met B., and we went to an eating-meeting in Annapolis to try to sell some tickets to a C.D.A. social function. Got lost on the way, and we were so famished that we ate half of the food we had brought with us before we got there. We really laughed it up in the car, sharing some old memories of when we would get the "munchies" and what we liked to eat, then. After arriving at the meeting, B. was asked to lead a meeting at a nearby rehab. So we left and went there. The rehab was packed with people from the outside. Since I had volunteered B. for the meeting, I thought I might catch some flak from her, but she handled the crowd like a real pro and did a super job.

B. and the other women I sponsor are so very important to me. We have become so close, this year, and have shared a lot of our pain and joy together. I feel a tremendous love and protectiveness toward B., and I am so glad that God placed us in each other's lives. I know that, without the people I sponsor, I would be thinking about myself nonstop. How boring!!

We got home around 10:45 p.m. I'm so tired, by now, that my words are starting to slur. Read (the last addiction I have left) until around midnight, then said a few quick prayers of thanks. Can't wait to close my eyes and drift off into the stillness of the night.

Wednesday

Up around 7 a.m.—feel weak and sick. Throat is sore. This might be the cold I've been fending off for the past two weeks. Made some hot tea with fresh mint and doubled up on my Vitamin C.

Got to work a little late, but don't feel motivated, today. When I get sick, I begin to obsess about how it's going to affect my plans for that day or, if I really want to project into the future, for the entire week. Back to "One day at a time"!

Ate some lunch. Tried to set up some appointments. Still no motivation. I feel too weak. I know, from experience, that my drive will return and that I can even ask God to supply some when I'm empty. That has also worked. "This, too, shall pass" applies in so many ways, during the course of a day. When I first came into the program, I used to think that a negative attitude would be there forever, that I had no way out of my depression or my moods. I know better, now.

Left work early. Came home and cancelled a visit with a new girl I have just started to sponsor. Felt guilty doing it, but I have to perform the program the way I would suggest it to someone else. And that means taking care of yourself.

Stayed in and did some paper work. Read a little, said my prayers, and went to bed early.

Thursday

Woke up early. Still feeling ill. Can't decide whether to go to work. The great debate in my head begins:

Voice #1: "Stay home. You're sick. You need a break; you deserve it."

Voice #2: "Faker, you're not that sick. See how you feel after you're up."

Got up, had a cup of hot tea and did feel a little stronger. Compromised with the two voices and decided to go in to work, but to leave early if I still felt sick after I got there.

Arrived at work and was extremely busy for the next seven hours. Didn't have time to think about "me." Left and went to meet a friend for dinner. Planned on going directly home after that, but stopped off at a store and bought some clothes for work. Home by 9 p.m. Read, said prayers, and went to bed.

Friday

Up early with my husband. He's going on some out-of-town appointments today. Reset the clock for my wake-up call. When it went off, couldn't get right up. I skipped some of my morning routine so I could sleep in a little and take care of myself.

Got up later and went to first appointment of day. That went well, and then went in to office. Only 10 a.m., and I'm thinking about catching a noon meeting, but I still feel weak, and there's a lot of paper work to do, here, and calls to make. Sometimes, I've gone to meetings at noon and let my work slide, but not too frequently, lately.

Decided against noon meeting, since I'm going this evening. Had some lunch and stayed in the office most of the day. Still catching up on work piled up while on vacation. Got to take this "one project at a time," so I don't become so overwhelmed I lose control.

Glad it's Friday. Looking forward to the weekend, primarily just to get some extra sleep. Plans for Sunday with S., to go to a meeting and a fair in town. Saturday, maybe B. and I can just be alone and see a movie in a theater. No telephone, no distractions.

Talked on the phone a lot. So many emotional crises going on. I'm glad I am trusted enough that people feel they can call and share with me. It means so much to me that I can be useful, today, and am able, perhaps, to lighten someone's load. I am also glad I've been given the courage to say "I love you" to friends because they need it. When I'm able to do that, I find I lose my own fear of rejection.

Worked out and then home by 5 p.m. Ate a sandwich. J. is picking me up for the seven o'clock meeting. She'll be here by six. Took out five minutes just to sit and relax. What did I ever do with my time before I came into the program? My life was never full, the way it is now. It was just months and years of playing out life as if it were a death sentence.

Saturday

Up at 7 a.m. Tried to sleep longer, but was unable to. It seems that once I'm up, my mind begins churning out an agenda of "things to worry about," and I can't fall back asleep. So I get up and start my day early. What a change from the old days of staying up all night and then crashing during the day, over and over again. I'm still not comfortable sleeping late in the day, because it reminds me of my using days.

Got up and showered and ate breakfast. Read my meditation books. One idea made a deep impression on me. It stressed how important it is to remember that God makes greater use of the channels that are the most willing and receptive. I have to remember how easy it is to become blocked as a channel if I become stressed out and out of control.

After meditation, exercised and did some chores. Finished by noon and took some time to relax. Spent the entire afternoon and evening with B.: dinner out and a movie at home. What a blessing—not one phone call during the evening. Glad to have this block of time to ourselves to strengthen our relationship.

To bed early. Lots to do, again, tomorrow!

Chapter 13

FUN IN RECOVERY

By now, you have come to the realization that there is much that must be given up in order to be a member of Chemically Dependent Anonymous. However, you will soon see, by reading many of the members' stories, that there is much more to gain than there is to lose from joining the fellowship. Yet when it comes to thinking about what life might be like in sobriety, you may be wondering if there is a life after addiction. C.D.A. offers a wide range of activities for all its members. We'll show you some typical examples of life's re-creation in recovery. Herewith, a C.D.A. play-by-play:

SOFTBALL
Big Al hits one over the fence for a home run for the C.D.A. Fun Bunch Twelve-Step Team. Coach Mike S. jumps for joy when Tim makes a double play look easy. John throws another pitch. Missy and Kim are both loved by their teammates for getting a hit and making a catch. Metro makes an unbelievable catch once again. Then Rick and Ken make still another catch. As Perry stretches on first for another put out, Jim and Greg make a pop fly look easy. Amy catches a pop-up. As Heidi, Mike B., Marlene, and Jeni cheer, the C.D.A. Fun Bunch wins the 1987 softball championship.

HORSEBACK RIDING
Cowboy J. T. can't get his horse to move, but finally Mike G. and Arundel get him to follow their horses. The horses are all glad to see the stables after one hour of hard riding by the crew of C.D.A.

VOLLEYBALL
Willy sends the ball Ron R.'s way for the slam. Brent taps it over the net for a point. Perry spikes another one. The C.D.A. volleyball team wins it all.

WHITE-WATER RAFTING
Mark R. is swept into the rushing waters; Ron R. falls into the rapids once again. Willy is carried along for a long ride. Gary has a close call, but keeps on going. The river is fast and thrilling. At night, Tommy has the big fire going for the bonfire meeting. Frank Y. talks about love in the fellowship. Kevin and Gwinn and Big Rob share their experiences. Brian and Dave put another log onto the fire. Lynn smiles and shares some of her love. Roy L. needs help getting his tent up.

GRATITUDE BREAKFAST
Brent speaks from the heart while Candy, Heidi, Maureen, and Marie listen and finish their coffee. Bobbi and Sterling smile and laugh as the speakers share their experience, strength, and hope with all of us.

SPIRITUAL RETREAT
The C.D.A. Men's Retreat is very special to us. It's a time to renew our relationship to our Higher Power, to share our God with others, and to grow closer to our fellow man. It's also a time for men like Allen to be used by God to serve Him and his brothers. Leaving the retreat is always hard, but we know we can come

back to Manresa next year. It's good to see the young ones, like Paul and Brian, praying in the chapel. Kevin and Sparks share their true feelings of joy. The retreat master is, as always, a joy to hear.

ANNUAL PICNIC
The C.D.A. picnic is always so much fun. Sterling shares from his heart and speaks in a low-pitched, soft voice as hungry people eat hamburgers. The food is wonderful, and there is plenty of it. We have games to play. Ron and Patti throw the water-filled balloons, but Missy and Rick are the winners. It's always great to get the volleyball games going. There's fellowship, caring, and sharing, the C.D.A. way, at our picnics. Denny enjoys the ride home on his big motor after snapping many photos of the event. Kevin also enjoys his motor on this hot summer day.

NEW YEAR'S EVE DANCE
It's 11:30 p.m., and the clock is ticking, the music playing. Heidi, Bucky, and Bev are getting down. Across the room, Lori and Marie kick up their heels. The clock strikes. It's midnight, and the kisses and hugs begin, as we say goodbye to the old and welcome in the new year.

Chapter 14

EPILOGUE: THE FUTURE

We know absolutely, without the slightest doubt, that God wills our recovery from the disease of addiction. This knowledge is not only based on our solid faith, but also on the history of so many chemically dependent people who have come before us and have stayed clean: first, by finally finding this program of Chemically Dependent Anonymous; then, by attending our meetings; and ultimately, by discovering a Higher Power to rely on in all situations as they work toward sobriety.

Our future as a recovery program remains uncertain only in that it is based on God's will for us and not our own. We can set no restrictions or limitations on His decisions. We can only hope and pray that our Higher Power will continue to allow us to be used as His instruments, in order to help still-suffering drug and/or alcohol abusers. We believe that this is our mission as individuals and as a recovery fellowship. And we know that our ultimate dream can become a reality with His help.

After ten years of dealing with our personal challenges, and those of other chemically dependent people, there is much we still do not know about this disease. But there is also much we have learned as a result of these experiences. We of C.D.A. will continue to keep coming back and will, we hope, keep growing as chemical-free adults, and as a fellowship, so we will be ready to help the next newcomer when he walks through that door, remembering always to "keep it simple."

We submit ourselves to the principles of our program, and to our Higher Power, as we say, "Here we are, God. Allow us to be used for Your will." We put our faith in Him, believing that He will continue to reveal to us how to seek the spiritual path and how to evolve better ways to improve our decisions and our direction.

PART II

PERSONAL HISTORIES

To the Reader:
 These personal histories were not meant to be read all at one sitting. Look through them (some are quite short) and find one that says something to you. Read others at your leisure. All come from the heart. Each is being shared with you by a recovering chemical dependent, with much pain and more promise, in the hope of reaching out to help you. If you are looking for a new, drug-and-alcohol-free way of life, these stories are presented as examples of how that goal can be achieved.
 Many of these stories repeat major ideas from the program of Chemically Dependent Anonymous. They are offered in the words of those whose circumstances may differ, but whose major life experiences often have much in common. You will recognize one or more of them. They are you. They are all of us.

Chapter 15
I FINALLY FOUND MY NICHE

After being brought up in an environment where alcohol use was prevalent and street drugs were used behind closed doors, I could not wait until I was old enough to partake of them. I related chemicals to having a good time. Any time my parents or older sister had a party, booze and other drugs were the main ingredients. I started experimenting with alcohol at a very young age and found that I didn't really like the taste. Every time I tried alcohol, I got drunk, and I would inevitably get sick.

Marijuana, among other drugs, was very popular in my neighborhood, and it was used by just about all the people I hung around with. The first time I smoked pot, I knew I had found my drug of choice. I liked the taste, I loved the feeling, and there was no sickness afterwards. The friends I was running with were the kind that my mother told me not to hang around; but what mom didn't realize was that I had become one of those people. I found much less pressure, a lot more fun, and I felt very accepted in this group of people. I didn't need to be intelligent; I didn't need to be good-looking; I didn't need to do anything or be anything special. All I needed was the honest desire to party hearty.

I had found my niche...

It wasn't too long before it became a real problem to use when I wanted and how I wanted. By now, I would use anything that changed my mood and the way I felt about myself. My preference was amphetamines. I think that, because I also smoked so much pot, I always felt ragged out. But I found I could drink enormous amounts of alcohol and not pass out or get sick. The problem came with not taking care of responsibilities I had, such as showing up for school—all day, every class. I flunked out of the ninth grade. It became a real job to remember what I told to which people. The alibis and excuses were running out. I was constantly in my parents' wallets and my younger brother's piggy bank.

I didn't realize that, after just a short time, I was using to live and living to use. Getting high was all I wanted to do. I might have some extracurricular activity, but I would not think of starting it without a buzz. As a young child, I had watched my family party it up; now they had all hit their bottoms. My parents were ready for divorce. My older sister was in one jackpot after another. I wasn't like them. I didn't have a girl to divorce. I could never get anything together to lose, or have anything in good enough shape to screw up. My situation was pretty hopeless, as well, but I didn't notice, because all the people I ran with were the same, or worse, than myself.

But, one by one, my family started attending Alcoholics Anonymous meetings. I was glad for them and thought that my parents were at the age when they should think about doing something about their problems. I was shocked when I found out that my sister was going to A.A., however. I couldn't understand why. I knew about her jackpots, but I had figured she would straighten that out. But not with A.A. I didn't know much about A.A., but I knew that if you went there, you couldn't drink anymore. My sister was only twenty-four years old.

It was not long before I was given this choice: "Either go to A.A., or get out and live on your own." My parents knew that I would never realize I had a problem as long as they continued to let me live at home and behave the way I was doing. They would no longer enable me to live life on my own terms. I didn't know where I was going to live or how I was going to support myself. I was only seventeen. I was still going to high school. I know, today, that my parents saved my life.

I went to A.A., begrudgingly. It was like jail for a whole hour. I felt humiliated. I realized that I seemed to be the only teen-ager around the meetings. I couldn't relate to the horror stories. After all, I had not yet wrecked cars, gone to jail, lost my wife, or ended up in an institution.

I heard about a new program that had just started, called Chemically Dependent Anonymous, so I went there. At that first meeting, I realized I was in the right place, with people just like me. The people in that room were talking about *me*. The majority of them were younger than the A.A. group and were sharing the pain that they had experienced. I remember someone sharing that he had felt like such a loser and had had no hope that the future would be any better. But after coming into C.D.A., all his problems had become challenges. He also said that, because he was not using any drugs and/or alcohol, he was starting to feel like a winner. Someone said, "Good things happen to addicts who don't use."

Someone else grabbed me, after the meeting, and we talked. He told me that all those things that had happened to the others didn't necessarily have to happen to me. But if I stayed chemically dependent, they would. And if I continued to use, I would die. I had a friend who had died from an overdose, and I had seen other friends locked up in jail. I knew that this guy was telling me the truth, and he seemed to care. After all, he had no reason to lie.

I had found my niche...

I kept going back to C.D.A., and I didn't get high—one day at a time. One second at a time. I have to say, after being clean and sober for over five years, that I've never experienced a bigger challenge than getting straight. I thought that there would be no life after sobriety, but much to my surprise, I have just started living. I have more material things than I thought could be possible in just five years. But I've found that those things don't, and can't, make me happy for long. My most prized possessions are the relationships I've developed since coming to the fellowship and working with the program of Chemically Dependent Anonymous.

The first relationships I had were with other people in C.D.A. who cared for me when I wasn't able to care for myself. The second was the relationship with God, as I understand Him, that people in the program told me I must have if I wanted to ensure my sobriety. Through the people who cared for me, and the God Who, I know, loves me, I have been able to get to know myself. I'm not the terrible, mean, uncaring individual I had feared I was. I found that I actually have the ability to care for another person. I do not try to harm others, mentally or physically. I know, now, that I was never a really bad person, but my behavior as a user was always in contradiction with my true self.

I do not behave like that, anymore. I have a love for life. I look forward to getting up in the morning. I love my job; I don't believe there is a better one in the world. I help people for a living. I enjoy watching, listening, and interacting with people. Today, I am able to go to the new guy in C.D.A. and talk with him. I let him

know I care, share with him my story, and tell him what I did, and still do today, to stay clean and sober. And that is:
1. Don't drink or drug (even if my ass falls off).
2. Go to meetings (my friends will screw it back on).
3. Pray.
4. Help another person.

It's very simple—so simple that I almost didn't make it. But I had, and still have, today, a desire for a new way of life.

    I've found my niche...in C.D.A.

Chapter 16
THY WILL BE DONE

I first started to use when I was fifteen. I grew up in a household affected by alcoholism. (My father is an active alcoholic.) So I convinced my parents to send me away to a boarding school for my sophomore year in high school. I was desperate to escape an emotionally chaotic environment. My first set of friends at school consisted of the campus potheads and acid freaks. I had never made many friends as a kid, and I wanted to fit in, to win the acceptance and approval of my new friends. So I did what they did—smoked a lot of dope, dropped a lot of acid. I was tripping every weekend.

The following summer, my father got me a job with his company. Since the job was out-of-town, I lived at the home of one of my classmates. During that time, my whole life revolved around getting high, doing as many drugs as possible, and running around. I'd go in to work high, if I went at all. I was ashamed of myself and how I was living, but I didn't know how to change it. My life was already unmanageable due to drugs.

At the beginning of my last semester at school, I was expelled for smoking dope in my dorm room. I was filled with remorse and guilt and self-pity over this. My parents were pretty easy on me—they knew I was remorseful—but this incident drove a wedge deeper between us. Fortunately, I had already been accepted at college, and I was able to start immediately. I was afraid the school wouldn't take me, but they didn't care about my expulsion.

Drugs weren't prevalent at college. Drinking was more the thing there. So I began to drink. In any case, I knew that I couldn't handle the drugs anymore. They were more powerful than I was. But I thought I could handle drinking. I remember my first hangovers—so mild, compared to the crippling headaches and nausea I would experience later.

After two-and-a-half years, I dropped out of college. I had started working as a waiter in restaurants. It was the perfect life for an alcoholic. So easy! Work in the evening, party until three or four in the morning, then sleep it off the next day, and do it all over again. Everyone drank on the job. When I first started coming to meetings, I heard people say that they were drinking in the mornings, or that they had become unemployable, and I didn't think those things applied to me. Yet I was always drinking within a couple of hours of waking up. It was okay because it was after noon, I thought. I was certainly incapable of working a responsible nine-to-five job, however. I could never have functioned on that kind of schedule.

I didn't have much self-esteem to begin with, but alcohol robbed me of the little I did have. I was incapable of setting realistic goals and then working a plan to achieve them. All I had were grandiose fantasies, and I was too physically and mentally debilitated by my using to put together a workable plan of action and stick to it. I knew I had some brains and abilities, but I couldn't seem to get out of the rut I was in. I became more and more frustrated by the lack of direction in my life, by my inability to get my life on track. This state of mind led to more self-pity and lower and lower self-opinion. It was a vicious circle.

But it was my blackouts, and a seemingly unstoppable month-long drinking spree, that finally got to me. Almost every night, I drove home from some bar in a blackout. I had become belligerent and vicious when I was drunk, particularly when I blacked out. Finally, one night, I came out of a blackout on the floor of my apartment, and someone I didn't know was kicking me in the face. If my neighbors hadn't intervened, he might have killed me. But I couldn't even remember how it had all come about. The next day, I went to my first meeting.

I was scared when I first came in: scared of going back out, scared of not being able to stay sober and clean, scared of everything. I didn't think I'd be able to make the program work for me. People who had stayed clean for a year were like gods to me; they were a different order of being from myself. I just clung to meetings and to the people I met, and I kept coming back. And today, as I write this, I've been clean and sober for over three years.

I've been through several different stages in my recovery. At first, I just operated out of raw fear. I lived from meeting to meeting. I could barely comprehend the Steps or anything else people told me.

Eventually, though, that same fear, along with a desire to have what others in the program had, compelled me to start trying to work a "program" of my own. I took a written and oral First Step, which helped in clearing away some of the guilt and remorse associated with my using days. I tried to tackle the Second and Third Steps. As I look back, my notions of these Steps, of a Higher Power and how It could work in my life, were very limited. I wanted to take the Steps because other recovering alcoholics and addicts told me I had to change, in order to stay sober. But I wasn't really willing to surrender to a God. I just didn't trust enough, yet.

In any case, I still wanted to grapple with the emotional garbage of my life, so I started a Fourth Step shortly after my first anniversary. I was as honest as I could be (which was not very), and I was sincere in my effort. I told it all to my sponsor, in my Fifth Step, and he helped me to dig a little deeper, to be more searching and less fearful. The Sixth and Seventh Steps were truly "The Lost Steps" for me, because I hadn't laid the groundwork, in the Second and Third Steps, for the close relationship with my Higher Power that these Steps demand. Finally, I wrote out my Eighth Step list and, over time, have tried to carry out the Ninth Step.

Then I basically stopped practicing the Steps in my life. I went to meetings, I associated very closely with some friends in the program, and I continued to try to develop my understanding of how the program worked. I don't mean to discredit my earlier efforts in recovery; I was sincere and earnest in my desire to grow. But mine was a selfish program in the worst sense—I wanted what the program could offer to *me*. I was only concerned with how it could get me the things I wanted. My own will was still the final arbiter of what I would do in recovery.

What was missing in *my* program was the spiritual: the active presence of a Power greater than myself. I hadn't let my God into my life. I guess I just wasn't willing to let go of my own will yet. But I finally became uncomfortable and isolated enough to hit a kind of emotional bottom that led me to reach out—to others in the program and to my God. That was a gift, His allowing me to reach a point where I was able to see and admit that my way didn't work. Through trying, each day, to surrender my will and my life to His care and by taking the daily action that is part of the letting go of my self-will, my life has been turned around completely in the past few months. The missing element has fallen into place. I've found a real joy in living and in sharing with others. It all goes to show: don't "pick up" before the miracle happens.

Chapter 17
OUT OF THE CRACK HOUSE

This is Vince R. My story is that of an addict and an alcoholic who always felt the need to be accepted. I took my first drink, a beer, when I was about seventeen years old. I was a senior in high school. When I took my first sip of beer, it didn't do anything to me. I don't even remember getting a buzz. But I do know that I began to feel a part of the group. During my final year in high school, I did what it took to graduate. My drinking was not excessive or alcoholic. I drank on rare occasions; if someone was passing around a six-pack and everybody was drinking, I would take a beer and drink it, too.

But my real, heavier use of alcohol began when I was in college. I went to a black college down South. It was my very first time away from home. I don't remember really wanting to attend this school. I kind of wanted to stay home, close to my family. But my father and his brother had attended this college. And when I was accepted, my father patted me on the back, shook my hand, and said, "Congratulations!" I guess, once again to feel a part of something, I decided to go to that school.

My freshman year seemed normal. My drinking was confined pretty much to weekends. And it felt good. For the first time in my life, I felt that I belonged. But within a short time, I began associating with people who drank much more than I did. And quickly, without really knowing it, drinking alcohol became a part of my social life. It got to the point where I didn't want to go to a party or a dance, or even to be with a bunch of the guys in a room, just sitting around shooting the breeze, without having something to drink.

So, my first year in college is when I consider that I started drinking alcoholically, although I wasn't drinking even as much as a pint a day. My drinking was born out of the continuing need to belong. I drank to suppress feelings of loneliness, and inadequacy, and all the problems that come with drinking. Needless to say, my grades, at the end of that year, were a little over a C average. But on the surface, things still seemed to be normal. My drinking did not start affecting me until the second year I was in school.

That second year, I began to associate with a different crowd of people, and I had my first experience with marijuana. It occurred when, again out of a need to belong, I joined a fraternity. I can recall how our fraternity used to march across campus in a line, singing songs. One day, someone at the front of the line had a joint. Since I was over six feet tall, and we'd lined up by height, I was near the back. I remember watching that joint being passed from the person at the front, all the way down that line. When it got to me, I assumed a kind of "Oh, heck, why not?" attitude and took a hit. Again, as with my first drink, I didn't feel any immediate sensation of getting high. It seemed like such a natural thing to do. Nobody made a big deal out of it. It was just part of being in the group.

After that, my drug and alcohol use escalated to the point where, by my third year in college, my grades were quite poor. In fact, I had quit attending classes and had dropped out of school. By this time, I was using THC, mescaline, all kinds of uppers and amphetamines, such as Black Beauties. On top of all that, I was drinking alcohol. At that stage, I really felt lost. I knew that something in my life was not right, but I didn't know what it was. It did not occur to me that using drugs and alcohol had anything to do with it. I was never much of a drinker, but when I found pills, and when I found the herb, that was my kind of high. I considered people who got drunk a lot real sloppy, so I would drink just enough to get a little buzz, to mellow off the drugs. The pills and the herb were my drugs of choice.

When I was about twenty-four years old, I married a woman I had met when I was in my second year of college. She had gone to the sister school across from ours. She was the type of person I had always wished I could be, and she still is. She is, and was, very independent, very intelligent, and popular. She knew where she wanted to go, and I knew she was someone I wanted to be around. We fell in love, we got married, and we had three children. By the time our first daughter, who is now nine years old, was born, I had been introduced to cocaine. I was still drinking heavily and using marijuana.

But when that baby girl came into my life, I told myself that I wanted to do things differently. I wanted to change. I wanted to make something of my life for her. Like a lot of other addicts and alcoholics, I had big dreams. I spent a lot of time in bars, thinking about big, big deals that I was going to make. And I had an idea: I wanted to own my own business. So we relocated back down South, leaving my home town, with our young daughter.

My wife's grandfather had owned a paint store for over twenty-five years, and nobody else in the family was interested in it. He was over eighty years old and was ready to give it up. Somehow, I got it in my mind that I could run this little mom-and-pop operation, despite the fact that, during this period of time, I was drinking daily, buying marijuana whenever I could get the money, and using cocaine. I was able to obtain a loan from a bank by persuading my wife's grandfather to cosign for the loan. For $25,000, I bought the old man and his partner out, and I became a self-employed person. I thought that purchasing my own business was the greatest thing that could happen to me.

But something funny happened. Soon after I bought that store, I realized that I had to go in and open the doors, sell the product, and actually work. Looking back on it now, I realize that I didn't want that. I did it just for the thrill of doing it. When it came time for doing the footwork, the hard work of running the business, I wasn't prepared, at all. In fact, within two years, because of my use of drugs and alcohol, I took a business that had supported a family for more than a quarter of a century and ran it into the ground, robbed it blind. During these two years, I was introduced to other drugs, and I think I used more cocaine than I had during the whole previous time I had been doing drugs. And yet, I still didn't know what was wrong.

Something else happened, though, one day during the latter stages of my owning that business, when it had become clear to me that I didn't want to be there, anymore, but that I didn't know what I did want to do. A cousin of mine came into the store. I think there had been one occasion, three or four years earlier, when he and I had gotten high together. He had been to a rehab and had just gotten out. He asked me, "Man, are you still using that cocaine?" I said, "Yeah, every once in a while." And he told me, and I'll never forget this, "You know, that stuff ain't no good for you. I went to rehab, and I kicked it, and I'm trying to get my life together." I looked at him, thinking, "Huh, what does this guy know? He's just somebody who couldn't handle it."

That's what I thought of people who were trying to get help, who were leaving drugs and alcohol. I thought they were weak people. This was a problem—if it was a problem—that I could handle, you see. I didn't feel that I had any problem, though all around me, my life was coming apart: my marriage was becoming strained, my business was folding. But I couldn't see it.

I remember the first time that I knew, or at least I had an inkling, that I had a problem with drugs. I had sold some paint, about $300 or $400 worth of it, to a friend. I took that money and went out and spent every penny of it on drugs, when I should have put it in the cash drawer at the business, to pay the supplier for the paint. I bought all that cocaine, and I looked at it and wondered why. I needed that money. How was I going to pay the supplier? I kind of brushed it off. But I think that was when I really began to have a feeling that this drug, cocaine, might be affecting my judgment, to some degree.

Then my business collapsed, and my marriage fell into real turmoil as my wife realized that something was very wrong. When we first met, she had dabbled in drugs, but she did not get into them to the extent that I did, and she was able to stop. Now she came to me and said, "Vince, I've had enough. I want you to do something about this." I had lost the business, and I was unemployed. I had lost my self-respect. I was bankrupt, spiritually and emotionally. But I was in deep denial.

My wife talked to other people about this problem of drug addiction, and what her husband was going through, and what was happening to her marriage, and then she told me, "Unless you get help, you've got to leave." I was more afraid of losing her, I think, than of anything else, because she was my only hold on the world. I had lost everything else. And so, with a great deal of anger and a lot of pain, I enrolled in a treatment program.

This treatment program was at a local hospital. It had been determined that I could go there as an outpatient, that I wasn't so bad that I needed to be hospitalized. I went in with a bad attitude. I really didn't want to quit drinking or using drugs. However, when I did go, I began to hear words like "denial," and people talked about the Twelve Steps, Alcoholics Anonymous, Cocaine Anonymous, and the other Twelve-Step programs, and I began to want what they were talking about. But there was a part of me, deep, deep down, that still wanted to use. And I did use. We didn't have sessions on the weekends, but we were supposed to go to A.A. meetings, or other Twelve-Step meetings somewhere. I remember using on the weekends, and coming right back to treatment during the week.

Occasionally, we would get so-called "surprise" urinalysis tests. I recall *wanting* to get caught because I did want help. I just didn't know how to get it. One particular time, they did a urinalysis, and a couple of days later, they came back and said, "Somebody in the group has been using." And it was another guy. I thought they were going to finger me. But they didn't, and I was pissed. I said to myself, "Why couldn't I get caught?"

A couple of weeks after I went into treatment, my counselor committed suicide. I was just becoming very close to her. I came in one day and learned about her death, and that was another excuse to use. But I made it through the treatment program and went into after-care, even though I used throughout the whole process. I know, now, that I went into treatment for the wrong reason.

When I came out of treatment, I discovered a new drug, a drug that really was what I was born to use. And that was crack. Back when I started doing crack, it was fairly new. It had just kind of hit the scene, and it was cheap. The high was intense. Crack took me places where I had never dreamed I would go. It was different from snorting cocaine powder. Crack was so addictive.

The first time I took a hit of crack, it was in what is called a crack house. That's just a place where addicts get together and use. They cook the crack up, they share pipes, and they sit there for hours and hours, until there's no more left. When I first went there, I went with a so-called friend. I thought I would only try crack a couple of times. I went back, the second time, on my own. I had just received my pay from a job that I'd had for a very short period of time. I went over one evening after work, about four or five o'clock, and I did not leave there until I had spent every penny I had with me. After that, I was gone. From that point on, crack ruled my life.

Since then, I've been in many crack houses. I was known as "Red" there. I don't know why, maybe because I'm a light-skinned black person. Or maybe because I looked kind of red, especially if you were looking at me through rose-colored eyes. In the crack houses, I was known as a person who, if he had money, would spend it all. And if he had none, he would stand around and beg. I begged, many a night, at the crack house.

I've seen people pull guns out at the crack houses. On several occasions, I've seen the police raid other units. The crack houses were not usually detached houses.

They were more often apartments. We would see the police out there, and we would refuse to move. I actually had the feeling that if the police came right in where I was, I wouldn't move. They could do anything they wanted to with me. I did not want to take the risk of getting up and leaving that crack house, leaving whatever chance there was for me to get high. It's the worst existence any person could have, being in a crack house.

I smoked crack for about a year. It took only that long for crack to totally destroy whatever was left of my life. My last drug use took place three years ago. By this time, my wife had become pregnant again, and we had just had our second daughter a couple of days earlier. I had no job. I had been stealing money from anywhere I could get it. I was stealing money from my older daughter's purse, from my wife's purse. I was getting money by returning items to stores. I was writing bogus checks. I would do anything to get my hands on crack.

I was going to take my wife home from the hospital the following day, and I had no money. Before I left the hospital that afternoon, my wife gave me a personal check, made out for $50, asking me to cash it so I would have some money to come get her the next day and also to pick up a few things we needed. I was due back, later that evening, for a steak dinner the hospital provided for the new parents. My wife's father and sister had arrived in town, she had a brother already living there, and they were all with her for the blessed event. I left about four o'clock with that check.

To show you how insidious the disease is, I cashed that check and went straight to the crack house. There had been no question, even as I watched my wife make out that check and hand it to me, what I was going to do. When I left the hospital, I knew right where I was going. I ran through the parking lot to get to my car.

My last drunk was terrible. I took that money and within thirty to forty minutes, it was gone. Fifty dollars' worth of crack was nothing, to me. I proceeded to go back to our home and unplug the stereo and take it to the crack house. At the crack house, you could do anything: You could pawn. You could have sex. You could get high. Sometimes, you could even find a place to sleep, but not many people slept, there. I got $20 or $25 for my stereo at the crack house and smoked that up. I went back home, again, and got our only television set and brought it back and pawned that. I had paid almost $600 for that set, a few years before. I got $25 for it, and smoked that crack up, too. I was off and running. By midnight, I had nothing left to pawn. And, of course, I was too ashamed to go back to the hospital.

When I arrived back home, I heard the phone ringing, but I knew what they were doing. My wife's family was looking for me. So I didn't answer the phone. I decided I wanted to end it. I felt so low. It's almost impossible to describe, except to another addict or alcoholic. Only they know how bad you feel at that point in your life. I didn't know what was wrong with me. I loved my wife. I loved my daughter and my newborn baby. I knew I did. I did not know why I acted this way, but I felt that I could not live this way, every day, for the rest of my life. I just could not go on.

So I thought I would kill myself, but I was too much of a coward to go through with it. I did take some pills, in a feeble attempt at suicide, but the pills were not really of sufficient strength to even render me unconscious. I did not want to face my wife and family the next day. There was no way I could hide what I had done, with everything missing from our house. So I went up to the attic, lay down on the cold wooden floor, and prayed to God that I would die.

I woke up the next day and went to pick up my wife at the hospital. On the way back, I explained to her how I had pawned all the items in our house. When we got home, she had this look on her face, and I could tell that she had come to a decision, that she had had enough. She told me, "Vince, I've got a newborn baby here, just home from the hospital. I can't take care of her and you, too. You've got to go." And I knew she was right. Something inside of me wanted to beg her to let me stay. But there was also something inside that said, "No. Think of somebody else, for a change." I agreed to leave.

And that day, I packed up and left. At the time, I had a six-year-old daughter, a two-day-old baby girl, and a marriage of almost nine years' duration. I was thirty-two years of age, and I was flying back to my home state to live with my parents. My mother told me, later, that when she saw me get off that airplane, she thought I was a ghost, I looked so pale. I had virtually no clothes, and I had just one bag with me when I arrived. And I had no hope; I didn't see how I was going to be able to live without my wife, my children. I knew I couldn't live with this disease—not here, at home.

So, again, I thought I would commit suicide. I had always been a gun buff; I liked to hunt. When I was a young child, my grandfather would take me hunting, and those were some of the most enjoyable times of my life. Fortunately, my father had kept my shotguns at home with him, so they were not at my disposal when I was going through my earlier decision to kill myself, down South. But when I got home, I knew they were there, and I felt that I didn't really see that I could survive here very long. My life was over. There was nothing left for me.

Once I was home again, my father laid down the rules I would have to accept if I wanted to live under his roof. He told me that he wanted me to go to Alcoholics Anonymous meetings, and I said that I would. I didn't have much choice. I don't remember much about the first meetings I went to. All I remember is that somebody got up and said, "Vince, we're going to love you until you love yourself." That was the first time anyone had ever said that to me. I grabbed hold of that.

But it wasn't quite enough to hold on to, so a guy came up to me at my second meeting, after hearing me whine and complain about how I'd lost my whole family and my life was over, and so on, and he said, "You sound like you need a sponsor." And I replied, "Yeah, I guess I do." And he said, "Well, I'm going to be your sponsor." Then he added, "You might need something to do during the day, so I'm going to give you a job, too."

This man not only became my first sponsor, he also became my first boss, in sobriety. He was in construction, and he hung sheet rock. We would go to jobs together, just the two of us, as generally this work, in a house, is just a two-man job. He would pick me up, because I didn't have a car, sometimes as early as five o'clock in the morning, and he would take me to work. We would work together all day, and we would talk about the program, and he would impart little mottoes, such as "First Things First," "Easy Does It," "One Day at a Time," and "No relationships in the first year," because, of course, as I began to feel a bit better, I began to want things. And I began to satisfy myself, but he would keep me straight on that. At the same time, he was teaching me a trade, and I loved him.

This went on for about three or four months, and that feeling of doom, and of wanting to commit suicide, began to go away. I still had compulsions to use, but eventually they subsided. I did a 90-and-90 [ninety meetings in ninety days], as it was suggested, and my life started to change. Now, some of these changes that occurred in my life were subtle. But others were drastically, terribly quick.

My sponsor and I split up, as far as the job was concerned. He remained my sponsor, but he got back together with his old partner, and I went on to another job. I was a courier for a while.

I had an idea in my mind, though, something I'd wanted to do, back when I was using, in the banking field. Of course, I had no hope of attaining it. I had no college diploma. I had left school after my second year. But someone in the program came up to me one day and said, "Vince, this might be something good for you," and set me up with a job interview. That interview led me to the career I am enjoying today.

The way this program works is truly wonderful, and my life continued to change really fast. I began to communicate with my wife, and we even started to talk about getting back together. I had been sober for about eight or nine months, and I was starting a new career. I was feeling good about myself and thought that I was accomplishing something.

Around this time, I was introduced to another fellowship, Chemically Dependent Anonymous. I had been going to A.A., but alcohol was not really my drug of choice; crack cocaine was. I remember someone pulling me aside and asking, "Hey, have you ever been to a C.D.A. meeting?" And I hadn't. So later on that week, I went to a meeting of C.D.A., and man, it is almost impossible to describe my feelings as I sat there and listened to other people talk about their experiences with drugs, their experiences with coke! You see, in A.A., we talked a lot about drinking, and I would have to try to substitute, in my own mind, the word "coke" for "alcohol" when people talked about their experiences. Sometimes I was able to do that, and sometimes I wasn't.

Not until I attended my first C.D.A. meeting did I realize just how much I needed that program. I needed to be somewhere around people I could sit down with and talk about how it *felt* to do drugs, what it was like out there. At my first C.D.A. meeting, I was really uncomfortable because I was hearing the God-honest truth about things. Somebody was telling my story, and it didn't feel very good when they were talking about drugs.

I talked to my sponsor, who had never done drugs (he was an ex-alcoholic), and he said, "Vince, if those people help you like that, it's a program you have to incorporate into your life." I began attending C.D.A. meetings regularly and got involved in the program. It was good for me because I was a newcomer, and C.D.A. was kind of a new fellowship. As the new kid on the block, it was easy for me to become involved because there were a lot of possibilities for commitment, but not so many people to fulfill them.

If it weren't for those first few commitments, through C.D.A., I don't know that I'd have had the courage to do some of the other things that I've been able to do since I have been in the program. C.D.A. and A.A. have been lifesavers to me. And the program, overall, has helped me to come to terms with who I am: that I am an addict and alcoholic, that I have a disease, and that there is something I can do about it today.

I'm happy to be able to share my story about my addiction, about my experience with crack, about my experience with alcohol, now. I'm coming up on my three-year anniversary this month—three years out of the crack house; three years out of hell. I never could have dreamed, in my using days, that I would be sitting here in a home with my family back together, with a two-week-old son born of the same mother as my first two children. Three years ago, but for the grace of

God and the fellowship, that would not have been possible.

Working the Twelve Steps of the program, getting involved, doing what I can, has made my life so busy that I often don't have as much time to spend with my family or on the program as I would like. But this program is the most important thing in my life. Without it, without the God of my understanding, the Twelve Steps, the people in the fellowship, I would have nothing.

I hope that the few things I have to say here will help someone else. God put me on this earth, and this program is teaching me the reason why I am here. I'm not on this earth to be a success in business, and I don't believe that I've been put here to teach everybody some new way of life. I think that God put me here to live a productive life and to do what I can to help another suffering alcoholic and addict. And if, along the way, He provides me with the things that I need, and throws in a couple of the things that I want, that's just icing on the cake.

Crack cocaine took me to the bottom, and now C.D.A. and A.A. have taken me up, almost to the top. I don't know how far I can go. I just know that I love the way my life is now. I want things to continue to get better. And I know that as long as I stay sober, one day at a time, as long as I don't take a drink or a drug, they will.

Chapter 18

THINGS I MUST EARN

When I heard the statement, at my first Chemically Dependent Anonymous meeting, "I was sick and tired of being sick and tired," I was startled into my first glimmer of hope. For three years, prior to coming into the rooms, I had suffered from anxiety, fear, bad nerves, diarrhea, loneliness, and despair. I was considering the possibility of suicide, as there seemed no other way out. Doctors had proclaimed me physically sound but suggested I see a psychiatrist. The psychiatrist proclaimed me mentally "loose" and promptly equipped me with medication to calm my nerves. Ironically, my nerves were shattered because of my abuse of drugs and alcohol.

The sedatives I was placed on I took only as prescribed, but I still suffered from fear, anxiety, loneliness, and emptiness. I had stopped doing most drugs, as oftentimes I would experience anxiety attacks from getting high, but I still drank alcohol and used tranquilizers to soothe my shaking insides. I would often hyperventilate, and I had an intense fear of going crazy. Life had ceased to be fun. All the good times were gone. I was just existing, and I wanted so much to feel normal again. I wasn't asking to get high anymore, just to stop hurting. Consequently, when I heard, "I was sick and tired of being sick and tired," I could really relate to that.

I met the people in the rooms, and they told me it didn't have to be that way anymore. They also told me I only had to get sober once. After some time in the program, I can truthfully say it's a lot easier to stay sober than to get sober. At first, I went through some horrible withdrawals and a lot of emotional pain, but the people in the fellowship told me to hang in there, that it would get better. And it did. I have wonderful friends in the program, and my life just keeps getting better. Sobriety is a gift, and I now feel very privileged to be a part of C.D.A.

In the beginning, I also experienced a lot of denial. Even though I was sick and hurting, I kept listening to the events in the people's stories, not the feelings. I consoled myself by claiming, "I'm not that bad." I had never had a DWI, I had never gone to jail, and so on. Therefore, I had a slip.

When I came back into the program, my sponsor told me to get honest and made me do a written First Step. I had to look at the unmanageability of my life caused by my use of all of the chemicals. I never got involved in my child's activities, joined P.T.A., or became a den mother because getting high was my top priority. Feeling the guilt, remorse, and anxiety from the "great" time I had the night before was another aspect of this unmanageability.

Spending the family money to party, wetting the bed, experiencing blackouts were part of this disease, too. My inability to stop using chemicals, even though I wanted to, proved that I was powerless. I had tried jogging, exercise, vitamins, and religion, and I still couldn't stay sober. The program was the only thing that worked for me.

Today, I am so grateful to C.D.A. for giving me hope and teaching me how to live sober, one day at a time. C.D.A. taught me not to worry about which chemical I was using. It was not what, or even how much, I used. It's what it was doing to me. I thought that I wasn't an alcoholic because I didn't drink every day. But this addiction disease is cunning, baffling, and powerful. For my slip, as it turned out, was on alcohol.

C.D.A. taught me to realize that, even though I wasn't a daily drinker, there wasn't a day that went by that I didn't put some sort of mood-changing chemical into my system. So I have to consider myself chemically dependent. Alcohol, tranquilizers (even medication), pot, and diet pills are all chemicals. In my case, using any kind of chemical is just feeding my addiction. Thank God, I stuck with the winners who were honest enough to tell me the truth about my disease.

Members of the fellowship also told me that if I wanted what they had, I had to do what they did. They didn't seem to be hurting the way I was. They were even smiling. They told me, "Meeting makers make it," and said that I should get to a meeting every day. Get a sponsor, get a Home Group, get involved—these were other suggestions for recovery. I did all these things because I was willing to go to any length to stop hurting. I was also told to pray to a God of my understanding. I chose a loving, caring God Who speaks through the people in the program, and my recovery was well on its way.

I would be lying if I said that, because I've been sober for some time now, everything is a bed of roses. However, it's much better than it was. I still go through a great deal of emotional pain, but I'm told that it's part of the growth. I do get glimpses of peace of mind and serenity. And, little by little, I'm beginning to get out of myself. My head still "thinks" too much, but it's not as loud or as frantic as it used to be.

The people in C.D.A. told me that it would take time to get well. I drank and drugged daily for nine years, so I have to be patient about my recovery. "TIME" stands for "Things I Must Earn," and as long as I trust in God, clean house (Fourth and Tenth Steps), go to meetings, and pray, I can get well. I also have to pass what I've received on to others, in order to keep it. I must do for the newcomer what was done for me when I came in. And it seems I feel my best when I try to give it away. All in all, I have a great deal of hope for the future because of the program. Thank you, C.D.A., for giving me back my life and my sanity.

Chapter 19
RECOVERED, NOT CURED

My name is Bill B., and I am a grateful recovered alcoholic. My father was also an alcoholic and, perhaps because of that, was physically abusive to me when I was a child. When I was seven years old, I made a decision that he would never again make me cry. This does not mean that I didn't use tears to get what I wanted, but I did turn off most of my feelings after that. I did not really cry again until I was thirty-one years of age and had been sober for a whole year.

I took my first drink when I was around nine years old. It was a swallow of whiskey, and it tasted terrible. But it felt great when it got down to my stomach. I took drinks from the bottles in the house over the next three years, but I never got drunk. When I was twelve years old, I took about a half of a fifth of rum to school with me. I drank most of it, but I did not get drunk. I just got a good buzz.

One New Year's Eve, I got a pint of whiskey and drank it in about ten or fifteen minutes. This was my first real drunk. I got sick and had a blackout. For the next seventeen years, when I drank, I usually got drunk and sick and had blackouts. When I drank, I usually got into some kind of trouble. I rebelled against all authority. For the next five years, it was great for me, but not so great for my family. My mother finally suggested that I get out of the house. So I joined the Army, also at her suggestion.

In the early sixties, I was sent overseas, and there the party started. I drank almost daily. I also started using drugs. I smoked grass and hash. I took speed while I was on leave, for about fifteen days. I also took a hallucinogen, for the first time, while I was in Europe. Alcohol and drugs made me think I was cool. I almost got kicked out of the Army, but I talked my way out of that, receiving an honorable discharge three years after I'd joined up.

I then moved back in with my mother and told her that I was a changed man. That made two lies. Lie number one: I had not changed. Lie number two: I was still a kid, not a man. For the next three years, I drank and used no drugs. Yet trouble was still with me. I had two auto accidents, caused by excessive drinking, in the same month.

I decided to go to college but quit because school got in the way of my playing. I thought of myself as Peter Pan. I did not want to grow up. I was arrested, many times, for drinking and being drunk in public, for disturbing the peace, and, one time, for trespassing—in a bar. I had been asked to leave and refused to do so. The police were called, and I was put in jail.

A friend bailed me out and took me back to my car. I drove around for about an hour, going seventy to eighty miles per hour most of that time. I really wanted a police officer to pull me over. On the seat next to me was a nine-shot, .32-caliber automatic. I fully intended to shoot any officer who pulled me over, to get even for having been arrested. Luckily, no one stopped me, so I just went home.

The next morning, when I woke up, I remembered

what I had done. Of course, I never even considered stopping the drinking, but I did give away the gun. I realize now that I was in total denial that I had any problem with alcohol at that stage of my addiction.

Near the end of the sixties, I took LSD for the first time, and I loved it. I ate LSD, on an almost daily basis, for four years. By now, I had started dealing drugs, too, and I tried just about every one of them. I loved PCP pills, speed, hash, and mushrooms, in addition to the LSD. I did not drink very much during this period. And I never got into needles—probably because my brother was a diabetic, and I had had to give him his shots when I was young. But I became a hippie, during the next year, and started mixing drugs and alcohol.

Then my life really went crazy. I won a court case and received a settlement of about $7,000, and I went on a very long binge. I started using PCP and alcohol daily. I was also snorting cocaine, to mellow me out. I bought the kind of car a teen-ager would love, although I had just turned thirty. The girls I liked were teen-agers, too. They liked money, drugs, alcohol, long hair, and fast cars. I was on top of the world because I had all of those things, and that made me cool.

During the next year, I had a lot of blackouts and woke up in some strange places. I would go to my brother's house and pass out on the couch. He told me that he was afraid he would wake up one morning and find me dead, but it meant so little to me that I didn't even remember his telling me that until he reminded me later. One morning, I woke up in a house and heard a man asking me what I was doing there. On the table was about a half of a fifth of Scotch, and I was in my underwear. I asked the man for a ride home, but he evidently had no sense of humor.

While I was hitchhiking home, I figured out what had happened. I had been with a friend, and we had gone to a bar and had been invited to a party. I remembered going out to the car to get another bottle of Scotch and taking a drink before going back to the party. I had obviously gone into the wrong ground-floor condo. Sometime during the night, I had taken off my clothes and passed out.

Another time, I came out of a blackout while I was driving and saw a car cutting me off. I went off the road, down a long hill, and stopped, luckily, without hitting anything. While I was walking back up the hill, I slowly realized that the vehicle that had blocked me off was a police car. I asked the officer why he had cut me off, and he told me that I had gone through a tollbooth without paying the toll. He had chased me across the tollbridge, going over eighty miles per hour, and had intercepted me when I still refused to stop. I really must have handed him a good line that night, because he only gave me a $17 ticket for my failure to pay the toll. Somehow, he let me drive away, despite the fact that I was wasted.

When I began to realize that I had only $900 left of the $7,000 settlement I had received less than two months before, I decided that I had better find a job. I began looking for sales jobs and, by the end of the month, had received an offer from a carpet wholesaler. The salesman I was to replace had made $35,000 in the previous year, I was told. I thought that this was the best day of my life. I went home, got all my PCP and cocaine, and went out to celebrate. I had almost a full fifth of Scotch in the car, and I bought a case of beer.

I celebrated getting that job from around noon until midnight. During the day, the police pulled me over twice and searched my car, but they let me go. I guess they were looking for drugs, but they never searched *me*, which is where my drugs were hidden. About midnight, I decided that driving home was not such a good idea, so I went for a long walk. When I got back to my car, a couple of hours later, I drove around the parking lot and felt that I was now able to drive. But on the way home, I was pulled over again. I was very upset.

When the police officer asked me to get out of the car, I said, "This is the third time I have been stopped by your police department today, and I don't like this harassment." I felt that I had been driving perfectly fine. The officer asked me, again, to get out of the car. I said, "You tell me why you pulled me over, and then I might get out of the car." I still refused to get out when he ordered me to do so a third time. He then said, "Mr. B., you were going five miles per hour. Now, please get out of the car." He seemed very nervous, so I finally got out. I agreed to take a Breathalyzer test and was taken to the police station.

There, I got into a fight with some police officers and went into a convulsion that was caused by the excess of alcohol and drugs in my system. The police called an ambulance, and I was taken to the hospital. In the next twenty-four hours, my heart stopped beating three times, but the doctors were able to bring me back to life each time. That was fifteen years ago. I have not had a drink of alcohol, or used any drugs not prescribed by a doctor, since that day.

I believe that I made a decision to live, at that time. I went to my first Alcoholics Anonymous meeting five days later, while I was still in the hospital. I have been trying, to the best of my ability, to work the Twelve Steps of the program ever since. Very early in A.A., I met a friend there who had drunk and drugged, just as I had. He asked me to identify with those people in A.A., and I did what he suggested.

I know, today, that I must practice the Twelve Steps, each day, if I want to stay sober and enjoy life. I want to have a good life, so I do what I believe my God wants me to do. I now have a house, a good job, a wife, a son, a baby girl, and lots of other *things*. But if we work for them, the program promises that we will receive even more important gifts: happiness, freedom, peace, selflessness, wisdom, security, and a sense of God's plan for our lives.

I was able to be in the delivery room when my baby girl was born, eight years ago. That birth coincided with the exact date of the seventh anniversary of my sobriety. I could not have made such a coincidence happen. I believe it somehow symbolized how God's plan works in my life.

This past year, a woman I grew up with asked me to take her to some meetings of Chemically Dependent Anonymous. She was a cocaine addict who had tried A.A. but had gone back to using drugs again. I began taking her to some of the C.D.A. meetings in the area. I thought I was "Twelve Stepping" her, but actually *she* "Twelve Stepped" *me* into C.D.A. Although she, unfortunately, did not stop using, C.D.A. was able to give me new insights into my own behavior.

Not too long ago, I had a spiritual awakening—the educational variety—at a meeting. I realized that the alcoholic part of me could be described as *over*sensitive, while my drug-addict side could best be called *in*sensitive. I have spent thirteen years cleaning up my alcoholic behavior. My Higher Power has now given me C.D.A. so I can work on the drug-addict personality problems that I had been ignoring.

I had never put *myself* on the Eighth-Step list of "persons we had harmed." Because of C.D.A., I now realize that I definitely belong on that list. I am working the Eighth Step on myself now, so I can better understand the relationship I should be having with myself. I intend to make amends to myself, and I believe that doing this will make me better able to serve God and my fellow human beings.

I know that I can only live one day at a time, but as it is my intention to stay sober in A.A., it is also my intention to stay sober in C.D.A., for the rest of my life. I need and want what both fellowships have to offer me.

Chapter 20
DREAMS COME TRUE

As a child, I was accustomed to being the center of attention. I was an A student, involved in music, art, ballet, and horseback riding. Our family had horses, ducks, chickens, gardens, and a vineyard when I was growing up. I was very happy, as I recall, but even then I had unrealistic expectations about life. I lived in a fantasy world. I was totally unaware of any family problems.

My parents sent me away, the summer of my eleventh birthday, to my grandmother's. When I returned, my fantasy world was shattered. Mom and dad had split up and were planning divorce. My father became obsessed with religion and the church, and my mother pursued her career. I was no longer the center of attention. I had to take on additional responsibilities around the house, since mom was gone, and I had less and less time to be a kid.

I started drinking and drugging when I was twelve, not as a rebellious act, but rather to escape myself and my life, and to gain acceptance. I went to great lengths to hide the fact that I was getting high because I knew that if my father found out, I would be severely punished. But I was soon getting high every day, before and after school. I was sneaking booze into my locker and peddling drugs. By the eighth grade, I was hooked. The school knew it and had me seeing a counselor on campus, but my parents were still not informed about my problem.

Dad noticed other things, though. I had changed my friends. I skipped school, was hitchhiking, and was picked up by the police when I was supposed to be spending the night with friends. Finally, my father decided there were certain friends I was not going to see as long as I was under his roof. I moved back with my mother. I was fourteen years old.

A new school, new friends, and a new environment did not change anything. I got worse. In ninth grade, I was asked to attend a private school, in hopes that it would straighten me out. I declined the offer. I was using daily and knew where to get a good supply. THC was my drug of choice at the time, but I did whatever was available. I quit taking care of myself, refused to ride the school bus, and skipped school, again.

My mother was at the school constantly, trying to salvage my academic future. I had special classes, special consideration, and special counseling—none of which worked. I was sent to child psychologists and a Christian youth organization. The only thing I had any interest in at all was my art, and my mother tried desperately to keep that part of me alive. But, eventually, I lost all interest in that, as well. I was only interested in using and whatever it took to ensure that I always had something available.

I don't really remember why I went back to my father. I was getting very "soul sick," and I was trying to get back to the "good times" I recalled from my childhood. I remember riding in the car with my dad one day and thinking that everything would be all right. It was him and me against the world.

But he had found someone else, my stepmother, and I became very jealous of her. It was at this point that I started using as a rebellious act. I wanted to hurt others, and I did this by hurting myself. I got into harder drugs and more trouble. I was expelled from school. My father took me to a girls' ranch, at this point, and tried to convince me to stay. I told him I would run away if I were sent there. We returned home.

Finally, dad could take no more. I constantly broke house rules. I had become defiant and rebellious. He told me to get out, and I did. I didn't need him, or anybody, I thought. I could make it on my own. What did he know about life, anyway?

I moved in with a teen-aged girl who also drugged. Through her, I was introduced to heroin and the crowd that used it. Still wanting to be accepted, I did as they did. But even though I looked "bad" on the outside, I was scared on the inside. During this time, I attempted to hold down part-time jobs, but failed. I had to have money, though, so I resorted to various methods to get it, all of which I had sworn I'd never do. By now, my values had deteriorated to that point.

I was sixteen. Everything I owned would fit into a grocery bag, and I was strung out. I rarely knew what day it was. I should have died; but, for some reason, God spared me. One day, during all of this, I woke up with no idea where I was, or with whom. I wanted to go home.

I called my mom. She said that she hadn't known if I was dead or alive. She came and got me. This wasn't the end of my problems, however. As soon as I was better, I was at the doctor's office, getting "scripts." Not long after that, I found a dealer and was on the merry-go-round again.

Mom got me back into school. I stayed only long

enough to finish drivers' education, and then I dropped out. There were also problems at home. I started coming home drunk, or stoned, all the time. Or else I just didn't go home at all, sometimes for days. I was selling drugs out of the house. Things just came to a head, and I left on my own.

I moved in with a dealer I had met a couple of weeks earlier. It was supposed to be a temporary arrangement, but it turned into three insane years. At least I was off the streets. I got my high school equivalency diploma and started junior college. However, my drug addiction only allowed for one semester of that.

I would do anything for my dealer, to make sure I had an ample supply. I risked my life in numerous ways: the guns, the robberies, the smuggling, the twenty-four-hours-a-day traffic, the junkies who would sell you their souls, the police, and the whole underworld scene. It was scary, and yet I felt a little superior to "ordinary" people because I was living precariously.

Things got hot, though, and my relationship with my dealer was going downhill, since neither of us could pass up a good opportunity. At nineteen, I decided it was time to move on. So, once again, I called my mother. Perhaps this time it would be different, I thought. I moved out-of-state to be with her. I tried to quit drugs entirely, but I never gave much thought to my abuse of alcohol.

At first, it seemed that things might work out. I got a job at a factory, making minimum wage. I met the beer-and-pot crowd. I swore off hard drugs, but soon I met "angel dust," and, very soon after that, my addiction was in full force again. I was on the phone to my dealer, begging him to send me cocaine and to take me back. I was drinking more and more and doing crazier and crazier things. I was losing my mother's respect rapidly. She had already bailed me out of jail once. I tried religion to straighten myself out, but that only lasted a few weeks.

Finally, I decided I would go back to my dealer, where I would be safe and taken care of. I rationalized the move back down South by saying I was going to college there because it was cheaper. But when I arrived, my real scheme failed. Someone else had assumed my role as the dealer's girl. I went on a three-day binge over this. The binge resulted in a blackout, during which I threatened the dealer's new girlfriend and broke the windows in his house. After that, most of my blackouts were violent.

Now I needed a place to live. That's how I met my first husband—a tall, handsome guy who needed a roommate, and who also drank and drugged. I had no intention of marrying him, at the time. It just worked out that way. Our life was pretty routine: We would sleep late, work, and party all night. I held down various types of jobs as a waitress or bartender, which worked well with our lifestyle.

We had many drunk-and-violent fights. I left my husband three times and divorced him before we had been married a year. I believed *he* was my problem. I had wanted to make something of myself, and he was in the way. I had landed a job as a courier with a major corporation and had started attending school again, since the company would reimburse me. I was tired of bailing my husband out of trouble. Of course, once I got rid of him, I had no one else to blame.

I started hitting the bar scene heavily. In the mornings, I ate speed to get going and looked out the window to see whether my car was in the driveway or not. I generally kept last night's last drink next to the bed so I could just roll over and get a little help for getting up the next morning.

One morning, I woke up and felt that horrible sense

of impending doom, of going nowhere and just not knowing what's wrong. I hated myself. I called a self-help hot line, and they recommended that I go to the local mental health institution. I was screaming for help, but I could not see that my problem was drugs and alcohol abuse. So the progression continued.

I met my future second husband in a bar, but, as fate would have it, we also worked for the same company. I thought that he was "Mr. Wonderful," that my ship had come in. He would fix all my problems, and we would live happily ever after. He had a job that paid well, a house, and prestige. I decided that I would marry him, and, a year later, I did. He liked me because I was wild. I liked to ride motorcycles, drink, and party. I kept a fairly decent house, so he overlooked my bad blackout sprees.

Once, before we were married, I drove off the road in his pickup truck while I was in a blackout. I blew out two tires and tore up one side of the truck. This episode landed me in jail for the night. I lay in bed most of the next day, feeling sorry for myself. When my husband-to-be phoned me, I explained what had happened. He immediately dismissed the incident as if it had never occurred.

There were many similar incidents, in the years to follow, which he similarly ignored. Since my husband was not into drugs, I became a daily drinker and only did drugs when I had easy access to them. He had asked me to give them up, particularly the amphetamines I had been using, daily, when we met.

Soon after we married, we were transferred to a large city up North. I really believed that life would be different there. Six months later, I woke up from another bad drunk, wanting to die. I couldn't stand to live that way, anymore. For the first time in my life, I realized that it wasn't my marriage, the people we hung around with, or the activities we were involved in that were the problem—it was me and my drinking. I really wanted to quit. That was my last drunk, and my bottom.

I admitted myself to a rehab program, which is where I was introduced to the Twelve Steps and the program. I showed up at my first meeting with a broken nose and a broken spirit. I was ready to listen. I would do whatever I was told because I knew that I did not know how to quit drugs and alcohol on my own. I had tried, several times, in the last fourteen years. I found a sponsor who had been clean and sober for some time. Together, we began working the Steps.

Things did get better, because I was getting better, but there were still major changes to come. When I was sober for eight months, I was still living with a practicing alcoholic. It was getting harder and harder for me to "Let Go and Let God." I felt that if I did not take action, I would drink again. I decided my sobriety was more important than anything else. So I moved out on my own. As time went on, I realized that I had to let go of the relationship entirely. I believe, today, that this was God's will for me, as He has opened up other doors in my life which far replace any void that resulted from this breakup.

I'm also in the process of changing my career. I was never very happy with my profession, but I had never felt I could do anything else. Yet the program outlined in the Steps of Chemically Dependent Anonymous and the encouragement of individuals in the fellowship have helped me to reach for my dreams. I'm not afraid, anymore, to try new things. I attend a university where I am taking courses for a degree which will get me one step closer to what I want to do. As long as I stay clean and sober, a day at a time, my goals are within my reach. Without my sobriety, I have nothing.

It has been over two years since I quit using drugs and alcohol. I'm twenty-seven years old now, and I'm living as God intended for me to live, for the first time in my life. I am happy—joyous and free! Throughout my using days I would always say, "I just want to be happy." The problem was that I wanted something outside of myself to make me happy on the inside. Today, I'm truly happy on the inside because I'm comfortable with myself. I could never begin to describe all the blessings which I have received from this new way of life, but they include friends, love, security, and, most of all, peace.

Chapter 21

RITES OF PASSAGE

Hi! My name is Max, and I'm an addict-oholic. I'm powerless over everything but my attitude and my actions. I'm also powerless over pot and hashish.

It has only been a year and nine months since I stopped using pot on a daily basis, and nineteen months since I stopped taking *any* mood-altering substance, except for coffee. My "clean time" has just recently entered a phase which I dare call recovery. I am very grateful to be able to come into these rooms and listen to myself and others share their hope and strength, the wisdom of all our experiences. I have become truly fond of many people in the fellowship and really feel as if I belong.

A relationship with my Higher Power is the most difficult, and at the same time, most rewarding, part of the program, or process, of working the Steps. Meetings like these are what I think I have searched for all my life. The subjects we discuss, the level of honesty, are what I always thought meetings should be about. But I never found them until I started coming into these rooms. When I don't get to a meeting for one or two days, I feel very insecure, not necessarily that I'm going to go out and use, but just spiritually "out of practice."

I come to Chemically Dependent Anonymous meetings because I need help. I come to C.D.A. to admit to myself, my sponsor, Sterling S., and the people in the fellowship of anonymous addicts and alcoholics, that I am powerless against the drugs to which I have become addicted, especially marijuana. My life not only had become unmanageable; it, like my body, was seriously, gravely damaged through years of constant abuse. I have lost at least two jobs (and perhaps as many as ten) and have ruined two marriages and several relationships. I have caused pain to my parents and have very likely inflicted psychological damage on my daughter.

I started drinking, with that old gang of mine, when I was a teen-ager. I was fifteen, in the tenth grade, when I began trying to get blitzed on malt liquor every weekend. But even before that, there was an incident. When I was fourteen, I stole a quart of bourbon from my father's cellar stash. He had cases of booze stored down there because it was cheaper by the case, and he was frugal. I was very sneaky about the theft of this quart, pouring its contents into a one-quart, aluminum Boy Scout canteen and throwing the bottle away. Then I went with my three friends into a nearby woods. One of them was coming along to watch and take care of us, in case we got into trouble.

The rest of us, in a puberty rite of passage, guzzled one-third of the quart each, in the manliest way we could muster. Well, we certainly got drunk, and sick, and crazy. I was hanging from tree branches like an orangutan, my friends were puking from other trees, and there were great, melodramatic groans filling the woods. I went out on the road in front of a liquor store and lay down to get run over. It was part of my *macho* merit badge requirement, to prove to my peers that I was suicidal, a rebel without a cause, outrageous and crazy.

The sober friend called my Boy Scout patrol leader and his girlfriend for help. When they dumped my body into the leader's car, I told his girlfriend that I loved her. She screamed, and my patrol leader came running to save her. He was tall, and blond, and very heroic-looking.

When I was seventeen, to impress my peers, I guzzled all of a large pitcher of beer at a bar in a college town. All of a sudden, my eyes got very big, and my face had the unmistakably worried look of someone about to barf. A path opened in the crowd, and I was hurried down the gauntlet into the men's room. I was very proud of *this* rite of passage.

At the age of twenty, I went to a lot of trouble to find pot and smoke it. I finally found some, and it didn't do anything the first couple of times, but I had faith and kept trying. One night, as I was supposed to be performing blues-guitar songs at a now-defunct coffeehouse, I smoked some strong pot, and it finally worked. A friend kept asking me what was wrong, as I giggled uncontrollably, my legs writhing spastically. He said, "Come on, Max. Let's do the song." "What song?" I asked. " 'Stagolee,' like we planned in practice," he said. "O.K.," I said. "How does it go?" "Like this," said he, with a disgusted look on his face, as he jogged my memory.

When I then had to ask what chord it started with, and how to make that "D" chord, he became more and more angry with me. I was scarcely able to talk, I was giggling so much. But he showed me how to start. "Oh, yeah," I said, "and what was that next chord?" He told me I was disgusting, and I apologized, but my ribs were hurting from laughing so hard. The crowd was spellbound at this display of dopey stupor and helplessness. I staggered to the door, out to the sidewalk, down the street, laughing my head off. "I feel sorry for you, you pathetic dope fiend," my friend shouted down the sidewalk. Of course, I didn't believe, at the time, that I was any such thing. But I was just getting started.

Seventeen years ago, I was foiled by U.S. Customs agents in my first, and last, attempt to bring marijuana into the country. In an absurdly foolish adventure with three other young men, I hiked fourteen miles through the desert, at night, with several kilos in a knapsack on my back. I was brought to trial and convicted of failure to pay the tax on a controlled substance, a felony. The judge sentenced me to three years, twenty-eight days of which I spent in a federal detention center. I was then placed on probation.

In spite of such extremely obvious warning signs, it was not until my own child was born, four years later, that I remorsefully came to realize that marijuana smoking was undeniably and absolutely self-destructive. I then tried, on my own, to break myself of the habit, but was unsuccessful. Shortly before my daughter's third birthday, I began attending a series of individual and group sessions at a pastoral counseling center. That process took four years, and ultimately did prove successful, in that it resulted in a change in my behavior.

I have always wanted to be a writer, I think perhaps because I always enjoyed reading books. In college, I had great ambitions of someday becoming a famous author. During that notorious decade known as the sixties, I was in my twenties, and the ubiquitous presence of all kinds of drugs, and most specifically, marijuana, was not the given fact of life that it is today. It was only in books that I had ever even heard of these exotic substances, and the very idea of partaking of them was extremely remote and confined to literature, as far as I was concerned.

When I was actually invited to try some marijuana, I was not even dimly aware that I was among the first few drops of what was to become a tidal wave of drug users. Back then, it seemed smart to disdain alcohol and prefer the "relatively harmless" and "creativity-enhancing" effects of marijuana. I was, quite honestly, ignorant of the very serious dangers, psychologically, physically, and socially, into which I was placing myself every time I indulged. I imagined that the things I wrote when under the influence of pot were profound, publishable descriptions of the new frontier of the mind. I would not heed the warnings of parents or of "straighter" friends; when they urged me not to jeopardize my life, I proceeded obstinately down my own path. I really believed that I knew better than everybody else.

I also used pot to escape having to deal with problems. It enabled me to procrastinate, indefinitely, doing the work on myself I knew needed to be done. It allowed me to tolerate intolerable situations. I was absolutely out of control in my never-ending lust for the pleasure of the high, the escape from responsibility.

But now I am ready to pay the price. I am ready to experience the pain of awareness: that I was mistaken and stupid to waste so much precious time of my life doing drugs, that I may have caused my child to have cerebral palsy, a wrong for which there could never be adequate amends. No matter how horrible I feel, no matter how guilty, I vow to myself, and to my Higher Power, to remain clean in my body and mind, each day, one day at a time. I am willing, wholeheartedly, to try the Twelve Steps to recovery. Just making this statement fills me with hope for myself and the ones around me.

At this moment, I have nearly two years drug free. My old resentments are leaving, fading. I am doing a great deal of reading, have organized a book club, and am trying to get a teaching job. Meanwhile, I am working every day as a trim carpenter for a home builder. I have a terrific fiancée, as well as my marvelous daughter. There is no desire for pot, or for any other drug, today. I feel "high on life" and enjoy each day with gratitude.

My great foe is laziness, spiritual and physical, the deadly sin of sloth. I am more afraid of it, in myself, than the compulsion to go out and use. Truly speaking, one leads to the other, and staying off drugs is the best way for me to combat sloth. Staying off drugs is my number one job, my priority, from now on. I need to remember that every day, to begin life on earth. One toke is no joke.

I pray to my Higher Power to be my guide. As Virgil guided Dante through the inferno, I humbly beseech *my* Guide to lead me out of the hell of marijuana.

Chapter 22
DARKNESS DISPELLED

My name is Anne L. I'm chemically dependent. And here's my story, as best I can recall it. I was the middle of five children. We moved, as a family, a total of six times by the time I was ten years old. So I didn't have any real close friends, growing up, or else I lost them when we moved. I became used to always being the "new kid." Out of all the children in our family, I was the quiet, studious one. You never had to worry about Anne, because she pretty much took care of herself. I remember reading and listening to music a lot.

I feel I grew up very quickly, around the age of twelve, because there was so much going on at home. My parents hadn't gotten along well at all for quite a while. There wasn't fighting, so much as silence, around the house. My mother was having emotional difficulties, and she would confide in me. I remember feeling helpless about the whole situation and wishing there were something I could do. Yet it was out of my hands. My mother ended up having a breakdown and going into the hospital. Once she got out, there was talk about divorce and where each one of us children would go. Everything was up in the air.

Shortly after this time, I was introduced to booze. I'll never forget the first time I had "enough," to the point where alcohol had any effect on me. The feeling I had was one of pure joy. I was elated at the tingling in my fingers, the light-headedness, and the *good* feeling I had from that very first time. It just grabbed hold of me. From then on, I took any chance there was to have a drink. I loved what it did for me. I wasn't shy and withdrawn, anymore. I felt O.K. about me, and it was fun being around people. There was no more discomfort. I was transformed, in some way, so I could be a part of things and could feel I belonged. From that point on, booze became a part of my life.

It wasn't too long afterwards that I was introduced to other drugs—to grass, and acid, and uppers and downers, and all the other things that were passed around in the crowd I wound up in. Everybody was doing it, and everybody seemed O.K., doing it. Drugs were nothing that I thought might harm me. They were just recreation—fun—I owed it to myself!

And so, throughout the rest of high school, and into college, I partied whenever I could, and the disease that I didn't know I had progressed. Looking back now, I can see that most of the symptoms were there from the beginning. I had blackouts. My tolerance was very high: other people would be stumbling and slurring, but I could handle it. I felt inwardly proud of that fact. But it was a sign. All along, I felt I could handle the drugs, that *I* was the master of *them*—until it turned around. It was a gradual turn, but one that picked up speed very quickly, once it started.

At first, it was quite gradual—shakes in the morning, blackouts where I didn't remember, even vaguely, what had gone on while I was out of it. I'd lose whole evenings; I'd lose whole days and weekends. There were feelings of just wanting to get away, that something was wrong. But I couldn't figure out what it was. So I wound up going to some shrinks. I thought maybe I was having some of my mother's emotional problems. Maybe it was hereditary. There was a discomfort, an unrest, a fear that was building, growing inside of me.

I dropped out of college, during my senior year, because of my growing anxiety and paranoia when I was with people. For the next two years, I had a job in an office where I was alone three days of the week, but I lost that because my performance wasn't getting any better. I moved back home and, after five months, hit bottom.

During those five months, I experienced a deepening depression, a growing hopelessness and helplessness, a confusion about what was going on. I really felt I was losing my mind, that the only thing keeping me together was the booze. By this time, I was drinking around the clock, yet it wasn't working anymore. I'd get up—and throw up. I wasn't eating right. I wasn't bathing. I was afraid to be around my mother and sister, and that scared me. I hated sunny days; I'd draw the curtains. I took the phone off the hook. I thought about suicide.

I had no idea what alcoholism or addiction were. I had been so wrapped up in myself for so long that, even if I had known someone (and I surely must have) who had a problem with booze and drugs, I wouldn't have seen it. About the only thing I could see, at the end, was that I was alone, and that I needed help and didn't know how to get it. I was too proud to ask. I was too proud to admit what was going on with me.

I didn't like myself very much, however, despite my pride. I didn't understand the creature I had turned into. I'd been through the one-night stands, waking up the next day not knowing the person who was lying beside me, not being able to find my car, not wanting to hear people talking about what I had done the night before. I didn't know how to get back to the real world. I wanted some*one*, or some*thing*, to just come along and take me away from the place I'd wound up in.

One night, I took a bunch of pills from the medicine cabinet, but I soon went and told my mother what I had done. She called the hospital and stayed up with me all night. I don't know where my head was when I took those pills. But it was clear that something had to be done with Anne. My family was disgusted with me. So, an appointment was made for me to see another shrink. I felt like a child. I thought, "Here we go with the shrinks, again. They didn't help before. How can they help now?"

The next night, two programs were on TV, back-to-back, that dealt with addiction. My head was clear enough that I could relate to the stories being told. In one of the programs, there was a person who was getting along in life all right until he stumbled across the whole drug scene. Then everything turned into chaos, and he was hurting. Yet, by the end of the show, something had turned things around so his life became O.K., again. One of the programs also mentioned Alcoholics Anonymous.

That night, evidently in a blackout, I called an A.A. Inter-Group. I don't know whether I reached a person, or a recording, or what. But the next morning, someone called me, and I found out about a meeting that was right up the road from our house. I called a sister to come get me, because I was not able to drive. I was too wired and filled with fear to get behind the wheel of a car. My sister agreed to take me to the meeting.

I don't remember much about that first meeting, other than the fact that I was made to feel welcome. The warmth and caring that I saw in those people's eyes was in such contrast to the looks of disgust and intolerance I'd received from my family. It was like sunshine coming in through the gray fog I had been in, for so long. And the people told me to come back. They told me I would be all right, that they understood what I was going through.

That meant so much to me, when they said that they understood, because I didn't understand, myself. I didn't think anybody could. I left the meeting, and I broke down and cried. My mind wasn't clear enough to analyze anything then, but I was feeling hope. I do remember, too, that I went home and poured out all the booze.

Someone from the group came to pick me up, the next day, for another meeting. There, the A.A. people said, "Don't drink. Just for today, don't drink." And I didn't. I went through the shakes, and the anxiety, with my mind going in all different directions. Yet I didn't even think about drinking. I can see what a real gift that was, now. But, at the time, I wasn't able to realize it. I was still in a fog.

In the beginning, people were driving me around to the meetings, and it was as if I were being *led*. I really didn't know what their program was all about. I just knew I was no longer in that bad place, and people were telling me that my life could be different. I wanted so much for that to be true. So I would listen, as best I could. And when they called on me, I would pass.

But I found people who made me feel comfortable talking with them. They came up to *me*, after the meetings. I would ask them what this or that meant, in the program. They gave me some literature, and they gave me phone numbers to call if I got into trouble or just wanted to talk some more, and they gave me love. Things gradually began to sink in, both what was being said in the meetings and what the fellowship was all about. I knew I was where I belonged, and I came to understand that I had a disease.

It was so comforting to know I wasn't alone. I wasn't to blame for what had happened, and there was a solution, a better way to live. And I was *there*. I was learning about it and was a part of it. I kept coming back, and I got a sponsor. I began going to Step Meetings and listening to things I didn't really want to hear, listening to talk about a Higher Power.

I'd shut off God a long time ago—when He hadn't mended my parents' marriage, when I saw that He left children around the world hungry and homeless, when I realized that He let so many innocent people go through suffering and allowed them to be killed. The people in the program talked about a God *as you understand Him*. I had to admit I didn't understand God, at all. But, by listening, I found out that I wasn't the only one who had that problem. As long as I tried to keep my mind open, was honest with myself, and was willing to find another way, I would make it.

And I didn't want to go back out. I was afraid, from the stories people told, that if you didn't work the Steps, if you didn't change, you would end up back out there. I knew what was waiting out there for me, if that happened. The certainty that I was an alcoholic and that I was in the right place, in the program, has stuck with me ever since then, except for a couple of shaky periods in the beginning where God intervened before I had even admitted that He was there.

Rather than face the darkness, I prayed, and there was always an answer to my prayer. There was always a better feeling, inside, that I was being taken care of. It might not, necessarily, always be in the manner that I would like, but I knew I was being watched over, and, no matter how tough the situation or how shaky I might feel, I would be O.K. And so I came to understand God, in a small, beginning kind of way, as a

Force which would help me and guide me, comfort and strengthen me. God became a friend. He was everywhere. But, most of all, He was in the rooms, where you people were talking. Because of Him, and you, that feeling of "O.K.-ness," that we can fight together, whatever the problem, was there.

So I proceeded through the Steps, and I began taking part in some service work: in making coffee, and then in answering the phone, in sharing at meetings, and then in sharing outside of meetings. And the program became more a part of my life as I practiced praying, in the morning and at night. Even though there were still some things I didn't understand, as long as I sat and listened, and kept that willingness to try, I found I was either able to understand better or able to accept that I didn't have to understand everything, yet.

Now my life is a whole lot better, much richer and fuller. It's not that I've been restored to anything that I was before. I feel I have been restored to so much more than I have ever been. I have learned that this disease I have is three-fold: spiritual, mental, and physical. As I make progress in recovery, I realize that there aren't any real limits, other than those I set on myself, in any of these areas. Through working the program, growth can be a constant—will be a constant—part of my life.

Although I started out in A.A., a great part of my story lies in Chemically Dependent Anonymous, and in being around and watching its growth, from the very first meeting in one man's house, to the many meetings of this group available today. In A.A., there were some old-timers who frowned upon talk about drugs. They would say that their meetings were for *alcoholics*. One of the first questions I asked, after being in A.A.'s program not too very long, and I asked it of a younger member, was, "Does this mean I can't have any pills, or smoke any grass, or whatever?" She replied, "I strongly recommend that you don't. Anything affecting you from the neck up is very likely to carry you back out."

The meaning of that was firmly planted in my mind when a fellow who had been secretary of the Young People's Meeting at A.A. shot himself in the head. After I found out what he had done, I went back to the member who had told me to avoid any substance abuse and asked her about this young man, a close friend of hers. She said that he had maintained his sobriety from booze, but he had been smoking grass, and he never really *got* the program. He couldn't; his mind wasn't clear. The whole thing can't work if you aren't willing to go to any length. It made quite an impression on me.

But there was also a disillusionment that this man had been in what he had thought was the perfect place for help. And, somehow, the message hadn't come across—a message that might have saved his life. The message is that it is not just alcohol that is dangerous. Anything you put into your system that is altering your mind is unsafe.

Rick R. was the one who really got C.D.A. started. He was my sponsor's boyfriend. I remember being at their house when he came home from A.A. meetings and seeing how upset he was that somebody had mentioned drugs and other members had made some derogatory remarks about drug users. I know, in my own case, how important it had been to feel that these people accepted me. If I had felt rejected when I first came into A.A., I might not have come back. Comments about my using drugs other than booze would have made me feel that A.A. was not the right place for me.

Luckily, perhaps, booze was the only substance I was using when I came to A.A., but I could just as easily have been on something else. There were many people who had come to A.A. for help, even though alcohol was not their primary problem, because there wasn't any other program around for them. They wound up back outside those doors because, for some reason, they felt, or were made to feel, that they didn't belong or were not welcome there.

And there were also people in the A.A. program, including the fellow who had committed suicide, who felt that they were sober as long as they didn't have alcohol inside them. The quality of their sobriety was very questionable. Rick felt, strongly, that you couldn't justify the use of any drug other than prescribed medication, and that you had better be sure you understood the medical need for even that use of drugs before you took them. An addict can't safely use any drug that affects his mind, and even prescriptions have to be monitored carefully.

That is the force behind C.D.A.—to help people who have a problem with addiction, regardless of what the drug is. C.D.A. was formed so these people would have a place where they could come and feel accepted. I decided I wanted to be a part of it, just from what I had seen and learned in the small amount of time I had been around the group. It is amazing how C.D.A. has grown since then, a definite proof that the need was there. I now feel very much a part of both fellowships, since C.D.A. is based upon the same foundations that A.A. has found to be effective.

And I think times have changed. The membership in the program of A.A. has changed, today, to the point where people are pretty comfortable in going back and forth between both meetings. There are so many potential candidates for either A.A. or C.D.A. out there, now. And, after all, both programs are really proclaiming the good news of the same hope and the same gift from a Higher Power that is there, no matter what you call that Force, to help people: to help them out of that dark place, to show them a new way of life, and to give them companions along the way. My thanks to all of you in C.D.A. Good luck, and God bless.

Chapter 23
GOING TO ANY LENGTH!

I believe "GOING TO ANY LENGTH" on a daily basis has been a very important factor in my recovery, in Chemically Dependent Anonymous. This concept involves several factors, which I will try to discuss briefly.

Sponsorship has been very important to me. I was scared to ask Danny to be my sponsor. But after I did, and we talked, I felt much better, and I have received good direction and suggestions from him. Having a sponsor has allowed me to let someone know what is going on inside of Brian. It has made me realize that I am not unique and that I am not alone.

I had to become willing to let go of the friends from my past who were still using when I decided to try for sobriety. I was very sick, and being around those people only increased my chances of getting loaded again. I was not willing to take that chance. Today, I have nothing in common with those people. They don't call, and neither do I. Some have died. Some have gone to jail. But I have become healthier—physically, mentally, and spiritually—and have more friends who love me than I've ever had before in my life.

I could not go to bars, events at the stadium, or

concerts after I first entered the program. Any time I had ever gone to these places, I had been loaded. I was afraid that the old tapes in my head would start playing if I went back, and that I would start using again. At the time of this writing, I have been to a few clubs and stadiums with program people, but I still do not feel really comfortable about it, after almost two years clean. I have not been to any concerts because of all the drugs that I would be around there.

In the program, there is a saying: "Meeting makers make it!" That has been essential in my recovery. In almost two years, I have missed meetings on only four days. In my first six months, I had strong compulsions to use, and the meetings saved my life. I would go to a noon meeting, and then to another one at night. Then, before I knew it, it would be midnight, and I had another day of sobriety.

Right now, I attend at least one meeting a day. When I can, I attend two or three a day, depending on how I feel. I have asked people who have gone back out and then come back into the program why they left, and every person told me that when they stopped going to meetings, they slipped. The meetings are where I learn to live clean. I never knew how to function in life without being under the influence. But, today, I am finding out how to do that, with the help of my fellow addicts.

Another suggestion I heard when I came to C.D.A. was, "Try not to get involved in a relationship for the first year." I did not even date anyone for eight months. It was hard not dating for that period of time, but I suffered from low self-esteem, anyway. I knew that I really didn't have anything to offer someone else, at that time.

I had gotten sober once before and had become involved in a relationship at four months into recovery. The end result was that I got loaded again. I had made that person the number one priority in my life. So I slacked up on my meetings, I stopped calling my sponsor, and I ceased communicating with people in the program. I believe, today, that when I depended on that person to make me feel good, I also gave that person the ability to hurt me. And, since I was still in early recovery, I did not accept rejection very well. Picking up that drink and drug was just the final act of the slip.

Also on the subject of relationships in recovery, I know, today, that I cannot give away what I do not have. Since I did not love myself, back then, it was impossible for me to love anyone else. A recovering addict needs time to acquire some self-esteem before he attempts a new relationship.

One final act of "going to any length" that I thought was necessary for me was not having a car. I felt that, with a car, I would probably have gone back to my old neighborhood to be around my old friends. That might have led to a loss of my sobriety.

I hope someone who reads this will find that he or she can relate to my story, and that it helps. I would like others to find what I have. I have been very lucky. If it were not for my Higher Power, the C.D.A. program, and the fellowship, I would not be clean today.

Chapter 24
GOD DOESN'T MAKE JUNK

My name is John E. I'm an alcoholic and drug addict. To qualify that a little bit further—I'm lucky to be alive, today. It's only by the grace of God, and the fellowship of Chemically Dependent Anonymous, that I *am* alive. I really thank God for the program. Before C.D.A., I felt that I didn't have a place in this world where I belonged, because my life was just one big mess. It was one big trial, after trial, after trial. And most of my trials were criminal ones.

Growing up, I was basically a fairly good kid. I liked athletics, and I played sports of all kinds. I dabbled with alcohol, a little, when I was a teen-ager. And it just got progressively worse. When it is said that addiction is a progressive disease, that is so true. I know that my addiction was.

I got in trouble at the age of eighteen, stealing a car—unauthorized use of a motor vehicle—and I was sentenced to one year in jail. It was the first time that I'd really been in trouble with the criminal justice system. I knew nothing about the court system, at that time. I went to court, the day after I got picked up, and the judge found me guilty of the charge and sentenced me. I couldn't believe it.

In that one year in jail, my disease really took over. I got involved with my cell partner, who was a drug addict. He used any kind of drug, anything that would change his mood so he could get high. So I tried it all, too.

The first drug I used was a nasal inhalant. You squeezed the cotton, and this juice came out, and you drew it up in a syringe and put it in your arm. My partner got really high, and he told me that it was very good stuff. Crazy person that I was, I said, "Let me try some." I did, and I fell in love with it. I started my drug abuse with it, doing that drug on a pretty regular basis, during my year in jail. I bought that stuff, and also cocaine. There was some heroin that came through there, so I did that, along with everything else.

When I got out of jail after doing my year, I fooled around with heroin for about another year. I liked it, but I didn't have a physical habit to the point that my body really needed it. I just used it on weekends, mostly. It was called "chipping"—recreational use. I liked the way it made me feel.

While I was in jail, I had learned how to open safes. So I now thought I was a safecracker. I broke into some places and got caught in one of them. When the police arrived, I was stone drunk on the floor, because I always drank when I wasn't using drugs. I kept coming back to alcohol, but my drug of choice was DRUGS in general; it didn't matter what they were. I think the main reason I got caught is that when I was drunk I had to do crazy things. And the thing I did, this time, made noise. I had set the burglar alarm off. So the police found me and took me to jail. I got three years.

I made wine in jail the whole time I was there. Homemade wine was called "jump-steady" in there. I used to stay drunk on it most of the time. Of course, I got caught. My mother tried to visit me once and was turned away, she told me later, because I was on lockup for ninety days for breaking rules forbidding the possession of alcoholic beverages in jail.

Confined to my cell, on lockup, I was allowed out only once a week to take a shower. My jailers even brought my food to me. They used to put it underneath the bars and kick it to me, as if I were a dog. At least, that's the way I felt. I sometimes used to throw my tray at the people feeding me. I told them to open the door and feed me, but what I wanted didn't matter. I was an inmate, and they could treat me any way they wanted.

I got off lockup, but I hadn't learned my lesson. I went right back to making that wine and got sick from drinking so much of it. But I did my time, and I finally got out. The first thing I did, after I was released, was get married.

I married for all the wrong reasons. Everybody seemed to be marrying, at the time. I figured it was the thing to do, so I did it, too. I don't really have any other explanation for my behavior. But the neat thing is that I'm still married to the same woman today, after all these years!

When I got out of jail this time, I kept on drinking very heavily, and I also began fooling around with different drugs. I experimented with PCP, but I didn't like that very much because, when I was on it, I couldn't operate. I couldn't steal; I couldn't do the other things I was learning how to do. Crime was a big part of my life, and I spent my entire adult life going in and out of institutions, as a result.

The next time I was caught, it was on a housebreaking charge, for which I got ten years in prison. I did almost four of that ten under the influence of all kinds of drugs. I was taking pills, barbiturates and speed. I was drinking, mixing everything. I stayed messed up.

When I got out of jail, again, I went home to my wife. She was hoping I would straighten myself out. But I felt that God had created me bad, even though I had come from a family where no one had ever before broken the law. I believed that there was no way I could ever get straight, do good, and stay out of prison for the rest of my adult life. I had been sent to a mental institution for the criminally insane, for about three months, while I was incarcerated this last time. That made me all the more certain that there was something fundamentally wrong with me. So, when I finished my time, I went right back into the same old drugs and crime.

But this time, I started fooling with cocaine. I used it for six or seven months on almost a daily basis, and I liked the way it made me feel, the rush it gave me. I liked shooting that dope. It was like a fantasy, sticking something into your arm that would get you high within a couple of seconds after you pushed it in. That was a lot better than waiting. Alcohol was too slow, even though I enjoyed drinking, too.

I was a beer drinker when I did drink. I got drunk quite often. And almost every time I drank, I either passed out on the couch or in somebody's car, or I had blackouts and couldn't remember where I had been or what I had done. My whole life was just insane, and I felt that there was no way out. But I didn't want to stop using, because I liked what it did for me.

By now, I was shooting heroin every day, too, doing anywhere from six to eight quarters daily. But I wanted to get off the heroin. I knew that it just made me do bad things. I did some boosting in the stores, and other stealing, to keep my drug habit going. I couldn't work. How could I hold a job? I didn't even want to *try* to work.

I talked to another addict, and he told me that there

was a methadone program available. He said I should try to go on that. It would eliminate my heroin addiction. But it didn't stop my addiction, because the methadone was a more potent drug than any of the heroin I'd ever been on. There was one good thing about it, though. It was free. I went in, every day, to get my methadone. I was on fifty milligrams for about a year. The first week I was on the program, I couldn't even function. I really liked that methadone high.

There were some outstanding warrants out on me, by this time, on several different charges. One of them was my second DWI, which had never been brought to trial. I couldn't go back to the clinic to get my methadone, for fear that the police would be waiting for me. They knew I was a drug addict, and they knew I was on methadone, so I was sure they would just come and pick me up there. I didn't want to go back to jail again. I kept moving, all around my local area, and to locations within a hundred miles of it, and then out into the surrounding counties.

But then I returned home to give my wife some money, and the police caught me at the house. In the past, I had been giving her $30 or $40 at a time for child support. My three children were all grown by now, but I still wanted to do my part. I found out, later, that $30 to $40 doesn't buy much, but I thought I was doing a good deed by coming back to give it to her. The police just happened to come over the day I was there, and they told me that they had an outstanding warrant on me and took me to the courthouse. I did thirty days on a shoplifting charge.

I also had that second DWI from another county. I was transferred there, and the judge gave me a year's sentence on that charge. I explained to him that this was not the first time I had been put away, that jail was not the answer. I had a problem with alcohol and a problem with drugs, and I just didn't know what to do about it. I said that I would like to have some help.

That was the first time I really surrendered and admitted I had a problem, even though I had realized that I was a drug addict and an alcoholic for the last few years. I had not been ready to stop because I liked the way I felt when I did the drinking and those drugs. I did not want to take responsibility. I didn't know what responsibility was.

The only things I did know about were the ins and outs of the institutions in which I had been placed for so much of my life. I had put guns in people's faces. I had robbed stores with a pistol. I had broken into many places. I had done insane things under the influence of drugs and alcohol.

When I told the judge that I needed help, he sent a counselor over from a drug-and-alcohol clinic in his county. The counselor told me that I certainly qualified for rehab, and I definitely had some kind of problem with drugs and alcohol. If I really wanted help, it was available for me. But it was up to me. The judge signed a court order and gave me a thirty-day leave to go to this rehab, but I was still under my year's sentence while I was there. I thank God for that program, because it taught me how absolutely powerless I am over alcohol and drugs. My track record shows that my past life was absolutely unmanageable. I had been unable to stay out of jail for more than two years at a time, up until then.

I think I may have forgotten to mention that I had been in a mental institution during my first jail sentence. I had stayed there for about forty days and was then sent back to jail to serve out my time. So, it had been noticed, long before, that I needed some kind of help. When I was sent to the rehab, this time, I really listened, though. I kept an open mind about it. I was honest, for the first time in my life, about being an alcoholic and a drug addict.

I found that I would have to go to a lot of meetings when I got out of there. I was told to go to ninety meetings in ninety days, and I did. But first I went back and did another month in jail, and then the judge let me off with time served and put me on probation. I'm still on probation, today. But my life is better than it has ever been because of the fellowship I go to, the meetings I attend, and the help of the Higher Power I choose to call God.

I'm in contact with God, now, as I pray on a daily basis. I try to help the newcomer, and I go to lots of meetings. I've had eighteen months of sobriety, the best months of my life. I have started to work—for myself—as a painter. I get a lot of work, more than I can handle. I try to do a good job, to show up on time and get the work done promptly. I am finally trying to take responsibility.

My wife and I are back together, again. Although we've been married twenty-three years, it's all really new for us, right now. My wife is in the fellowship, and I love her to death. I have a better relationship with my three children, and I'm communicating with them. They understand, now, and they are so glad I am in the program. They know there's a big change in me because I go to the meetings, even if that change is almost unbelievable. It's a miracle to me, too, especially when I recall that I once had no hope that a person as bad as I was, a person born bad, could ever reform. But I found out that God does love me and that He doesn't make any junk.

I'm beginning to notice things that I'd never paid attention to before. I see flowers blooming, notice the change in seasons, realize that there's snow on the ground—all the things I've ignored all these years. For me, life had always been just one, big, gray day.

Without God's help, my way was destructive. I didn't care who I hurt, what I stole, how I acted. I would go to any length to get money for my addictions. I fed on other people and loved to manipulate them.

I am not that way, now. I believe that God had a plan and that's why He spared my life. I was involved in so many situations where I should have been killed. Many times, I barely escaped being shot. And, in fact, I was shot, once. I even shot myself, on one occasion, when I went to draw my pistol and hit myself in the leg. Today, such things never happen. I don't even own a pistol, anymore. The only thing I like to carry is my Bible. I keep it with me and read it, daily. My power, today, is God.

I attend C.D.A. meetings, now, and I really like their fellowship. I don't feel bad there, as I do at some other meetings, because I know that I can share about my drug addiction and my alcoholism with these people. My problems don't offend anyone. C.D.A. is a good program for me because I know that the people really love me, and I surely love them. They have listened to my story, and they really do care. They are interested in me.

At one time, I didn't care about you all. I didn't care about anybody. Money was only for getting high. Now, I worry about my next dollar so I can pay my bills and, maybe, give some of it to others, to help them.

People who have more time in C.D.A. than I do say, "Keep coming back; it keeps getting better," but I can't imagine that my life will be any better than it is now. My wife and I do things together, and we've been to new places and done many new things since we've been in the program. We've gone horseback riding. I've been white-water rafting. I've been to a dance, the first I've ever gone to while sober and without any drugs in my system, and I have found that I can actually dance, something I had never realized before. It's really neat!

Being clean and sober is the miracle that has happened to me. But I see the same miracles happen to many other people, in and out of these rooms. I thank God, every day, for those miracles of sobriety, for myself and for those others.

If I can say anything to encourage anybody to try the program, it is that C.D.A. does work. But you've got to want it. I wanted it because I was tired of hurting. I was tired of the institutions. I was just sick and tired of being sick and tired. I decided to give the program my best shot, and I'm going to keep coming back. I hope that the newcomer does the same.

If there was hope for a hopeless case like me, there is hope for you, too. My parents were once ashamed of me because I was always in trouble. I left them as soon as I was eighteen and only disgraced them more as I got older. But now my whole family is proud of me.

I'm straight, today, because the fellowship works, and because God has been on my side. He has opened a lot of doors in my life. He never left me; I left Him. Now, I just want to get closer to Him. I know that God is great, and good, a loving God. I just can't say enough about my Higher Power. I asked Christ to come into my life, and He has. He has shown me ways to better my life. I still have a long way to go. I have many character defects that I have to improve. But I'm working on them. Working the Steps has been an important part of my program, a big part of my being where I am, today. If I can help anyone with their own programs, I'll be happy to, because it helps me to get, and stay, better.

I thank you all, in C.D.A., so much. And, most of all, I am grateful to God for my new happiness. I'm happy to be a husband. I'm happy to be a father. And I'm happy to be a child of God.

Chapter 25
I AM

When I came into the doors of Chemically Dependent Anonymous, I was spiritually dead. I had no desire to stay that way, though. I was finally ready to look inside, to find the stranger I never knew. Once the fog began to lift from eleven years of drugs and alcohol, the true feelings started surfacing, and they were painful. But C.D.A. deals with feelings, too, and not just substance abuse. The most important thing I did was to make a decision not to go back to the way I had been living. I knew I had that choice. I never had to go through that again. When I realized that, I felt a warmth inside, for the first time in a long time.

I never thought I'd find people like myself, but C.D.A. is open to all addictive people. The first few meetings, I saw people of all ages. And they, too, were looking for a better way of life. They were willing to give living a chance. Their love is what kept me alive for the first month.

Before I came to C.D.A., I had tried finding a Higher Power. I would get stoned and try meditating. But there was a fog between me and my Higher Power. Now that I am straight, I feel that Power even when I'm down. It's a feeling of calmness I never got from drugs and alcohol.

I still have a strong urge to explain who I was, and who I am now. But that's the old tape playing. I recognize that my past is why I'm here today, and I accept that I can't change the things I did because they were meant to be. Those past events brought me down so I could look inside.

Today, I feel so strange and confused, at times. It's as if I'm meeting a new person in myself. I'm scared, happy, sad, lost. In my mind, the new person can see what the old person couldn't, however. It's a different entity from the old one. It's as if I'm being drained of old ways which only leave room for new ones. I know the soul remains constant, but it is what I never listened to, before. Now, it speaks strongly (though not all the time), but my head is still trying to convince me that my soul is wrong.

All my life, I searched for the truth outside myself. Not willing to make my own decisions, I put my world into the hands of others, only to realize I was stagnating when I did so. My relationships led me to self-destruction because I'd let people, places, and things control my happiness. I had no foundation of self. Once I finally made a decision for myself, however, I discovered that foundation of self, and it began to work for me.

Never knowing the self is spiritual death. That realization was the turning point that brought me to C.D.A. Now, I live my words. I stop to feel the pain. I have no choice: My self has finally caught up with me. But I've found out that I'm O.K. After I go through the pain, I reach the other side, which is growth. The only way to understand, honestly, the mistakes I've made is to see them as part of my growth. Letting go of my past has been worth it.

My old friends and my lover are in some other place in their own journeys. Now, I have true friends who go out of their way to help me love myself. I work, every day, to find the true self within. There are no guidelines, other than honesty with myself, that I use to do this. Most of all, I try to find that fine line between self-abuse and self-love.

Some days, all I can do is say the Serenity Prayer, over and over. But the most amazing thing happens when I do: The pain goes away. I know I only get what I can handle, even though I sometimes think my Higher Power might be pushing it too far. If it didn't push me, though, I wouldn't grow.

I'm here to live day by day, to learn *who I am*. And, in doing that, I become closer to my Higher Power, which has been with me always. Now, I MAKE A DECISION, every morning, to work with my Higher Power. Because of C.D.A., I have a chance to start my life over, to become friends with my Higher Power.

I AM . . . .

Chapter 26
MY LOVE FOR C.D.A.

Since I am a garden-variety alcoholic/drug addict, Chemically Dependent Anonymous appealed to me from my first meeting, seven years ago. At the time, it had been almost eleven months since my last drink/drug. However, I had no idea it would be my last, as I still had desires to use when I joined the fellowship. Prior to this time, I had been to some Alcoholics Anonymous meetings, my first being four years before, when I was in an alcoholic treatment center which was basically a halfway house. Before that, I had been committed to various mental hospitals, the last time for almost two years.

By the time of what has turned out to be my last use of any substance, I had been drinking for thirty years, and using drugs, off and on, for twenty-five. My addiction reached its peak in the late sixties/early seventies, when I resigned my job as an assistant vice president in public relations and advertising for a large corporation to become a "beach bum," occasionally working as a bouncer in nightclubs. I began to put anything available into my system, resulting in what I then considered to be my death when I was incarcerated, supposedly permanently, in a state hospital. I really thought I had died, and that I was in the eternal living Hell the preachers talked about.

For twenty-three days, I was in seclusion, in a concrete room 6 feet wide by 8 feet long. My clothes were removed the second day; my rubber mat disappeared the third. By then, I was refusing all medication and food. My attendants cooperated, and, except for one elderly, crew-cut, white-haired gentleman, they left me alone. He was the only one I wouldn't bite and hit at, and he brought me water often enough so I didn't truly die. Somewhere along the line, I began beating my head against the door and the wall, knowing only that I wanted to stop thinking. Were you supposed to think when you were dead?

Five years later, I was called upon to "think" when I was offered some vodka and mixer. Very little thought actually went into the process, however, although it had been, perhaps, four months since I had last "injected" chemicals. Six hours later, after only one drink, I was arrested and escorted to a waiting cruiser. My arrogance on the way to jail caused a police officer to strike me with a blackjack, very neatly removing what had been my left eye.

Yet this was a tremendous benefit! Two months later, upon my release from yet another hospital, I was directed to a mental health clinic, where I was to meet what have come to be long-time friends (strong members of A.A.) and eventually to hear of C.D.A., my long-sought-after, beloved fellowship.

Although I had a good and loving mother and father, as a child I showed every sign of becoming a juvenile delinquent. I loved adventure and needed to prove how tough I was. My dealings with the Man in Blue included shooting out street lights with a BB gun when I had reached the very grown-up age of nine, and stuffing mud in the gas tanks of city buses when I was ten.

Somehow, I managed to avoid reform school.

In the fifth grade, I overreacted to the experience of moving to a smaller town. On the first day at my new school, I felt compelled to fight it out with the class leader at lunch break. When he announced to the gawking kids, "It's a draw," my reputation was made, even though he had been demolishing me until a teacher mercifully broke up the fight.

I always knew what alcohol was. My father was a moderate drinker who imbibed only on holidays or special occasions. My mother used liquor sparingly, medicinally, in a hot toddy, for colds or flu. And we, like many children, were given a mild version of this remedy for the same illnesses. But neither my environment nor my genetic inheritance led to my disease of alcoholism, and certainly not to my drug addiction. Chemical dependency was, and is, all mine.

My teen-age years were typically small-town and middle-class, with no great trauma or dramatic happenings. But, as I examine the events of my life then, and how I reacted to them, I can see, now, the pattern being established for my addiction to chemicals, which began when I stole my first bottle of bourbon from our basement. I spent a lot of my time in solitude there, fantasizing, during puberty. My dad, who did some carpentry, kept liquor locked up in one of his tool chests down there. I thought, "How could the old man miss just one?" It never occurred to me that my dad could count. As a result, no matter what else I have done in my life, I have never stolen that particular brand of bourbon again.

To my friends and me, words like "snow," "grass," "acid," "buzz," and "toot" were familiar, but with far different meanings than those I was to later discover. Beer, cigarettes, or corn liquor; sniffing glue, gasoline, varnish, or shellac; or the dizzy kick from aspirins in a soft drink were all we knew in those days. A particular addiction I had, as a teen-ager, was to laxatives. It seems that I was always constipated because I didn't want to take the time to go relieve myself. I was too busy having fun: contemplating a high, planning some destruction or a theft. For stealing was another of my addictions. I even stole coins from a wishing well that earmarked its proceeds for charity. This vice continued into adulthood, where it took the form of padding expense accounts.

Childhood ended with high school graduation. As for adulthood, where did that begin? Maybe, in my case, with registering for the draft. Or could it have been when, at eighteen, my friends and I proved our manhood by guzzling a quart of beer in less than twenty seconds? With a freshly killed, beer-soaked rabbit roasting on the open flames, and a supply of beer and corn liquor, we juvenile neophytes of the adult world were just having innocent fun.

Of course, night hunting was illegal. Twenty-one was the legal age for drinking, locally. And bootlegging, since we bought our beer across the state line, along with possession of moonshine, could have brought the revenuers down on our heads. But laughing at the law was all part of growing up! We loved drag racing and stealing watermelons, too.

Being eighteen also meant that we were expected to work on the family farm, or to get some other legitimate job, if we were not going to attend college. I compromised. Hoping to avoid being sent to the Korean conflict, I enrolled in an apprentice program for draftsmen at a shipbuilding company where aircraft carriers and other warships were being built. Unfortunately, no program such as A.A. was offered along with the apprenticeship, because I was really abusing alcohol, by this time. None of my friends knew it, nor did my family. And what's worse, neither did I.

Some of my associates from the year I spent as an apprentice provided guidance and examples that eventually played a significant role in my reentry into the world of the living, and my successful introduction to A.A. But it is also important to recall that my parents had provided warm and strong training, as well. They were loving, but strict. My disease didn't arise out of a lack of parental compassion or a reckless, wild childhood unchecked by parents or teachers. My mother was, herself, a teacher. Helping others was important to her. Dad loved his family and all mankind. I was given a strong foundation by more people than I can count: neighbors, teachers, ministers, and employers. I don't think I ever really lost that, no matter what I did.

None of these people contributed to my self-inflicted corruptions. They helped to give me something to return to when everything else around me had deteriorated. That is an important fact to remember. And I'm bringing it up because I want to convey this message to everyone reading this book: There is much in your life to be grateful for, just as there has been in mine.

My drafting instructor is a case in point. He was as kind and patient a person as I have ever met, and our short association has proven fruitful for me, especially in these past few years of attempting sobriety. But sobering up after heavy drinking was my way of life while I was under his guidance, unfortunately. My drinking finally got me into real trouble when I got very drunk at my high-school class reunion. While trying to "get it together," I was careless and received a facial injury that resulted in a blood clot and hallucinations. My parents and my brother had to admit me to the psychiatric ward of a hospital for several weeks of shock treatments and therapy. Of course, alcohol had nothing to do with it! Afterwards, I went back to work for a few months.

But now that the Korean conflict was winding down, four of my hometown buddies and I had decided to volunteer for the draft. I was assigned overseas to the U.S. Army Corps of Engineers' Stock Control Division. My job was to transfer the old wartime stock numbers to a new system, paving the way for later-to-come computers. I also quickly mastered some other numbers, such as the exchange rates on all foreign currencies, and became a runner for an Army Department civilian employee who dealt in the black market, primarily in currency. Running PX-bought and bartered cigarettes, cameras, and small appliances increased my ability to count quickly.

I spent my earnings, both legitimate and illegal, on beer at the enlisted men's club. There, a buck and a quarter would buy a scrumptious steak dinner with all the trimmings, including a bottle of wine, and the price for alcoholic drinks was ridiculously low. Even before my overseas stint, the on-post clubs in the U.S. allowed a soldier to booze it up cheaply. During basic training, and a subsequent two months of school, I drank more than I care to remember.

Drugs were widely available, too, both at home and abroad. My overseas assignment came at a time when I had not smoked cigarettes for over eighteen months. An excursion to the capital city of the country where I was stationed led me to the streets, looking for some action. When I was offered what I wanted, by a young woman wearing only a raincoat, the transaction included the smoking of something called the "steek." It didn't resemble any brand of cigarettes I had ever seen before. But one long drag, and I knew I had found wings to fly. That was my first taste of marijuana.

I wouldn't take a million dollars for the experience, the discipline, the travels, and the friendships I acquired in the service, although I would not want to do it again. I, and only I, abused my time in the military. My superiors were trying to tell me something when I was hospitalized, over the Christmas holidays, due to alcohol abuse. But I thought that I had just drunk too much wine—bad wine, at that. I celebrated my release from the hospital by marching right back to the enlisted men's club for shots of bourbon washed down with beer. No more of that rotten wine for me! At least, not that night.

I managed to go AWOL several days before I was to ship out, back to the States, and that cost me a stripe. But I was able to con my way through the finance and personnel offices, before the regimental commander's action made it through the normal red tape, so I was given an honorable discharge, and was able to spend six years in the inactive reserves, and, furthermore, to receive veteran's benefits that allowed me to attend college, later, under the GI Bill.

When I got home, I had money to burn. I hung around the bars, showing up around noon or so each day. My dad suggested to my mom, gently but firmly, that shoving me out of the house would be a compassionate, and necessary, act of parenthood. Six children had been brought up within the walls of that home, and all of them would make our parents proud and pleased some day, one way or the other. I just took a little longer than the rest. Mom was the softy, and dad the tough guy. But when I wrecked the beautiful new car my brother and sister-in-law had presented me when I came home from the wars, my father gave me his old car and went out and bought a new one. It took all of eighteen months for me to junk my second gift vehicle, too.

One of my brothers has always been the towering strength of our family. He was, by now, living in a neighboring state, in high-middle-class suburbia at its best. He and his wife offered to let me move in with them, since I said I was going to enroll in college somewhere in the area. I got a part-time job selling books, mostly encyclopedias, door-to-door. The job was mostly a con, offering books that could have been bought at a much cheaper price at a bookstore. Next, I sought more legitimate employment, in the world of finance, with a loan company. After about a year, I was promoted to supervisor and sent out-of-state to initiate a new credit-card system in thirteen Southeastern states.

No one would have guessed that I, at the hardened-bachelor age of twenty-three, would meet a Southern belle who would transform my life. She had everything, both physical and internal beauty. Unfortunately for her, I was a self-made, rotten con artist, by that time. My alcohol intake was astronomical, but I could talk almost everyone, including myself, into believing that it was normal. I'm sure that I didn't fool my girl, though, because she suggested that it might be a good idea if we both abstained from alcohol, especially since her parents had died from alcoholic complications. I agreed. No problem! I welcomed the thought of a completely new life with her.

My girl had decided that we should get married on the Fourth of July, as a symbol of her independence from her wealthy, high-society grandmother. I had met my future wife in a bowling alley. She avoided questions about her background for more than a month after we met, even though we were seeing each other three times a week, by then. At first, I didn't want her to know that I was living at the YMCA. But she was even more fearful that her lifestyle might frighten *me* away, as it had so many others. On dates, we would meet at prearranged places, or she would pick me up at the Y in her car.

When her grandmother became curious as to why my girl was so secretive about her new friend, she had her granddaughter ask me to dinner. Not until that night did I discover what I had let myself in for. These people were in a class I never even knew existed. I had been happy to accept the dinner invitation, excited to finally learn the truth about my girl and to shoot down the "princess" fantasy I had built up in my mind about her.

I was overwhelmed from the first moment I saw her grandmother's residence. The old lady had had my background thoroughly checked out, and I was not her idea of a good catch. The evening was a nightmare. But if she thought that she could prove to my girl that I was an unacceptable choice, she was sadly mistaken. My girl wanted a more normal life, and a regular guy.

After our wedding, we lived comfortably, if not very extravagantly, while I attended school. We were healthy, busy, and productive for the first years of our marriage. My wife worked at her chosen profession, and we were active in church and civic affairs. We participated in all sorts of volunteer work. I even gave up smoking, cigarettes included, as well as the alcohol. But I didn't attend A.A., despite my past record of abuse, because that was for winos, or those who had a real drinking problem. I know, now, what a mistake that was.

But, remember, at the time I still thought I was *normal*. My father had never believed in mental illness. With his philosophy of hard work, I guess it was difficult to find time to drink or be depressed, or to become a schizo, or paranoid. Somehow, despite his example, I would find the time.

When my oldest brother hanged himself, in the early sixties, it was a complete shock to my family. But my mom, at least, was able to accept it as the Lord's will. My brother had been a minister, and a good one. He had left a lucrative career and, after fifteen years of marriage, had packed up his wife and three children to take up a rural pastorate. When he left for a larger city ministry, and to further pursue his studies, something went wrong. But seeing this happen didn't help to refocus my life, as it should have.

I was a lay speaker in my own church, at the time, dry and free from drugs, but far from all right. For a long time, I was unable to speak of my brother's death and the problems resulting therefrom. His youngest son became close to me, but I was incapable of showing him proof, in my life, of a better way to live. His own life later became one of grief and pain, too, because of drugs. I pray that he can find the light that I have, and that he will be able to overcome his difficulties. My church work was another influence that saved me, I am convinced, and led me to accept the help that I sorely needed, later.

I wish that I had been more teachable when I attended my wife's *alma mater*, twenty years ago. I managed to graduate through my usual deceptions and con games. I cheated, cut classes, and induced instant recall with the aid of Black Beauties and other little goodies of the day. I also used my office, as chapter president of the business fraternity I belonged to, as a lever against professors and deans. With the additional help of the GI Bill and part-time jobs, I got my degree in business management, although it took five years.

After graduation, I worked in a variety of fields. But success was never in the forefront of my mind, perhaps due to the realization that my wife would someday inherit a fortune. While everything appeared to be going well, our life was not really what it seemed to be on the surface. My reentry as a user had begun with an occasional beer at frat parties. I was now spending more time playing golf and drinking gin than I was at working. My wife and I had both become hooked on pills, not the street variety I was to sample so abundantly in future years, but on prescribed dope, the upper-class scourge.

During my final semester in school, my wife had had a complete nervous breakdown and had to be hospitalized. Doctors had offered little hope of a cure. I was given medical, legal, and family advice to have her declared mentally incompetent, in order to facilitate the settlement of her grandmother's estate, as well as for other business reasons. A lawyer was appointed to handle her affairs.

In the ensuing six months, I really went off the deep end with my carousing. I felt fully justified in doing so because of my loneliness. When my wife finally came home, we attempted to live a normal life again. Before the year was out, however, she had left me. I then moved into my frat house on campus and became a real rogue about town. I went so far off the deep end that I was actually relieved when my wife called, a little over a year later, and asked to visit my parents. She, too, was hurting. But she could admit it, as I never would. I couldn't stay with her, because I had since graduated and had gotten a job, but I spent weekends with her there.

On one of these trips, I was offered a job in public relations and advertising, as assistant to the vice president, for a major tourist attraction. The deal included an apartment in a management-owned motel. My wife and I were offered the additional opportunity to manage it for a year, which we accepted. It was more work than we had bargained for. When my mother died, later that year, we moved in with my dad awhile.

The following summer, my wife left me again, but I was able to keep track of her through old friends. State law forbade divorce, at the time, because of the earlier court ruling on her mental competency. Although her mental health seemed to improve, after she got home, she remained under a doctor's care. The laws in her state were finally changed, and a divorce decree was issued five years later. She remarried, but, sadly, eventually took her own life.

I kept my job at the tourist attraction, even though my vice president was, by now, well aware that I "occasionally" drank too much. I even passed out at a travel council annual meeting, one morning, at nine o'clock. I hadn't started drinking in the morning, yet; I had simply never stopped from the night before. But I convinced myself that I had just been sleepy because I didn't have any Black Beauties with me on this trip. My boss's wife convinced him that everyone drinks too much, once in a while, so I was not fired. In fact, I was given even greater responsibilities.

My job was promoting the tourist attraction and the surrounding area, and much of it entailed traveling. My trips were carefully mapped out by my boss in advance. But I would always find some way to manage a side trip to a certain town where an old fraternity brother owned a bar. That "some way" was often by means of a feigned illness, sometimes even requiring a supposed three- or four-day hospitalization, so I could have my fun, as well as make my calls. And, of course, the best way to entertain business people is with booze. I traveled with a very well-stocked portable bar. Seventy-five percent of its contents, at least, was for my own private consumption, however.

After about three years on the job, I began having "accidents" with company station wagons. I wrecked two cars in two months' time. In the first such incident, I rammed three other vehicles waiting at a red light and sent several persons, myself not included, to the hospital. Thanks to certain influential help, I was convicted only of failure to keep a vehicle under control and was given a $50 fine. After all, the gas pedal had "stuck" (weighed down by the heavy foot of a driver who had just finished about ten double martinis).

If only I had realized that my life was as out of control as that car had been, I might have avoided my second accident. This time, the car struck a light pole. I had been drinking just about the same amount, of the same substance, again. I was thrown into the mirror and windshield, receiving a major gash in the side of my head. An unknown good Samaritan wrapped my head in a towel. Doctors later told me that this person's action had kept me from bleeding to death.

But several days of hospitalization had not served as a warning about the growing severity of my disease of alcoholism. In less than two weeks, I was off and running for a winter-weekend funfest filled with eating, fishing, and much boozing at the seashore. I think that this was when my dependency on alcohol really took a grave turn for the worse. My badly deteriorating brain thought about booze while I was sleeping, and, I truly believe, even when I had passed out from drinking. Thinking about liquor certainly filled my every waking moment.

My father passed away just after the new year began. And I was roaring drunk, at the time, at another one of those travel council annual meetings. By this time, I was always drunk, no matter where I was or what I was doing. But my dad and I had become so much closer, the last four years of his life, that I got even drunker, if possible, the night before his funeral. My sisters were understandably upset and now realized I had a problem, but they waited, patiently and supportively, several more years until I recognized that fact for myself—and even more years until I actually started to do something about it.

The next nine months are still foggy in my memory. But my character defects were in full bloom, by now. During Easter week, I abused not only alcohol and drugs, but also many human beings. I persuaded a young woman to spend the weekend at the shore with a sick friend—me. I then conned her into flying off to an island in the Caribbean, where we joined an old fraternity brother of mine in his decadent lifestyle. My chaotic life, after that, led me steadily downhill, until I found A.A. and, finally, C.D.A.

Chemically Dependent Anonymous made no distinctions, in the recovery process, when I cried out, "But I'm twice as old as most of you;" "My Higher Power is called 'Gohonzon,' not God" (I am a Buddhist); "I've been to meetings for years, and I can't make it;" and, my last resort, "I only have one eye." No, all you people said was: "We love you," and "Keep coming back."

Yes, it took me a long time to get to the Twelve Steps, and almost as long to grasp them. But, with the help of my Higher Power, my sponsor, co-sponsors, spiritual advisors, and the newcomers, I'm here, one day at a time, for the rest of my life.

You see, now I, too, can say, "I love C.D.A.," and "We love *you*. Keep coming back!"

Chapter 27
IN GOD'S OWN GOOD TIME

My name is Bobbi, and I'm a grateful alcoholic. I couldn't have conceived making that statement until about seven or eight years ago. My life is wonderful today, really beyond my wildest dreams. I know none of this would be a reality without Chemically Dependent Anonymous and Alcoholics Anonymous, and C.D.A. wouldn't be part of my life had I not gone through the hell of active alcoholism.

I grew up in New England, in an upper middle-income family. I certainly never lacked for anything, in terms of food, clothing, toys, and so forth. Somehow, though, I grew up feeling I was always on the outside, looking in. I felt I just didn't fit in. When I was young, my family moved frequently. One of the effects of moving was that it seemed that whenever I started to get comfortable in any place, we were up and gone again, so I was always the "new kid on the block," which fueled my feeling of always being an outsider.

At any rate, I always believed that the best was expected of me, all the time—in athletics, school grades, you name it. And I was pretty successful in many ways. The thing is, I never stopped to take any pride in my achievements, because I was off and running to the next thing. So, I never felt successful, and I was constantly afraid of failure. But I kept that feeling to myself. Now, anyone looking from the outside would have thought that I was one of the happiest, most well-adjusted and mature kids (for my age) around. I was pretty good at putting up a front.

I picked up my first drink when I was fourteen years old. Normally enough, it was at a party, it was with my boyfriend, and his family was there. It was not just a bunch of kids having a rowdy time. I was given a beer, and I had no idea about the effects of alcohol—what it could do to you. I'd never thought about it. So I drank the beer that was given to me at this party, and then I stood up, and I had the most wonderful feeling. I really thought this was liquid gold.

And I know, looking back, that I was an active alcoholic from that point on. I had just been waiting for the drink to get in me, because I certainly had all the symptoms, up to that time, in terms of personality. From then on, I went to all the parties I could and became a weekend drinker; I drank as much as I could, whenever I could.

On the outside, my life continued to look pretty good. I still got straight A's in school and participated in activities. So nobody, of course, suspected anything, least of all me. I wound up skipping my senior year of high school and going right on to college—which, looking back, I can see may have been ill-advised. In college, away from the family, my alcoholism began to progress much more rapidly because, all of a sudden, I didn't have to conform to parental guidelines. I could set my own. I wasn't wild and crazy, but I wasn't an angel, either.

During my first two years of college, I was a math major. By the middle of my third year, I had decided I didn't want to do whatever math majors did after they got out of college, which, as far as I could see, was basically confined to teaching or working in an insurance company. So I decided that I wanted to be an architect. I liked the results of what architects did. I had no idea how they actually did it, though. A university accepted me into their school of architecture, and off I went.

I still can't fathom why they let me in, because, during my first semester there, I realized it was more of an artistic endeavor than I had anticipated, and I absolutely didn't have that kind of talent. So, I went trotting off to the engineering school, which I'd always figured I'd fall back on if things got too rough. But I had failed at something—my house of cards was beginning to wobble. One of the effects of failing in architecture was that my drinking increased. And my fears increased. Deep down inside, I knew that there was something different about me. But I certainly wasn't near a point of admitting to myself that I had a problem with alcohol.

And it wasn't just alcohol, either. I abused other chemicals, from time to time. However, alcohol was my drug of choice. If you laid out every drug known to man on the table, and alcohol was in there among them, that's what I would have gone for. I guess it's because I knew what it did. I felt I could control its intake to some extent, whereas the drugs frightened me. I always had the feeling that, once I put them in my body, I couldn't control where they would take me. But if there had been no alcohol on the table, I would have picked up something else. I think it would have been marijuana, or some sort of sedative-type of drug. I know that I would have substituted something for the alcohol.

By this time, in college, my boyfriend had caught on to the fact that I had a drinking problem. I denied it up and down, and made excuses all the time. (One of the things that helped fool him was that he was going to school in another city, so I could keep my drinking hidden much of the time.) My parents were back home, but, after he realized how bad things really were, my boyfriend alerted them to the fact that I seemed to be drinking too much. When I came home for vacations, they began to watch their bottles, and they picked up on my problem, also. Now I felt that everyone was on my case. I took it very personally.

Back then, I thought that if I was an alcoholic, it was my fault—and that it indicated that I was very weak of character. And that was totally unacceptable, in my mind. On the outside, I seemed to be always the strong person. I was emotionally stable, or so it appeared. The truth was that I was a wreck on the inside. Eventually, I got rid of the boyfriend who was on my case for my drinking. I more or less had to, in order to keep drinking!

In my last year at the university, my drinking had reached a point where it was now affecting my schoolwork. I could no longer study. And it was affecting me physically, because I'd reached a point where I was often so sick in the morning that I just literally couldn't get out of bed and face the day. So I was missing classes and having to catch up with the work later.

I now had a new boyfriend, a classmate and a civil engineer, like me. He and all my friends were successful in life, well-adjusted, and stable—all the things I wanted to be. For some reason I still don't understand, he really loved me and tried to help me. Were it not for him, I would never have made it through my senior year of college, and I would never have graduated.

Some of my professors knew I had a drinking problem, but they also knew it was my final year. They just wanted to pass me on and not get involved with my problems. My grades, in my senior year, were all down to C's. But my grade-point average had been so high, up until then, that I graduated *cum laude*. That's something that still looks good on my résumé.

When I left college, I took a job with a consulting firm which is considered a leader in environmental engineering. Once out of college, without the pressure of schoolwork, just having to be someplace from 8 to 5 o'clock, my drinking took off as it never had before. By this time, the physical effects alcohol produced in me were becoming much worse. I became a binge drinker. When I'd get too sick, I'd dry myself out, and I'd stay straight until I felt I had it under control, again. And then I'd go on another binge. And it was always bingeing, now, because once I'd started, I couldn't stop until I was too sick to keep on drinking.

During all this time, I embarrassed myself. I became irresponsible. I couldn't follow through on all the things I wanted to do because I was physically unable to do so. My free time, unless I was in one of my dry periods, I spent drinking. And when I was in a dry period, I had to patch up my life from the binge before. The job lasted two years, and then I got fired because of "absenteeism." I don't know if anybody there really knew about my drinking. I expect a few did, but absenteeism was a good enough reason to fire me and yet not get involved in dealing with my alcoholism, and I can't blame them.

I got another job, somehow, working for the Department of Transportation back in my home state. I moved back into my parents' house. Since I was living in their home, I couldn't drink the way I wanted to. So I was always trying to find some place else to go. Consequently, I'd wind up driving around and drinking. It is a miracle that I never killed anybody, or hurt myself, and never got into any serious accidents doing that. I did crash into objects quite a bit, though. My car looked as if it belonged in a demolition derby.

Well, naturally, my parents noticed that things weren't right. And my whole alibi system began to fall apart. The excuses I made up began to sound wild, even to me. I can imagine how they sounded to people who were looking at this a little more objectively, with a little bit clearer mind.

Then followed my round of rehabs. I went through several of these for treatment of chemical dependencies—four, to be exact. The first one I went to was renowned, on the East Coast, for its celebrity clients. My parents thought it had to be good, if it attracted people with a lot of money. And I was covered by insurance if I went there. After a few days, once the alcohol was out of my system, I began to feel pretty good, again (as I had in all my drinking/drying periods), and I also began to deny that I was an alcoholic, again. And, once again, I told myself that the next time, it was going to be different. That is the insanity of this disease—that I could, over, and over, and over, do the same thing and expect different results, every single time. But the results were always the same, and always devastating.

I got out of that rehab and, naturally, started drinking again. And, within a couple of weeks, I was right back to where I'd started. But, by this time, I was not liking myself a whole lot, because I couldn't live up to my ideal of the kind of person I wanted to be. Alcohol really had me. I just couldn't consider living without it. I couldn't imagine what I would do without alcohol. That was something that frightened me to think about, living my life without *ever drinking again.*

I was getting worse, physically and mentally, and my relationships were all lying in tatters: those with my boyfriend, who still kept hanging around, and with my parents, and with the people at work. I was just so ashamed about my behavior that I didn't even bother to try to get close to people, because I knew I would somehow embarrass myself, and hurt them, and it just wasn't worth it. So I became rather isolated.

In my rural home state, female professionals were relatively few. The combination of being a professional in a male-dominated field and being an addict made me feel that I was truly unique. Hiding my addiction was paramount, so I continued to drink by myself. I'd long since stopped going to bars. There was no evidence of alcoholism around me; no one else in my family was an alcoholic. (Or so I thought. Since I have been in the program, however, I have found out that I do have an uncle, my mother's brother, who is an alcoholic. He's been recovering for the last five years.) When I was younger, there was no role model of addiction for me to play to. I was the only alcoholic I knew: a pioneer, so to speak. But I didn't want to be a pioneer in alcoholism. I thought that it was absolutely the worst thing that I could be.

When I was, again, feeling really sick, my parents convinced me to go to another rehab, a place which wasn't quite as ritzy as the first one, but the facilities were still pretty good. I went through the same thing, again. I started feeling better, and I thought that things were going to be different, this time. So I got out and, within two months from the time I went in, there I was again, hurting. Needless to say, by this time I wasn't working. Things kept on in this vein, and I went to yet another rehab. This one was state-run, but it was kind of nice, up in the mountains. When I started feeling good, I was able to go hiking and do some rather enjoyable things there.

After I got out of this latest rehab, I did things a little

bit differently. Somehow, one of the biggest consulting engineering firms in northern New England had gotten hold of my name, given me a call, and hired me. It was a very good job, in another part of the state. I moved there and was staying sober during this period. But shortly after I found a place to live and became a little settled in my new job, I started drinking, again. It was just a matter of weeks before I was even worse than I had been before. The progression of this disease now really made itself known to me, and I immediately felt the physical effects. I wasn't able to get up and go to work every morning, and people at the office took notice.

For some reason, people at this particular company were a little more willing to deal with my problems. They confronted me, and I was told, "We know what your problem is, but you'd better straighten out, or you're going to lose this job." They gave me that chance as a sort of warning shot. So I did the only thing I knew to do; I went to another rehab. This one was located very close to the office, another state-run facility, but not at all as nice as the last one.

Right before I decided to go there, I was out drinking and driving one night, across the state line, and I got picked up for DWI. This wasn't my first such offense. It was in the middle of the night, and I was far from home. The police just threw me in jail. No one cared what I said, and they weren't going to call anybody. They would let me call, but who the hell would come? The only person I could think of, at that point, was my father. I couldn't call anyone where I was now residing; I didn't know anybody well enough to feel I could ask them for anything. I hated to phone my dad, but I did. Of course, he wasn't going to come at one o'clock in the morning. He said that I would have to wait until the next day.

So I spent the night in jail. And that was one of the most frightening experiences I have ever had. I was totally alone. I was caged like an animal, and I felt like one. The thing that I had feared the most, throughout my life, was now happening: I had lost my freedom. This was one reason I had always denied having a drinking problem, all those years that people were on my case. I was just so afraid that they would take all my alcohol and lock me away somewhere and throw away the key.

And I think that was the beginning of the end. Right after I got out of jail, I made the decision to go into rehab. I had reached the point where I was about to lose my job if things didn't work out. My parents had cut me off. They weren't going to help me out of my scrapes, anymore (something I now realize they should have done a long time before). My boyfriend had just about left me on my own. He told me that I could call him if I wanted to, but he wasn't going out of his way for me, anymore. He was dating other people, by this time.

On my own now, I was alone and scared. I was full of remorse and self-loathing, and I had absolutely no self-respect. I had reached a point where I felt the only alternatives were death or getting sober. And I didn't believe it was possible to stay sober. I really wanted to die, but I lacked the courage to kill myself.

I went into the rehab with this attitude: If it works, fine; but if it doesn't, then I *will* kill myself. But I decided to turn my life over to the care of the counselors there. I surrendered; I gave up control. I knew I hadn't been doing a very good job on my own. And it was with that attitude that a feeling of hope was somehow able to get through. When the counselors introduced me to Alcoholics Anonymous, I listened, and I learned. And I did whatever those people told me to do, because they were being successful at life, and I was a failure. They had what I wanted, what I had chased after my whole life but was never able to attain. I had been miserable, all this time. So now I was just surviving, a day at a time. But I wasn't drinking, anymore.

When I got out of the treatment program, I went back to work, but I was never given a clean bill of health by the rehab people. By that, I mean that they were good enough to keep me there on a halfway-house basis. (I was the first one they allowed to do that. And, to my knowledge, they have never had anybody else since then on such a basis, because they are, actually, an inpatient center.) I am so grateful because I know that if they had just let me go, I probably would have wound up drinking again, as I had all the previous times when I was feeling much better, physically. It's so easy to fool ourselves that we're cured when we feel well again. I needed a place to go home to that was clean and safe. So I lived there for three months, and I went to work every day and to meetings every night. I did what everybody told me to do. I even got a sponsor. When I was ready, after about three months, to leave and move into my own apartment, I still went for weekly counseling.

One thing I've left out is that, during all my drinking, and up until I went into the rehab this last time, I'd always believed that I was master of my own destiny. I was an agnostic. I had never truly believed that there was a Supreme Being, and all that "stuff" I'd been taught in church. I never even gave it a lot of thought. Once in the program, with the words "Higher Power" and "God" being thrown out in every other sentence, I couldn't ignore these concepts too much longer. And so, after about six months of being sober, I was talking to my sponsor about it, and she pointed out to me that I now had these months of sobriety, something I'd never achieved before. And she asked me how I had done it. In all honesty, I knew I could not give myself credit for that; I had not done it under my own power. And that was the first step, for me, in coming to believe.

Looking back, I realize, now, that I had turned my will and my life over to the care of a Higher Power that I didn't understand, at the time, and I was using the fellowship as my "Higher Power." Since that time, however, my concept of a Supreme Being has developed to the point where, today, I have a relationship with a Someone whom I choose to call God. And I still don't understand Him! But I pray daily, and I don't think my prayers go unheard.

My life improved, as I began to live in sobriety. My health improved. I acquired a sense of self-respect that kept growing. I even began to like myself. I also began to have friends, not only in the program, but relationships outside, as well, that were healthy. And I became very active in Alcoholics Anonymous.

But my story doesn't really end there. I still had my job with the consulting firm. After I had about four years of sobriety, we got very busy at the office, which wasn't unusual. But this time, the busy period lasted about six months. I was working really hard, putting in a lot of overtime, working many weekends. And I began to stop going to my A.A. meetings. Although I'd missed meetings in the past, I'd never attended meetings sporadically for as long as this.

After approximately half a year, the busy period was over; the work was done. But I didn't start going back to meetings, as I had always done before. And I don't know why. I guess it's that it is so easy to take sobriety for granted, to really forget where our priorities are. (Our priorities *should* be our recovery—first, and always, and foremost—and going to any length to keep that. And then should come everything else because, without our sobriety, we can lose it all.) I gradually removed myself from the program. At first, people from the fellowship would ask me what I was up to, and how I was doing, but they were pretty much concerned with their own lives, as they should be. And after a while, they just stopped bothering with me.

About three months before my fifth anniversary, I was no longer going to meetings. I took a new job, one that entailed a move to another state. So there I was, again, all alone. And when the job didn't go as well as I had expected it to, and things just weren't as hunky-dory as I wanted them to be, I did what is very natural for any alcoholic to do. I picked up a drink. Within three weeks, I returned to the point where I had left off and was going far beyond it. I was missing work. Physically, I was sick as hell. Emotionally, I was much worse, because I kept thinking that I'd thrown away all that recovery time.

I'd only been on the new job a couple of months (I had, when applying for it, sent out many résumés—really flooded the market), when a company in the state where I now live called me and asked if I were still interested in working for them. I was more than happy to get out of where I was, so I accepted the job offer and moved, again. But I was still drinking. I was back to my old pattern of bingeing and drying out. Knowing everything I did, I still used all of the old excuses to myself.

When I became established a little bit, the people at the office picked up on the fact that I might have a drinking problem. One day a woman at the office, a member of Alcoholics Anonymous in the local area, confronted me. And all of my defenses came down, then and there. I knew I couldn't go on. I knew what lay ahead and that I wouldn't be able to survive it if I kept on going the way I had been. And I knew that I needed something more than just going back to the program, so I went to another rehab. And I'm glad I did.

In a lot of ways, I could easily be considered a so-called "high-bottom" drunk. But as an engineer, my chemical dependencies were highly visible. Active alcoholics are easy to spot, and they are not well-tolerated in my profession. My job required me to be alert all the time. I couldn't be drinking at noon and come back to the office and get away with it. My colleagues were going to notice when I was drunk, not just because they smelled it on my breath, but because it would be apparent that I was sloppy and not on the ball.

The company I worked for, or at least the people in my branch office, were good enough to work things out for me so I could be gone for a month and not lose my job. I have to point out that my second recovery (I'd only been drinking for five months, this time) was the most difficult thing I've ever done, much worse than my first. And statistically, the chances for somebody to recover a second time, after a length of sobriety such as I had had and then lost, are very, very slim.

When I got to the rehab, there were wonderful people there to help me. What they pointed out was that, before I could begin recovering again, I had to forgive myself. And that was so difficult. I just couldn't do it. I read all the A.A. literature that was handed to me. I had already read a lot of it before, but now it had new meaning. I found the words there that I needed to comfort me. It took a lot of work, and most of the month I was there, but I was finally able to forgive myself.

One of the things I learned was that out of all bad can come good, if we're willing to recognize the ways to make that happen. And the options and the choices are always there. It's just up to us to do something about them. Thus my relapse became an important part of my recovery.

When I got out of that rehab, where I had been introduced to local chapters of both Alcoholics Anonymous and Chemically Dependent Anonymous (a group I had never heard of, up until that time), I felt so comfortable with C.D.A. that, although I continue to go to A.A. today, I have more or less adopted Chemically Dependent Anonymous as my home, so to speak. All my close friends are in C.D.A. And my whole social life, today, revolves around that fellowship. I get not just what I need, but what I want, from their program.

Shortly after I became involved in C.D.A., I met my husband-to-be. We got married three years ago, and my life really is, today, beyond my wildest expectations. I have a wonderful job, a new one. My career is going well. My relationships with my family couldn't be better. And I have a new family, my husband's, which is now mine, as well. I have so many things to be grateful for, so many blessings. My new life is a real gift from God.

Today, my priorities are in order. Today, my recovery comes first, above my husband, above everything else, because without sobriety, all of this would be gone. I've already proved that to myself, once. When I look back on my relapse, now, I see it as a blessing. I guess I needed that, and I believe God knew that I would somehow survive it. Since choices are ours to make, He knew that if I wanted to, I would make it through.

I can't think of any way I could improve my life as it is now. It's not that I don't have problems. Of course, there are problems. But the point is that now I am *living* life, on life's own terms. I'm dealing with my problems, and I'm walking through them. I'm also dealing with the good times and walking through those.

Everything passes, everything changes, and it's just a question of taking it a day at a time. We plan for the future only in such a way that we have direction, some sort of path to follow, today. And if we do our best, today, we'll have a good tomorrow. I know that, because it's been happening for me, day after day after day.

What I've learned, through all that's happened to me, is that if I'm not spiritually fulfilled, I won't be happy. If I'm not continuously paying attention to my spiritual health, and trying to further develop my relationship with God, all the material things in the world aren't going to matter. I have material things, and they improve the physical quality of my life, but they certainly aren't the basis of my life. Without my relationship with my God, I wouldn't have the contentment that I always feel, the deep-down faith that, no matter what, everything's going to be all right. I have peace of mind, and that's what I never had before. That's what I never dreamed I would ever achieve. And that's what I'm truly grateful for, today.

Chapter 28
LOVE SET ME FREE

I had seen drugs around my neighborhood for a couple of years, but I was nearly eleven years old when drugs first began to interest me. I saw other, real big-shot guys around town smoking dope, and laughing, and having a good time, and I wanted to do that, too. I tried to talk them into giving me some dope. None of them would. But after a while, they finally decided to let me try it.

They let me smoke pot and drink wine. It got to the point where it was a little entertaining for them. When I'd get high, I'd play around and make a fool of myself. But I was having fun, and I liked that and the attention it gave me. From then on, I started smoking pot and hash, and then I would just about do anything else to look cool, because I wanted that. I wanted to be someone who was looked up to by other people.

As a kid, my goals were not to be a straight-A student, or to be a very successful businessman and get rich, because I always did badly in school. I was the class clown. I liked getting into trouble and being a smart aleck. When I found drugs, and the different world that drug people are involved in, I said, "Man, this is it!" There are a lot of people who say they didn't want to become addicts, and they didn't want everything that went with the drug scene. But once I got into that world, that's exactly what I wanted—to get loaded every day. I thought I was going to make my money selling drugs and become a big-time dealer with sailboats and houses around the world—all the dreams that don't really come true.

I lived in a place where there were all sorts of drugs to be had, so I started to use different types. Within a very short while, by the time I was around twelve, I began taking pills. I was snorting heroin by the time I was thirteen. Within three years, I had used all the drugs I knew about.

I found certain ones that I liked more than others. I knew, right from the beginning, that narcotics were very addictive, and I didn't want to get hooked. I wanted drugs that I could have fun with. I had fun, all right. My addiction lasted for sixteen years, and, for the first ten years of it, I had great times. Of course, there were some bad experiences. But, all in all, it was good, and I loved it. I thought of those years as a happy and successful part of my life.

It was a long time before I started to have problems, but then I had them for a lot of years. I lost my wife. She left me over my insanity with drugs, crime, and crazy people. But I didn't think that was any big deal. At the time she left, it hurt, but I accepted such things as just part of life.

I never thought of myself as a criminal, even though everything I did was illegal. I wasn't wrong; the laws were. I wasn't out there robbing stores and doing things like that. But I was involved in drug deals, and guns were a part of my life. I began to get arrested for stupid things, and I accepted that. It was the way I chose to live.

It wasn't until I was about twenty years old that

everything in my life seemed to fall apart. My friends, and I had lots of very close friends who cared about me and loved me, began to look down on me. Every time I was around them, they'd be lecturing me, saying, "You're ruining your life. You can't use those types of drugs. Why don't you just smoke pot, and do a little coke, and drink? You've got to leave narcotics alone." But I had fallen in love with heroin—that was now my drug of choice.

I left the West Coast and moved east. But on the East Coast, I didn't find the drugs as good. I didn't like the heroin I found there, but I was introduced to a lovely pill called Dilaudid. So I fell in love with that, instead.

Since I didn't know all the right people or have the connections to get the money and the types of drugs I liked, I started committing bigger crimes. I carried out armed robberies and burglaries. Then I realized that the best way to get big money and lots of drugs was to rob dealers. So that's how I made my living. Ripping off dealers was easy because they didn't dare to call the cops. Some people got shot, but I didn't care. I was at the point where I didn't care if I lived or died, so I didn't care if anyone else died, either. I just felt nothing. All I wanted to do was get loaded. I was depressed most of the time, and I used to think, "I wish it would just all end."

By the next year, I was in the hospital. That wasn't the first time, but it was one of the times when things started to work. I was sent to a detox, then to a rehab, and I learned about the program of Alcoholics Anonymous. I went to lots of meetings. I liked them, and I liked the people. When I'd hear them talking about looking into medicine cabinets for drugs at parties, I knew exactly what they meant. But I thought I was worse than they were. My self-esteem was so low. I was sure that if everyone knew what I was like, and what I had done, they wouldn't want me there. So I went back out, and I used for three more years.

In those three years, I went places, emotionally, that I had never been before. The darkness and the depression were just constantly with me. I was a blackout user. I would go for days without knowing what had happened. I wasn't just using recreationally, now. I was a daily maintenance user. I would wake up in the morning and shoot dope so I wouldn't go into withdrawal. Steadily, throughout the day, that's all I would do. I worked, off and on, but nothing in my life mattered. Eventually, I went into three more hospitals and detoxes.

There began to be a pattern to my behavior, and, each time, I would be told that I would never make it because I was unable to be honest with myself. And the terrible thing about it is that I knew they were right. Coming in and out of the program, for about five years, I began to learn some things. I started to pick up values, and I began to feel worse about myself.

I was strung out badly, I was physically shaky, and I was having persistent convulsions. I couldn't even get loaded. No matter how much I'd shoot, I would either pass out or still be in withdrawal. I hated it, so I checked myself into another hospital. I thought, "This is it. I don't like this, anymore. It's no fun." I went through detox. Halfway through, I started to feel, again, to come to and realize what was going on. And I was filled with fear because I thought I would have to live without drugs, from now on, and I was afraid I couldn't. Because I felt I was such a failure, I thought I might be the type of person who couldn't make it without them.

When I got out of the hospital, I went to a rehab. But I was soon thrown out of there because I wasn't cooperative. When I was alone with the counselor, and I felt pain, I could talk to him about it. But when I was around other people, my ego wouldn't let that happen. I couldn't let anyone else know how badly I hurt.

So I started using again, and I used for four months. It was the worst it had ever been. I didn't shoot dope for the first three-and-a-half months. All I did was drink and smoke pot every day. I became a blackout drinker. I would black out in the mornings, and I'd come to the next day. Then I'd drink and black out, again.

Now, for the first time in my life, I began to think about killing myself. I was just so miserable. I was afraid to live, but I was not afraid to die. Somehow, I did start going back to meetings, again. I knew everything about the program—I'd been going for so many years. But this time, I went in with this attitude: If my life doesn't get better in a year, I'm going to kill myself, because I *cannot live* like this any longer.

That was eight years ago. I haven't picked up a drug or a drink since then. That's a miracle. What worked is that I tried to listen to what the people told me. I knew all the Steps, and I knew all the clichés, and I knew everything about the program *except* how to do it. I looked back over my life, all those years of going in and out of the program, and I knew I had to do something different, or it wouldn't work for me this time, either.

I started meeting some people, and, I guess because I was at such a terrible point in my life, I decided, "What the hell. I'd better trust these people." And that was very hard, learning to trust *anybody*. I went to meetings every day. I got a sponsor, and I hung out with people after the meetings.

But I didn't want to do those things, and I didn't like the people. Everyone was always so happy and positive. I thought if they just knew how awful I felt, and how much I hurt, they couldn't be in there laughing. Of course, I wasn't going to tell them that. I couldn't admit to them that I was in pain, because I didn't know them. It seems so stupid, but I believed that these people would recognize me as the failure I was if I let them know where I was coming from.

The first four months I was in the program, I didn't talk at the meetings. I couldn't bring myself to open my mouth because I was afraid of what I might say, and I didn't want to humiliate myself. But I would talk afterwards. My sponsor and Jack, another member, would talk to me for long periods of time after the meetings, and they taught me how to have fun. Jack openly spoke about a Higher Power, and he made it easy for me to learn to start praying and to begin working the Steps.

I got another sponsor after around four months, and I went to his house every day. We would just talk for hours and hours. I got rid of some of the nonsense and a lot of the fears that I had bottled up. I learned to become comfortable with myself. I started living for today, instead of in the past.

After I was in A.A. for about six months, Chemically Dependent Anonymous was started, and that was where I began getting involved in the program. I started by making coffee, and I felt responsible for that duty. As I saw that I was doing my job well, I came to realize that this was the first time I had ever done anything well. My sponsor and I continued to talk about working the Steps.

I was told, in the beginning, that the Steps *are* the program, and that the only way I was going to get better was by following them. But everything I had to do, in the beginning, was completely against the way I had always lived. I didn't like doing most of it, but I found out that when I did what C.D.A. said to do, things were a little bit easier. I didn't get a job for the first year or so in the program, mostly out of laziness, but partly because I was too burnt out to think. I had a lot of time on my hands. So, if there were three meetings a day, I'd go to three meetings.

When I did start to work, it was with my sponsor. He taught me that it was O.K. to screw up in the job I was doing. He used to tell me, "That's why they make erasers on pencils." What he did for me, and for my program, was that he gave me permission to make mistakes. I had been so terrified of doing things wrong that I often wound up not doing anything. Now, I could start accepting the fact that I am human. Therefore, I will, at times, be less than perfect.

Everything that I had, when I came into the program, began to get better. The relationship I had been involved in took a long time to turn into a healthy one. I had been told, in rehab, that if the girl I lived with and I wanted to stay together, we were both going to have to get lucky. I know why they said that. It is much harder for two addicts to try to recover together than it is for each of them to try to do it alone. But, for some reason, it has worked out for us.

The turning points in my program came when I would get backed up against the wall. I'd hurt so badly that I would be willing to go on and do a next Step. I did my Fourth and Fifth Steps when I had about eight months in the fellowship. These Steps allowed me to just let go of my past and stop living in it. They gave me that time in the present, without the drugs and the alcohol and all the crazy behavior, to look back at the eight months and say, "Well, I haven't done all these things in eight months. I'm just not that same person."

And they let me go on. Instead of basing all my decisions on my sick past, I began to make decisions about myself and my life according to my life in the present. I started to build a pathway of program action, and that opened up the world for me. My first couple of years were hard and painful, but the joy I got out of them was well worth it.

Then, after a year or so, everything stopped being *new*. The first time you went to the dance without drugs, the first time you went to the job without using —all these first things—were old hat, now. The excitement had worn off. I had to start looking at just living, one day at a time. Going through the Steps, though, caused most of my fears to ease, and I did begin to live.

I no longer looked to other people for my standards for growth. I looked at myself and saw that I was O.K. I had come a long way! I had been taught not to judge my insides by other people's outsides. And the true miracle that had happened in my life was that I had really tried to work the program, this time. And even though I had gone back out so many times before, I was now clean and sober.

Going on into the Steps opened up all the doors. I started to let go of my character defects, something that was very difficult for me. I began to look over my day, each evening, to see if there were things that I had done wrong. I tentatively made conscious contact with my God. When I first came into the program, I just believed in anything. But, after a long time, my definition, or my concept, became more particular. I found more faith, and that faith kept me going.

Slowly, I started to feel more a part of the world. I was told, when I first came into C.D.A., that it had taken me sixteen years to get there, so I wasn't going to be able to change overnight. I accepted that, from the first day. It helped me, too, not to have expectations that when I had one year in the program, I would have this, or that after three years, I will have that, and after five years, something else. I didn't go by such guidelines. If I had, I would probably have gone crazy and gotten loaded.

Instead, I went to the meetings, and I worked the Steps, and I lived just one day at a time. Just give me one day, and I could succeed. I did the very best I could, but some days that meant just staying in bed—not getting out, but also not getting loaded. And some days, that meant going out there in the world and doing everything I could to live normally.

I came into the program unfeeling and uncaring. Today, I have all the feelings any other person has. I care about people. I have learned how to love people. I've even learned to like them. And that is one of the greatest gifts I have received. My life has changed completely since I started working the Steps. People in the fellowship told me that happiness comes from within. And it is from within that I am happy, now. I have a successful life, but my happiness is where my true success lies.

C.D.A. has given me many other great gifts in my life. When I first heard the saying, "With responsibility comes freedom," I thought, "I don't want to be responsible. Freedom is in the back of my backpack." But I have found that freedom does come with the responsibility that I accept. I am employed, now, and I'm responsible for my job. I go to work—even though I don't *like* to work, and I don't like *going* to work— because the things that I get from working *are working for me*. And the job gives me the opportunity to do other things that I like to do.

I've got a commitment in life, not only to the program, but also to my wife. We've been married for five years (and have been living together for seven). That's a real commitment, one that gives me freedom— freedom to love. I don't have any of the bad feelings I had with all my other past relationships because I know I am being true, this time.

My wife and I have bought a house. It's not a house

at the beach, or a mansion. It's just a little place, but it is ours, and it's not going to be taken away because of the next drug deal I blow. I'm living a life I had never thought possible, and I owe all of that to the program.

I believe, at this moment, that my Higher Power gave me the people in C.D.A. I'm very grateful for them. They have helped to make me into someone I never thought I could be. I owe God, and them, everything. I have to have people in my life, and that's great. I used to think that not needing anyone was the way to be. Today, I know better. The people I sponsor give me so much, too. To be able to watch them change and grow is a truly wonderful gift. The miracle is that I haven't had to have a fix, a pill, or a drink for six-and-a-half years. I couldn't have done that alone. I just put my little part in; I did a little bit of the footwork. The program and the people of the fellowship are responsible for the rest.

Anybody who wants this program can have it. It states: "If you want what we have, here it is—just take these simple Steps. And, one day at a time, your life will change."

C.D.A. saved my life. It can save yours, too.

Chapter 29
MISERABLE MIKE

The story begins in the Midwest. Mother was a Lutheran, and father was a Catholic. The move to dad's home, down South, was short-lived. Mom became unhappy and left my father. She then took custody of her son, me, returned to the Midwest, and remarried.

My entire family, and most of our friends, drank on a daily basis. Some of us drank more heavily than others, and, as a result, had to pay the consequences. My stepfather died from an alcohol-induced seizure, in the late sixties, when he was only thirty-nine years old. A brother-in-law got so depressed while drinking that he blew his brains out onto the living room floor one evening, much to the horror of his wife and two young children. An aunt drank until she passed out in the bathroom one afternoon, never to regain consciousness. My stepbrother partied so hard that he overdosed and died when he was just eighteen. Both my stepsisters still like to drink socially, and are married to men who use chemicals, on a regular basis, in order to function. By the age of thirty-six, I was suicidal, wondering why I had to endure the pain of this life twice as long as my little brother, and knowing that I could not survive as long as my stepfather had.

I remember being melancholy as a child. I didn't like attending the Lutheran grammar school. The teachers said that I had the intellectual potential, but that I just would not apply myself. Maybe that had something to do with my stepfather. He was a bartender who was absent from home much of the time. Or maybe it was due to the fact that we had a well-stocked bar at home. As the oldest child, I was responsible for acting as the family bartender. I could make all the house-favorite cocktails by the time I was eight years old. I had to attend summer school more than once because of my bad grades. As a cute little kid, I sometimes drank until I passed out. And sometimes I awoke in my own vomit.

Things began to change when, due to financial pressures, I had to attend a public high school. Now I had peers who liked to drink and smoke. I got my first pair of contact lenses, shed my thick glasses, and discovered girls. I played football and loved the hard physical contact at the defensive position of middle linebacker. It seemed as though I had died and been reborn. I was enjoying life. I seemed to be so much more capable of doing things. I was even studying. In fact, I graduated as a member of the National Honor Society. But as my drinking increased, my blackouts were not all at home, anymore, and my driving record proved it.

After graduation, I got a job working for a large corporation as a computer operator/programmer, and it was here that I met the young lady I was to marry within a few years. Her family lived on the other side of town, but they loved to drink as much as I did. All our dating and social engagements revolved around alcohol.

Somehow, it was decided that I should resume my education, and, the following year, I enrolled in a Christian university. Of course, I pledged the fraternity that had a beer machine hidden in the basement. College football was intimidating because it seemed as if everybody but myself had put on about a hundred pounds. But unfortunately, sports had now started to interfere with my partying. Disciplinary problems ensued, and I was asked to leave school during my sophomore year.

When I joined the Army, near the end of the sixties, it seemed to be a big mistake. I didn't like the barracks life with the guys, so I married right after basic training. Eventually, I secured a position as a computer programmer, and everything seemed fine until my wife, who must have gotten tired of living with my self-centeredness, began to have affairs. I believe, now, that she was merely seeking the love and attention that a practicing alcoholic cannot give. But, at the time, I just consoled myself by drinking more heavily.

I received orders for Vietnam, but was instead diverted, purely by chance, to duty in a state far to the north. My wife and I tried to make the relationship work again, but neither of us had changed, and her affairs continued. Flying was now my big love, and I received my private pilot's license. I began to experiment with marijuana socially, at this time, since it was legal in that state.

I was given an honorable discharge from the Army, after two years, and returned to college. But my finances dwindled until I was forced to seek employment. Now living out West, I had a real "Catch-22" experience. I found that I couldn't get a position in the computer field without a degree, and that I couldn't get a degree without a decent job. The Air Force Bootstrap Program appealed to me, so I was off to the West Coast, where I majored in psychology, visited the local wineries, and cultivated my own herb.

After completing my bachelor's degree requirements, as a distinguished graduate from the School of Military Sciences, I was commissioned as an officer. Neither my wife nor I appreciated my assignment back East. Since she had continued to seek love outside of the marriage relationship, it was decided that she should stay behind and seek legal separation.

My next relationship lasted approximately five years, during which time I drank daily and smoked grass on occasion. I carried the scars of my broken marriage, and I found that, besides not being able to love, I was now unable even to trust. So I began cheating, in order to keep from being hurt again. I enjoyed the status of being an officer, and during this time I returned to college and took some undergraduate pre-med courses. At twenty-seven, I was too old to be accepted by a medical school, so I completed a master's degree in business management and supervision. It was really an extension of my psychology degree in counseling, but I just couldn't see working with a clientele of emotionally disturbed people every day.

One dreary morning, I returned home to find my girlfriend in bed with my best friend, a fellow officer. Of course, I reacted immaturely, and, as a direct result, both my best friend and I were subsequently released from active duty and honorably discharged. Somehow, the Air Force decided that our using marijuana constituted conduct unbecoming of officers and that our behavior was not that of gentlemen. My sick relationship with the woman was renewed, however, and continued until she again had an affair. This time, it was with my *new* best friend. She eventually married him.

On my own, with no woman to give me any heartache, was how I started my career as a federal employee. I was still in the computer field, and I was determined to work hard and play hard. I was finished with formal education for a while, but I became an avid student in the field of parapsychology. I bought my first house. I had been addicted to running, so I was in relatively good health. Now I added weight training, in order to become more *macho*.

It was while working a part-time job with a company running weekend ski trips that I was introduced to cocaine. Initially, it was used as just a stimulant, to allow me to party all Friday night, ski all day Saturday, party all Saturday night again, ski all day Sunday, and then keep awake for the drive home Sunday evening. I enjoyed this drug so much that my next part-time job was that of a nightclub bouncer. The fringe benefits included free drinks, better coke, and exposure to opiated hash, mushrooms, PCP, barbiturates, and other drugs, as well as lots of fun-loving women.

Although my absenteeism from my government job increased, and my ability to function as a computer specialist was becoming more and more impaired, my capacity to fabricate stories grew to meet my needs. It was at this time that I was introduced to freebasing cocaine, and I fell so much in love with this new high that I became a dysfunctional addict. It wasn't long before I experienced every symptom of mental illness that I had studied in abnormal psychology: schizophrenic paranoia with full-blown audio-visual hallucinations, the overdoses, the sweats, the shakes, and, finally, the deep suicidal depression and complete inability to cope.

My roommates feared that they might be in danger, so they volunteered me for treatment on an outpatient basis. I was able to quit freebasing, but I continued to drink and use coke and other chemicals, daily, for another year. My last weekend binge, six years ago, started at an office picnic. I knew I had a problem, but I was still trying to find out how I could drink socially. I figured one hot dog or hamburger per beer would be a safe ratio. But, after the first beer, I was unable to stop. And, eventually, I had to score some coke, too. The usual blackout ensued, and when I came to, on Sunday, I did a line of coke and began to cry.

This was the first time that coke had let me down, and I was embarrassed because there were people around. I dropped back to "old reliable" and drank a fifth of 100-proof vodka straight down, but that, alone, didn't help. Next, I grabbed a quart of rum, downed it, and faded into oblivion. When I was revived, I found myself wrapped up in my own vomit and bleeding from both ends. I showered and went to work, came home and vowed not to drink again. The D.T.'s were very bad Monday night, and I found no rest amid all the horror of the hallucinations. I returned to work the next day, only to have a mental breakdown. I finally sought medical help in a hospital with a detox ward, and this is where God introduced me to Alcoholics Anonymous.

My only prayer, up to this time, had gone like this: "Look, God, if You don't allow me to quit hurting so bad, I'm just going to kill myself, and You're going to lose one of Your little experiments down here." I guess this concept of God was left over from my parapsychology days. But now, in A.A., I was being told that I no longer had to drink or use drugs, that there was a program designed to show me how to live a better life, and that I didn't have to die. I wept. It was too good to be true.

I went manic-depressive in detox and was sedated with antidepressants for two weeks. After release, I was too depressed to return to work, but I started attending local A.A. meetings. There I was told about another fellowship for people who used drugs, as well as alcohol, and I started attending Chemically Dependent Anonymous. I went to one of their meetings at a local rehabilitation center and apparently was still in bad enough shape, after thirty days clean and sober, that they admitted me for twenty-eight days of inpatient treatment. Here, I received the tools necessary for success in my recovery.

I learned that I needed to get down on my knees every morning and ask God to remove the compulsion to drink and use drugs. I was told to return again, on my knees, at night, to thank Him for another day, clean and sober. The medical aspects of what I had done to myself, and valuable lessons on the importance of fellowship; keeping honest, open-minded, and willing to try; and the Twelve Steps were slowly absorbed as I began to work the program.

After returning to work, I found that I had changed one addiction for a much healthier one, and I began to attend meetings as if my life depended on them. I was allowed to go to lunchtime meetings. With the one or two meetings I also went to each evening, during my first ninety days, I managed to make it to about two hundred meetings. The emotional high I was on is called a "pink-cloud," and I enjoyed it until an incapacitating depression brought me once again to my knees, around six months into the program. I just could not stop crying, so I called in to work, explaining my embarrassing condition. Then I sought medical assistance.

The empathic physician who patiently listened to my predicament said, "You're just lazy, and what you need is a good swift kick in the ass." To this kindly statement I replied, "But I'm going to die." He referred me to a psychiatrist, who also listened patiently (for $100 an hour) and explained to me that I was having a normal reaction. I had lost my best friend and lifelong companion, Alcohol, who had always been there to help me to celebrate, or to console me when I was down.

I was just undergoing a mourning process, and once it was over, I would be a lot stronger psychologically. Once again, I stated, "I'm going to die." But he said he couldn't help me, or give me anything to ease my pain, because I was an addict.

Now just about ready to give up and take my own life, I stopped in at a meeting place. One of the guys there came to my assistance and told me that this sort of depression sometimes occurred as part of a protracted withdrawal, as was explained in *Under the Influence*, by James R. Milam, Ph.D., and Katherine Ketcham. This volume showed pictures of healthy blood samples and compared them to the electron microscopic views of the alcoholic's, with the organelles and mitochondria all blown apart and oozing their life-sustaining properties. In the sequel, *Eating Right to Live Sober*, by Katherine Ketcham and L. Ann Mueller, M.D., it was shown that a nutritional approach, eliminating caffeine, nicotine, sugar, and red meats, was indicated for recovery.

Being compulsive, I eliminated even the legal stimulants from my diet. I went so far as to fast regularly and eat nothing but organically grown, fresh, raw fruits and vegetables for a period of one year. After dropping from one hundred and eighty-five pounds to one hundred and twenty-five (with my friends fearing I had contracted either cancer or AIDS) I added whole grains and, occasionally, some meats to my diet. I then regained a more healthy one-hundred-and-fifty-pound-average weight for one who is my height.

During this time, I had what I choose to call my "spiritual awakening." While attending a seminar on the Book of Revelation in the Holy Bible, I accepted Jesus Christ as my personal Higher Power. My first year of sobriety was filled with some six hundred meetings, three spiritual retreats, and one baptism. The sponsor I've had ever since I first went into treatment was a real blessing through all this. He listened to my crying, and, although he had never personally gone through the deep depression I was experiencing, he encouraged me to stick with not picking up, to continue to attend the meetings, and to keep on praying. Seeking his approval, I told him that I had answered an altar call and was going to be baptized. He confided in me that he had already done the same thing and said that it was O.K.

Having God in my life is not a universal panacea, but it does provide me with strength to carry on, with the help of the fellowship. God works through people. But, even though life in recovery is a series of relationships with other men and women, sometimes there are heartaches that only God can heal. Some of your buddies, or members of your family, won't get the program, and they can end up in jails, institutions, or even the grave. An intimate relationship breaks up, and you can't use to relieve the pain, as you used to do.

There can be other heartaches, too. After buying that new house and a new car, and after years of being clean and sober, you lose the job you've had for ten years, and your confidence is shot. It's not always easy to remember that the Lord gives, but that He also takes away, that all things work together for the good for those who love the Lord and are called according to His purpose. Thank God, though, there is the program and the words of encouragement that are found in the Holy Bible.

The opportunities I have for growth are always there, as long as I continue to show up and reach out to help someone else. It might be through sponsorship, speaking on radio talk shows, doing TV commercials, leading out in Bible studies, sharing in meetings, listening to a troubled friend, or in sending cards and letters to loved ones. Faith, without works, is dead.

Working the Steps to the best of my ability is a major challenge. A crying man wrapped in his own vomit and blood knows that his life is unmanageable, but I had harbored such resentment against God that coming to believe that He had my best interests at heart was extremely difficult. Taking a personal inventory was something I had never done before, and I was afraid that I would not like what I was going to find out, let alone be able to share it with another human being. I still struggle with character defects; but, today, I ask God for help in eliminating the ones He points out.

Personally making amends to people wasn't easy, either. But even though they didn't always accept me or my apologies, I felt better for having tried. I remember, in particular, making amends to my beloved grandfather. When I blurted out that I hadn't visited him for a few years because I was too embarrassed about my alcoholism and my drug addiction, he said, "It's been more like five years, and, even then, it wasn't any fun to have you around." But on my next visit, when he saw that I was still sober, he was so impressed that he took me around to his friends and showed me off. Continuing to take a personal inventory and admit my wrongs allows me the opportunity to grow spiritually.

In making decisions, I use the Third and Eleventh Steps, trying to seek God's way, praying that He will close the doors where He would not have me enter in, and open those doors where He wants me to proceed. To me, prayer means talking to God. And meditation means that I have to listen: at meetings, in Bible studies, or in church, and that I have to keep an open mind as to what God's will is for me each day.

A.A.'s *Dr. Bob and the Good Oldtimers* has shown me where the Twelve Steps came from, and the importance of studying the Bible and applying what I learn to my daily life. The slogan, "First Things First," refers to seeking first the kingdom of God and His righteousness, after which all other things shall be gathered unto you. And "One Day at a Time" means that we are not to worry about tomorrow, for today has troubles enough of its own.

Today finds me between relationships, unemployed, melancholy from time to time, but strong in my faith that God can still use this beaten-up, tired shell of a man to help someone else in recovery, to be of service to someone in need, to encourage the less fortunate, or to pray for a brother's salvation. I enjoy reading the Scriptures, and sharing the light that I find, so much so that I've applied to a small Christian Bible college to study pastoral counseling. I'm not sure where tomorrow may find me, but I'm sure that God will be with me, and with anyone in C.D.A. who is looking for Him, always, even until the end.

Chapter 30
A SIXTIES IDEALIST

During the sixties, like many drug-experimenting members of my generation, I believed that taking psychedelics and smoking pot were positive, beneficial things to do. I thought that if the whole country would "turn on, tune in, and drop out," America, and the whole world, would be a better place in which to live. In my mind, my drug taking was connected with being for the civil rights movement, civil liberties, and environmental protection; and with being against war, racism, and classism. Most of the people who were part of the counterculture, in that era, also smoked marijuana.

Therefore, it was very difficult later, in the eighties, to admit that I had become an addict. To make such an admission, to finally acknowledge that marijuana was addicting, seemed also to mean that I had sold out all my values, and that I was renouncing my ideals and my politics at the same time. Fortunately, attaining sobriety, which was the most difficult thing I have ever done in my life, did not require that I become a conservative.

I was born on a farm. I received a nurturing and stable upbringing from my liberal parents. They inculcated in me the idea that, as an American, I had a duty to oppose the government, or any authority, whenever it was wrong or interfered in my right to privacy, provided that my opposition was peaceable and within the system.

In college, in the late fifties, I was introduced to marijuana, which was very rarely used, at that time, on campuses. I was also given pure Sandoz LSD once, in my sophomore year, at a time when it was still legal and had not yet received attention from the press. The acid trip (and the state of consciousness which I experienced during the trip) was the most significant thing that had ever happened to me. After this experience, I found that I was able to understand certain mystical poetry and philosophical writings which had previously been incomprehensible to me. I was also able, for the first time, to appreciate modern art. This led me to believe that the path to greater intuitive insight, as well as wisdom, and even spiritual enlightenment, lay in experimenting further with psychedelics and in finding other psychedelic devotees.

So, two years later, when I graduated from college, I headed for the West Coast city known as the world capital for such experimentation. My most hopeful expectations were fulfilled when I had a spiritual experience while under the influence of a psychedelic. During this epiphany, I felt a union with the One and understood, completely, the first chapter of the Gospel according to St. John.

After that revelation, my life seemed changed, as it is when a person has a religious conversion, except that I wasn't converted to any specific belief system. I just felt at peace with the Universe, as if my own individual wants and needs were not so important, and everything was O.K. I thought, "God's in His Heaven, and all's well with the world." I stopped doing psychedelics after about ten or twelve trips because I ceased to have new experiences or breakthroughs, and I thought that was what these chemicals were for. They did not seem to be the types of drugs one would want to get high on.

I went to law school and became a lawyer, and I did very well. Not only was I successful financially, but I was able to become involved in various types of "movement" cases that would allow me to attack, and help change, the system. I smoked marijuana and considered that it helped me to be creative. Often, I edited things I wrote when I was high on marijuana. Although I drank heavily, off and on, I considered marijuana my drug of choice, and I considered myself a "head," not a "juicer." Because I believed strongly that more widespread use of marijuana would help society, I actively and publicly worked to repeal laws prohibiting *Cannabis sativa.*

In the middle seventies, following the breakup of my marriage, I began to drink in the morning, and this really alarmed me. I went to see a highly regarded psychiatrist and told him I was afraid I was becoming an alcoholic. He said, "No, you just have a lot of anxiety, and you are self-medicating. If you come to therapy and get to the root of your problem, your anxieties will diminish, and you will not need to drink so much."

While in therapy with this doctor, my drinking and marijuana use increased; I would get up at 6 a.m. feeling acutely suicidal and would often cry out, "I want to die." Then I would have two martinis, follow that by smoking a joint and, by 10 a.m., after a couple more martinis, I'd go to work. If I had to go to court, I would forbear smoking the joint.

After two years of therapy, my psychiatrist started showing up late for my appointments and then began not showing up at all. I got very depressed and concluded that psychiatry was a sham and that my real problem was America—and practicing law. So I closed down my practice and went to the Far East for eighteen months. There, I stopped drinking in the morning, stopped smoking grass every day, and stopped feeling depressed and suicidal.

When I moved back to the United States, I decided the answer to my alcohol and drug problem was to get out of the fast lane, mellow out, live on less money, and work fewer hours. With a smaller amount of stress, I would not abuse alcohol and drugs. But even though I wasn't working and was leading a very laid-back lifestyle, as soon as I came back to America, I began drinking compulsively, beginning in the morning, again.

I went to a couple of Alcoholics Anonymous meetings and identified and bonded with my brother-and-sister alcoholics right off. But I didn't like the fact that the A.A. program involved total abstinence. I walked out of my first meeting chuckling to myself, "Of course they can solve their alcohol problems, if they don't drink anything at all." It seemed much too simplistic a solution. "A well-rounded individual must drink," I thought, "and I would be a failure at life if I admitted I couldn't handle booze and recreational drugs." There must be a therapist, or therapeutic method, which would help me get myself together so I could drink as I had in the good old days of my late twenties and early thirties.

While I was searching around for a solution which would not require abstinence, I met and fell in love with a beautiful young lover who thought everything I did was just great. This person was especially impressed with my ability to debauch, which my lover regarded as some sort of achievement. Being involved in this affair, and traveling around the country reenacting Hunter S. Thompson's *Fear and Loathing in Las Vegas*, kept me from feeling I had a problem, for a year. But when the affair broke up, I found myself staying high on pot continuously. So back I went to the therapists.

I even paid a nice sum of money to go to a six-week workshop which promised to teach people how to smoke marijuana moderately. Until that time, I hadn't known other people who felt they were addicted to marijuana, but at this workshop I met some people, including other professionals who, like me, were still "functioning" and practicing their vocations. I was particularly startled to meet a psychotherapist who was a pothead and who went to her sessions while she was high. The workshop used behaviorist methods to cut down, to set goals, and so on. I found I could cut back and control my marijuana use, but when I did, my alcohol consumption shot up. Although a local newspaper article touted the workshop, and the psychologists who ran it, as being 90 percent successful, my research on the people in my group revealed that, several months afterwards, all were back to smoking as much as they had before the workshop, if not more.

I continued to drink more and more until finally, after a ten-day binge, I went to two A.A. meetings and stopped drinking for thirteen months. During that time, I didn't continue to go to A.A., however, because I felt I didn't really need it, and I found it too corny. What would my sophisticated friends think if they knew I was getting together with a group of losers at life, holding hands and saying the Lord's Prayer?

Although I used no alcohol, I continued to use marijuana. I attempted to control my use of grass in various ways. I would only buy nickel bags or joints, and I'd have a friend hold my marijuana for several days so I could get temporarily clean. Rarely did I get really stoned on pot, and seldom did I smoke more than one or two joints a day. I smoked just enough to get high, and stay high, with a mild buzz. Of course, as I had throughout my life, I would, every so often, take coke, MDA, opium, or hashish when they were offered in social settings. But I seldom bought or used them by myself.

Being off the alcohol completely, I became very healthy, physically, and I looked great. I ate health food and did yoga. But I was increasingly panicky and anxiety-ridden. It was a big effort for me to do any work, or to do anything except party and have sex. I did less and less legal work and made less and less money. Increasingly, I felt estranged from people and alienated from society. More and more, I became depressed as I realized I didn't really care about anyone or anything except, "What is wrong with me?"—and whatever therapy, therapist, religion, lover, sex practice, career change, or new political cause could provide the answer to that question.

I felt like a fraud as a human being. When I told people I loved them, I suspected I was lying. When they told me they loved me, I thought there must be something wrong with them, or that they must have some hustle going or have some grave, sick dependency, if they could care for me. To bolster my eroding self-esteem, I sought to encourage people to think that I was the answer to their problems, the fulfillment of their fantasies; but then, if my self-promotion efforts were successful, I would feel trapped by the very demands that I had worked to arouse.

Also, I no longer had any real interest in participating in any political causes or professional associations. I felt society's institutions were hopelessly corrupt and decadent, and there was no way I could relate to any of them. Secretly, I believed a nuclear war might not be so bad, after all.

Then, after thirteen months, I started drinking again. I thought that drinking would be preferable to using marijuana all the time because I might be able to work better on booze. Using marijuana was inconsistent with trying to make a living at doing "left-brain"-type mental work. Even if I didn't use every day, I knew that there was a fuzzy-brain aftermath for several days after use of pot. Never did the idea that I could, or should, come off all mood- and mind-altering chemicals occur to me; instead, it always seemed a question of which ones, in what combination, to discontinue.

I then began to drink and use grass, as well as coke and speed, for four months, in an increasingly compulsive manner, before, in complete despair, I decided I must stop everything. I realized that, whatever joyful, enlightening function alcohol and marijuana might have played in my life earlier, I was now at the point where my usage of drugs and alcohol was solely for escape and avoidance of reality. It couldn't conceivably be thought, at that juncture, to be mind-expanding or beneficial in any way.

So, to start, I came off the alcohol. I knew I could stop the alcohol use because I had done it before, but I could not imagine how I'd ever be able to stop marijuana. I knew no one who was in Narcotics Anonymous, nor did I know anything about its program. But out of desperation, five days after I stopped drinking, I called N.A. (the city where I started to get clean and sober didn't have Chemically Dependent Anonymous) and asked, "Do you take people who only have a problem with marijuana?"

I was embarrassed to ask this because I felt ashamed

that I was addicted to such a mild drug; I thought that if I was going to have a drug habit, I ought to be using something like heroin or cocaine. But to be addicted to pot was ludicrous. The person on the telephone said, "Yes," and I went to my first meeting seven years ago. I have been clean and sober ever since.

Well, actually, I did have three or four Dalmanes after that meeting. I had persuaded a doctor to write a prescription for one hundred of them for me before I stopped using, because I couldn't imagine how I was going to sleep if I gave up both marijuana and alcohol. When I mentioned to my first, temporary, sponsor that I had some Dalmane in case I couldn't sleep, she informed me, "In 'The Program,' we don't do any drugs at all." I asked, "But how will I sleep?" and she said, "You may not sleep for a while, but eventually you will."

This advice, at first, seemed dogmatic and fanatical, since I had never had a problem with prescription drugs, although I had taken them, off and on, to ease off alcohol and street drugs. Furthermore, I had proved, so I thought, that I was not generally an addict, since I could take or leave cocaine, barbiturates, and even opiates. So some wimpy, boring drug like Dalmane certainly wasn't going to get its hooks into me. But I decided to do it the way "The Program" suggested, and I got rid of all my sleeping pills and tranquilizers. And I have not used any drugs since that time.

In my first meeting, I announced myself as a "marijuana addict," and, afterward, a young man came up and told me he had had the same problem. He said he had never seemed to get addicted to the stronger drugs, even though he had used them off and on. He had figured he couldn't have an "addict personality," or he would have become addicted to the so-called addicting drugs. And, he had asked, "Who can be addicted to marijuana?" He, too, reported that he'd spent a lot of time and money on therapists because he seemed to lack the motivation and the ability to get his life together and to use his creative potential. Finally, it had dawned on him that his marijuana use might be "The Problem."

So that night, I had another spiritual experience, a blinding revolutionary insight: *My* "Problem" was caused by my use of drugs! Before that, I had thought that my compulsive drug use was a result of my screwed-up psychological state and that if I got cured psychologically, my drug problem, my work problem, and my motivation problem would all be solved. But I had it backward: So long as I kept using, I would have work problems, anxiety, and feelings of alienation from people and society.

The first priority was to stop using all drugs and alcohol. And I knew that there was a power in the room, a force tapped by a group of addicts with a common desire to stop using. While I had not been able to stop by myself, with the power that was accessible through the group, I would never have to use again. I was free.

As the sedatives, marijuana, and alcohol gradually left my system, I experienced a succession of anxiety attacks and rages. These emotions had been there all along, but my "self-medication" had prevented me from feeling them. While the cravings for drugs and alcohol were lifted from the very beginning, I felt I was on the verge of insanity, most of the time, for well over six months. But the people in "The Program," by now, C.D.A., kept assuring me that my reactions and anxieties were not atypical and that I could survive it all, clean and sober, one day at a time.

The anxiety provided a great incentive to do the Steps and gain some insight into why I was so upset. I would then be able to change some of the maladaptive patterns which had resulted in my putting myself in no-win, stress-producing situations. A lot of my anxiety centered around my fear that I was permanently brain-damaged, because I found that I couldn't concentrate. I was afraid I would end up having to give up my profession and take a menial job for the rest of my life.

When the anxiety became so great that I decided, "To hell with it all! How do I know that it is not best, in the total scheme of things, that I be poor and brain-damaged?" my anxiety subsided, and my concentration improved. Eventually, after several years, my full mental capacity returned. As long as I was so attached to my intellectual ability, I was prevented from using it. I had to "Let Go," and put it in its proper perspective, before I could use it again.

C.D.A. has allowed me to live the life I had always wanted to live and to relate to people the way I had aspired to do when I was a flower child and peacenik. I now have a set of guidelines to live by: the Steps. They are nothing more than a compendium of principles found in many religions, philosophies, and psychologies from both East and West. They are not a mere gimmick that some self-help book writer has just discovered. I also have a group of people who are attempting to practice the same guidelines for living to talk to, to be with, and to turn to when I feel overwhelmed. By working with others, especially newcomers, I am relieved of the hell of self-preoccupation.

I feel that, initially, I turned to drugs because I wanted a fuller, richer, more deeply conscious life. Perhaps drugs do, in the beginning, open the doors to perception. But as I increasingly used them for escape, the result was that my life became narrower, poorer, and less conscious. And when I became addicted, no amount of personal effort or self-discipline, no new religion, or therapy, or lover was able to remove my craving and compulsion. Since coming to C.D.A. (and the other Twelve-Step programs) and doing the Steps, my desire to use any mood- or mind-altering chemical has left me. I hope that someone may read this story and see that there is a way to freedom from slavery to chemicals in this program.

Chapter 31

EVENING THE ODDS

My story is just like a lot of others. I never had any intention of growing up to be a drug addict and an alcoholic. It just seemed to happen that way.

When I was fifteen, I took my first drink. Not long after that, I became drunk for the first time. Three friends and I got hold of two fifths of wine and had drunk about half a bottle when one of the kids bet me that I couldn't finish the rest of that bottle and drink the other one, too. That was a 75¢ bet, and I won it. As a result, my first experience with alcohol was that I had a total blackout. I was sick, I began vomiting, and I woke up the next morning with a hangover. That should have told me something, but the next weekend, I got drunk again. This time the effects weren't quite so bad. I actually enjoyed drinking. And this was the way I started off my career of chemical dependency.

During high school, I was an athlete. I played varsity sports, track and football, and I really didn't abuse full time. But every weekend, I would go out and drink, and I would always get drunk. Everybody I ran around with did the same thing. We had a lot of fun; we were wild and crazy. But, from the very beginning, the only thing I associated with drinking was getting stoned.

Alcohol allowed me to do all those things I couldn't do, or didn't want to do, when I was straight.

At the end of my senior year, I thought I was going to get a football scholarship to a small university in the South. The recruiter came over to my house and talked to my parents, but when the school looked at my academic record, my grades just didn't cut the mustard. The following fall, I received my draft notice to report for a physical, and I was classified 1-A. Two months later, I received another notice to report to the Army.

The Army is where I found drugs. I was introduced to people who had been doing drugs since they were thirteen years old. I had never even seen any before I entered the service, when I was nineteen. Now I learned about marijuana, speed, rug cleaners, cough syrup. And I immediately became an abuser. I decided that I wanted to live my life using drugs as much as I could, whenever I could. I heard Timothy Leary say, "Turn on and drop out," and I was very ready to do that. The only problem was that I was in the Army. I couldn't drop out.

When I was discharged two years later, after almost getting busted for possession, I decided that I was going to live my life exactly the way I wanted to. And that was to do whatever I wanted to do whenever I wanted to do it, to have fun, to do everything in a different way than my parents had.

I had a girlfriend back home; I had kept in touch with her while I was in the service. We now decided to move in together. We got an apartment, and I enrolled in college, with the GI Bill paying my tuition. She was a schoolteacher, so she worked. I supported myself by dealing marijuana to supplement my GI Bill money.

I grew my hair long and did everything hippies did back then, going to concerts, demonstrations, and parties and getting high. I had a great time. I even went to

Woodstock, a fantastic experience. I tripped, the entire time I was there, on acid, mescaline, Dolophine, and any other drugs I could get.

Basically, I was tripping all the time, anyhow. After Woodstock, I went back to school. I got through college only because a good friend of mine supplied me with speed. I took it not only for exams, but just to be able to go to class. And, of course, I was smoking grass, too. It's a miracle that I managed to graduate.

When I got out of college, I found a job in sales, which has turned out to be my lifelong profession. I had a friend, about my age, who owned a factory where they silk-screened T-shirts, and he offered me a job selling these shirts. Everybody who worked at the factory was also young, and we all got stoned.

My job was to call on head shops, surf shops, and department stores. The majority of our shirts were drug paraphernalia lines in a wide variety of designs. They appealed primarily to people who were users. This was just when customized, silk-screened T-shirts were becoming very popular for advertising, and bar owners liked to order them to promote their establishments. Most of the people I called on were also getting loaded.

I remember the first time we had a boutique show in New York, shortly after I was hired. We had just set up an elaborate display. And my sales manager pulled out a bag of pharmaceutical Black Beauties and gave them to everybody. I was even more certain that I had found the perfect job.

And my alcoholism started to take shape, too, because of the calls I made on the bars. I'd be speeding, and then some of the bar owners and managers I had become friends with would give me free drinks. I would sit and drink in the bars all day, not making any sales calls. It progressed to where I was doing this on a daily basis. Sometimes I wouldn't leave until eleven o'clock at night. I'd call my girlfriend and tell her I wouldn't be home for dinner. As a result, after almost nine years of living together, we broke up. And I felt that this was the best thing that could have happened to me.

By now, my addiction was really taking a downhill course. I was getting DWIs. I started losing things, like my relationship with this girl. And I wasn't feeling too good about myself. I quit the job selling T-shirts and sold drugs for a few months, while I was unemployed.

I finally got another job, a really good one, selling ladies' sportswear. A head shop owner I did business with introduced me to another drug addict, who hired me. This user couldn't cover his whole territory, and he was still making $100,000 a year. The potential was there for me to make a lot of money, helping him. All I had to do was take samples to stores and show them five times a year. But I couldn't do it.

By this time, I had been introduced to cocaine, and I was also doing barbiturates and Quaaludes when I would go on the road. My routine was to take about an ounce of coke with me, and some speed. I would get a motel room, go to a liquor store and buy a fifth of liquor, come back to the room, and start making my calls. After a couple of trips, I no longer made the calls, though. I would just sit in the motel room and get so strung out that I'd be wired from all the drinking and drugs.

Needless to say, that job didn't last very long, and I found myself unemployed, broke, and addicted. I decided I would just deal drugs for a little while, again, before I found something else, but I wasn't a very good dealer. It seemed that everybody was willing to front me the drugs, but I would use them myself and then have a very hard time trying to pay back the man who fronted the dope. It got to the point where I owed thousands of dollars to my drug dealers, and they refused to give me any more.

I was still in the bars every day, acting like a big shot, pretending I had money. I cashed checks at the bars for $10 and $15, wondering where I was going to get the money to cover the checks. I borrowed from everybody I could think of, from my friends to my mother, until nobody would lend me any more money. At that time, I was living with two practicing drug-and-alcohol addicts. We were renting a house together. I was even writing bad checks to one of them to pay for my rent.

Then one of my roommates decided that he was going to leave the country, and, since the lease was in his name, the rest of us had to find another place to live. I kept putting it off, but finally a guy who frequented one of the bars I hung out in said that I could move in with him. Although I felt that the move would be good for me because I'd be away from my former roommates, it proved to be the beginning of my bottom.

I had found another sales job, but everything else was getting worse. I became more and more paranoid. I experienced more despair than I had ever known before. Yet at no time did I associate those feelings with drugs and alcohol abuse. I was not ready to quit, yet.

Then something happened. A former roommate, my best friend, Ronnie, was someone with whom I'd always compared myself, but only to the extent that if I ever got as bad as he was, I might think about doing something about myself. He was a *real* drug addict. He hadn't worked in about a year, and he had become totally unemployable, except for selling and manufacturing PCP. He was doing every kind of drug imaginable. He was the person I got many of my drugs from.

Then, all of a sudden, he decided to quit using drugs and alcohol, and he joined a program called Alcoholics Anonymous.

And here he was, staying straight! He would tell me about A.A., and how he hadn't done any chemicals for two weeks, a month, two months, three months. He started calling me all the time to tell me what was happening with his life, and I saw a miraculous change take place in him. I truly believe that there are miracles in these programs. But you have to experience them, sometimes, in order to start believing.

For me, it had to be the combination of hitting my own bottom and seeing this miracle happen to my friend, Ronnie. I saw someone who was so nonfunctional that he had barely been able to talk completely change within a three-month period. He began to look better. He started sounding really good. He actually got a job and worked, something I had never thought he'd be able to do. Ronnie was the one who took me to my first meeting.

At that meeting, I was given a copy of the Big Book of Alcoholics Anonymous, and I was told to keep coming back. I took the book home, but I didn't even open it up. I just put it in a closet somewhere and forgot about it for a couple of months.

In those months, my life got worse. I started experiencing physical, as well as emotional, problems. For the first time in my life, all these drugs I was doing started affecting my body. I began having mini-convulsions, but I didn't know what was causing them. My emotional state was really bad. I was experiencing more and more despair and paranoia. So I decided maybe I should do something about myself.

My friend Ronnie said: "Well, O.K. You don't have to go to meetings or anything. But I'll bet you that you can't beat this on your own." That was just what I wanted to hear. I had been brought up to believe that if you put your mind to it, you could do anything you really wanted to. "And I've got plenty of willpower," I thought to myself. It was a perfect opportunity to show him, and myself, that if I wanted to do something about my problem, I could.

So I took the bet. It was for $50, a lot of money at that time, and I was thinking, "If I don't win this bet, I don't know where I'm going to get the money to pay him." I locked myself in my room and just didn't go anywhere. Those thirty days were the hardest I've ever gone through in my entire life. But I won the bet! I went thirty days without taking a drink or any drugs.

I was very uncomfortable without those chemicals, though—one mean, miserable person. So after I won the bet, I went out to a bar and drank six or seven vodka gimlets, right straight down. Then my roommate came in with a sheet of LSD and gave me a hit of that. I remember staying in that bar until it closed. I had a pretty good time, that night.

That bet played a very significant part in my recovery, because it showed me the difference between drying out by simply not using and becoming sober through working the program. However, that was something I would not recognize until later on, when I had experienced true sobriety. I wasn't ready to quit for good, yet, even though I'd been able to do it on my own, to win the bet. I went right back to where I had started and continued to use on a daily basis, getting loaded to the max. I didn't hit any gigantic bottoms. I didn't get busted and go to jail, or anything like that.

Something did happen that brought me up short, though. My best friend, since childhood, had spent quite some time traveling, and I had not seen him for six or seven years. He got back in town and called me up and suggested we get together. So we went out to a bar, and we both got drunk. Then we got into an argument. I had been so glad to see him, after such a long time, and here we were, arguing. I can't even recall what the disagreement was about. But he said something to me that really caused me to hit my emotional bottom that night. "You know something?" he told me. "You think you're better than everybody else."

And that proved to be my moment of truth. I had never thought I was better than anybody else. I didn't think I was as good. But I had always presented an image that I was O.K. I think the big lie of my addiction had finally caught up with me. I had been using the chemicals to change my mood, to make me believe that I felt great when I actually didn't. My friend's words now made me realize that I needed those drugs to get up, to talk, to do so many things. That hadn't changed since the first time I had used them. But they were not working anymore.

I felt maybe there was a better way of living. I thought of Ronnie, and of the changes that had taken place in him, and I said to myself, "Well, maybe I'll give this program thing a try. Maybe I can get my act together. Then we'll see what happens from there." I still hadn't made any real decision to quit my drug use, but I had at least made a decision to try.

I let Ronnie take me to some meetings, and he introduced me to people there. I started listening to what they said. We had a mutual friend who had come into A.A. the year before, and there was a miraculous change in him, too. He and Ronnie reinforced what I was hearing about the need to get a Home Group, so I picked a meeting not too far from where I was living and signed up to be on their Home Group list.

That was one of the most important things I did in my early recovery: I made a commitment. The people in the group gave me the job of cleaning up after the meetings, emptying ashtrays and coffee cups, things like that. I had to be there, every week, to do my job, and that's how I began to get into the routine of attending meetings. In my Home Group, I started meeting people, and I was soon venturing out to other meetings in my area. I met young people, with lifestyles just like mine, who had experienced many of the same things. I found myself relating to them. I didn't just listen, however. I went home and found that A.A. Big Book I had thrown in the closet and started reading it. For the first time in my life, I began to understand the concept that alcoholism and drug addiction were diseases.

But the fellowship is what really put me on the road to recovery, the people who reached out and helped me, especially those in my Home Group who made me feel so comfortable there. I began to realize so many things. First of all, I had to share what I felt with other human beings, something completely contrary to what I had been taught. I was one of those people who kept everything inside, who never shared anything with anybody. But the program said that I would have to let people know me, in order to recover.

I first started letting people know me in my Home Group. I started to talk about feelings, because that's what I heard other people talking about, and that's what I related to. I can remember going home from those first meetings, after having heard things that just turned a light bulb on in my brain, saying, "Boy, I feel the same way." And that was how recovery started. I found people who were happy and content, with smiles on their faces. And I said, "I want that, too."

But there were a lot of obstacles, both within me and in front of me, if I wanted to continue in A.A. I had so many reservations. I could not comprehend how I would ever be able to abstain from using drugs and alcohol for the rest of my life. How could I have fun without drugs? How could I go to work? How could I be in any kind of a relationship? I had been using drugs and alcohol since I was fifteen years old, just so I could do all these kinds of things. And now I was being told that I had to give up my crutch.

I discovered that you only have to do it one day at a time. That was the most important thing I ever learned, because that made it all possible. Everything else, about working, about having fun, I could find out about later. But that "one day at a time" was the beginning of my recovery. It gave me the means, intellectually, to make it. I knew I could go one day at a time without using.

The next thing that really perplexed me was the concept of God in these Twelve-Step programs. I had rejected God at the age of about sixteen, because of the influence of my alcoholic older brother. He explained to me, one day, that there wasn't any God. I immediately latched on to that point of view. It appealed to me because of the injustices I saw in the world, and because of the strictness of my Catholic upbringing. Not believing allowed me to be free of guilt; if I didn't believe, then everything I did was O.K. My life, and what I made of my life, depended on me. I was in control. It was up to me to decide for myself.

I really had a hard time, coming into the program, when I found out that God was mentioned in the Steps and all throughout the literature. When the group said the Lord's Prayer at the end of the first meeting I attended, I couldn't even remember the words. I cringed when I thought about the very idea of God. But then I heard somebody say that you can believe in the God of your understanding. That means that He doesn't have to be the God that you were brought up with. He can be whatever you want Him to be.

Looking at it that way made it so much easier for me to find the God of my understanding. At first, I used the group, because that was a power greater than myself, and I saw how God worked within it. Then I found the Serenity Prayer. And finding out how effective it could be was another great influence in my recovery.

My earlier physical problems, caused by taking too many drugs, had included over-amping. When I took too much speed and cocaine, I would often get so high, be so wired out, that my heart would be jumping out of my chest. The only way I could bring myself down in a hurry was to take some alcohol or some kind of a barbiturate. When I was about three months into the program, I had a similar reaction, despite the fact that I was no longer drinking or drugging. I was driving on a major highway, at the time, and I had to pull over to the side of the road. I later discovered that what I had suffered is called, when it happens to someone who is straight, an anxiety attack.

While I was hyperventilating, I said, "Well, I can't go to the liquor store, and I don't have any drugs." And then I remembered the Serenity Prayer. I said it over and over. In about ten minutes, the attack went away, and I became normal again. That was the first time in my entire life that I had used a prayer and found that it actually changed my mood, just as the chemicals had done in the past. A very important part of my finding my Higher Power was the realization that prayer worked. Through further investigation, and reading A.A.'s *Came to Believe* and a few other such books, I found a Power, a God of my understanding, which I still use today.

Another of the stumbling blocks I had to overcome, in order to stay in the program, was that old question about how I was going to be able to function without drugs and alcohol. I had invested some time in the program, by now, and I was beginning to wonder about such things. After about six months, that question was answered when the compulsion to use finally left me. I realized that I could do what I needed to do. I could go to work, and have relationships, and even live with myself without the chemicals. It was a tremendous breakthrough, one I had never thought possible.

About ten months into the program, though, everything came crashing down on me. I had been working the first three Steps, and I now faced the Fourth, or inventory, Step. I had looked at it when I first came into A.A., and it had really scared me. But I knew that I just had to get honest with myself. I had to look at, and find out more about, who I really was. I had been avoiding that introspection for so long. I had been putting up walls, my entire life, refusing to face the real me. I finally came to the conclusion that I desperately needed to do my Fourth Step when I woke up one day feeling as bad, both physically and emotionally, as I ever had when I was using.

I went to my sponsor and told him how I was feeling. He agreed that it was time for me to do my Fourth Step. I always did whatever my sponsors told me to do, but I didn't know how to go about it, at first. I went over to my sponsor's house for a couple of hours, one night, and he explained to me about the various methods for working this Step recommended in program literature, which he suggested I read: the A.A. Big Book, the A.A. *Twelve Steps and Twelve Traditions*, or the Hazelden *Guide to the Fourth Step Inventory*. I decided that I was going to do it all three ways. I wanted to make sure I did a thorough inventory.

The first time I sat down to do my Fourth Step, I began to lie to myself on the paper, especially as far as fears and resentments went. After a half-hour or so, I put the pen down and thought to myself, "This is really ridiculous. Here I am, trying to do this Step, and I'm lying, instead of trying to help myself." I tore up that sheet of paper and said, "I don't care how painful this is. I'm going to write and be honest and fearless."

I started writing the truth, and even though that was uncomfortable, it was the most valuable thing I have ever done. For the first time in my life, I looked inside and put what I found on paper. It took me as long as two months to complete my Fourth Step, and I covered about twelve yellow, legal-sized pages. I did the entire Hazelden guide, as well. I really reached down and did the best job I could.

I called my sponsor after I had completed my inventory, and he asked me to come right over and do the Fifth Step. His house was on a military base. It was a spring evening, and while I was driving there I saw kids playing tennis and softball, all sorts of people having a good time. I thought, "I'm going to have to tell this person things I've never told anybody in my entire life." I was really scared about it. But people in A.A. had told me that this Step (admitting my faults to God, myself, and another human being) would set me free, and that is what I wanted.

When I reached my sponsor's house, we got into his car and drove out to a lake on the base, to be alone together outdoors. All of a sudden, it got really cloudy, and the wind started blowing. Then it began to rain, and the temperature dropped. So I had to do my Fifth Step in the car. It took about three hours, from beginning to end. And when I was finished, it felt like a great weight had been lifted from my shoulders.

All the fear and anxiety I had anticipated were unfounded. I had trusted my sponsor. He had shared his experiences with me. A wonderful feeling of fellowship had developed between us. After I completed my Fifth Step, my sponsor told me to go home to a quiet place and meditate on what we had just done. By then, it was getting quite late, so I went home and did exactly what he had said to do, and then I fell asleep.

That was the most restful night I had ever had in my life. When I woke up the next morning, it was as if a whole new world had opened up to me. I had now become a part of this program of recovery. I felt that I finally fit in, that I had really done something important toward changing my life. And since that day, my life has gotten nothing but better.

I continued on, working the rest of the Steps, and got very involved in a newly established fellowship, Chemically Dependent Anonymous. I became committed to service work, did Twelve-Step work, took meetings to hospitals and institutions, became part of Inter-Group, and took on all sorts of responsibilities. I was willing to be the secretary at meetings, to do anything I could, because I realized that you do have to give it away in order to keep this program.

Today, I still make it a habit to do whatever I have to do to grow in my program. I sponsor many people. I go to retreats. Even things I don't want to do, I do, anyway. And that seems to be what makes it work.

Since the time I came in for help, with nothing but misery, despair, and fear, my life has turned 180 degrees. I have everything I need, now, and almost everything I want. I have peace of mind. I have love. I care about all of *you*. And it's all a result of working this Twelve-Step program called Chemically Dependent Anonymous. When I came in, I was told, "This is not a program for people who need it. It's a program for people who want it." That is so true. I really believe that anyone who wants it can get what I have received from C.D.A.

And if I want to continue to grow, to get closer to my

Higher Power, and to maintain some semblance of the serenity that I have experienced so far, I have to keep wanting it, too. Just because I've been clean and sober for a while, I can't expect that, in order to live happily ever after, it is enough to simply stop doing what I did before I came into the program. I know that the addict in me will always be too strong for that. If I stop going to meetings, stop praying, stop helping others, and stop reaching out and sharing with others about myself, I'm going to revert back to that miserable, fearful person I was before I came into the fellowship of C.D.A. And I don't want to go back. I'm not taking chances with the life I have today.

Chapter 32
HAPPINESS, TOO, IS INEVITABLE

As far back as I can remember, I always looked for a way to avoid the reality of living in the present moment. Life was scary and unpredictable, and there was nothing solid to hang on to or believe in. I was a great dreamer, as a child, and I would fantasize for hours about being in a different family or a different city, looking prettier and being anyone other than the person I was. I thought that there was something wrong with me, that I was not a worthy person.

Our house was not a happy one. There was constant fighting and tension in our family. My mother would close the windows so the neighbors wouldn't hear what went on behind the normal-looking facade of our family. I often felt that I was the cause of my parents' unhappiness and that they, therefore, could not love me. I stayed awake, many nights, thinking of running away so the pain would stop.

Growing up continued to be difficult, particularly in school, where I was picked on and frequently rejected. I thought that if I weren't so skinny and ugly, I would be accepted, and I would feel normal. I turned the hurt and anger from these experiences onto myself. Believing that I wasn't "as good as" other people, that I was unlovable, I began to hate myself for what I saw as my fault. That feeling became ingrained in my mind, and I carried it with me into adulthood.

Somehow, I was ashamed to communicate my sense of rejection to my parents. The few times I did talk about it didn't bring me the support and reassurance that I needed to overcome my burden. I began to hide my feelings, eventually to deny them. I'm not blaming my upbringing or my childhood for being the reasons for my addiction. However, those experiences do explain the insecurity and low self-esteem, and the desire to escape reality, that led to my later problems with drugs.

Around the age of eleven, when I began junior high school, I started to develop problems falling asleep at night and staying asleep. I was hanging around with a crowd of people who were, like me, a little bit different, people I thought would accept me. I became what they call, in the program, a total people pleaser. To speak my true feelings, or to confront anyone when I didn't like something they said or did, was a struggle for me. I wondered if life was painful like this for other people, but was too ashamed to ask anyone else.

When I was around fourteen, my parents sent me to the first in a long line of psychiatrists, to be treated for insomnia and depression. The only thing I remember of my relationship with this first doctor is that I was given sleeping pills. I loved the way they changed how I felt, and I began to stay up and nod out, instead of sleeping. I found that I could manipulate the doctor to get more, and I quickly built up a tolerance. It became a pattern—going to doctors and getting pills.

My father was a pharmacist, so if I needed additional pills (and I always did), I could call him and he would bring them home for me. Our relationship became centered around the drugs, but we pretended that everything was normal—the typical denial of the disease. I believe, today, it was out of fear I would get drugs from someplace more dangerous that he enabled me with the pills. It was not because he didn't love me. My addiction had now become a "family disease."

When I was sixteen, I finally began to attract the opposite sex. However, I didn't date then, or for many years, for fear of getting close and letting someone get to know me. That developed into another pattern—of not letting anyone get too near, or of ending a relationship as soon as I felt exposed and vulnerable to pain.

Fearful and depressed, the only thing that got me through this time was knowing that I would soon graduate from high school. I was going to college, where I could further my love of both writing and photography by majoring in journalism. I was always waiting for something to change my life, and I thought that once I got away from home, everything would be all right. Never once did it enter my mind that I was addicted to pills, in any *negative* way. They were medicine, something to help me sleep. The pills dulled the edges of reality so well that I started to feel that this was how life was supposed to be.

College wasn't what I had hoped it would be. I was very unhappy there. I felt I was an imposter amidst the human race. Drugs became even more important to me, because now I had to hide from the shame of not being, or so it seemed, accepted again. At that time, drugs on campus were not as popular as alcohol. I lived in a dorm, so I had to hide my drugs. I smoked a lot of pot, and I took large quantities of sleeping pills. I also started taking Valium on a daily basis. I experienced hangovers in the morning, and I lost my concentration. I walked stiffly and slowly. My reflexes were off.

I went home on vacation, one semester, and it became evident that I had a serious problem when I couldn't wake up one morning. I was in such bad shape that my sister and my mother became hysterical, trying to get me up. They called the psychiatrist, and he had them pour coffee into me and walk me around the bedroom until I was finally alert. It was a very bad experience for all of us. The family could no longer deny my drug abuse.

Unfortunately, this experience frightened them a lot more than it frightened me, because I wasn't awake for their ordeal. At first, they thought that I had tried to commit suicide. I assured them I hadn't, and that was the truth—then. I had just forgotten how many pills I had taken, another pattern that would become more dangerous as I began drinking, along with the pills.

When I came home from college, the next summer, my life and my addiction took a turn for the worse. A friend and I went to the beach to get summer jobs. I held my job for a couple of weeks, but I was getting too high to keep it, so I quit. I began to meet people who were using narcotics, and, for the duration of the summer, I did nothing but fire or snort dope and nod out, completely unaware of what was going on.

My parents attempted to intervene. They knew that I was using drugs from the way I talked on the phone. One weekend, my roommate and I had a surprise visit from our mothers. They pleaded with us to come back home, but I wouldn't go. Rebellious as ever, I stayed the summer to finish out my rampage of drugging.

When I returned home, I discovered a crowd of people who liked to get down. We all became addicted to cough syrup and Doriden sleeping pills, and we would drive to a nearby city, every day, to cop cases of syrup. At the time, all you had to do was sign a book, and you could get quite a few bottles. You could also go to some doctors there and get prescriptions for Dolophine very cheaply. Just "living for the high" became a way of life.

Nothing else existed. But something was still wrong, inside. The only time I felt O.K. was when I was high. And even then, I wasn't happy. I just didn't feel pain.

Not long after I had a serious car accident, caused by my drug use, I went into my first mental institution. I was sent there by my psychiatrist, who believed my depression was too severe for him to treat. He was not then completely aware of the severity of my drug problem. I was almost eager to go, because I felt so suicidal. However, the hospital, like my psychiatrist, never addressed the problem of addiction. They just gave me more drugs to fight my depression.

Eight months later, I left the hospital as depressed as the day I had walked in. I had no idea how I was going to live out the rest of my life. I came home and tried to do all the right things, but I had no fervor for life. The only thing I looked forward to was the temporary escape that drug use afforded me. What followed, until the time I finally came into the program, was a series of jobs, attempts to finish college, different apartments, many psychiatrists, a hypnotist, two more mental institutions, many failed relationships, all adding up to a dreadfully lonely existence. I had become someone I hated so much that I didn't want to live.

When I was twenty-six years old, my father died after a long illness. That was a very significant event in my life, as it was also the beginning of the end of my addiction. My feelings were very mixed about my father's death. I was grief-stricken, but there was also a sense of relief, not only because he had been so ill, but also because I felt that the chain of my dependence on him had now been broken. As long as dad was alive, he had picked up the pieces of my life, even though he knew he couldn't put them back together. Scared and depressed, I needed the drugs more than ever.

Later that year, I got a job as a technician in a

pharmacy, the worst place I could have been. I stole drugs and was totally out of control. One of the employees started to suspect me, and I knew it was only a matter of time before I was caught. I quit shortly thereafter, with a sense of relief. The amount of drugs I was taking had begun to frighten even me.

After leaving that job, I went to work in the mental health field, in a day-care center. Many of my so-called "normal" friends were also employed there. I was able to maintain this job for a few years, even though I was still getting high. I rationalized that now was my chance to have a normal life.

Of course, it didn't work. I found it harder and harder to get to work in the morning. The hangovers were just incredible. It was as though I were sleepwalking. My supervisor, a very kind woman, found it difficult to confront me about these situations. Once again, I was able to get away with addictive behavior and keep my job.

When I eventually left this job, I took another one to see if that would fix me. I was even more miserable. I would go to a bar after work, or sometimes I would take home a bottle and drink, take more pills, and smoke some pot, alone. Many nights, I would fall down in the apartment and wake up later with bruises.

Then the drugs and the alcohol stopped working. The feelings of pain just wouldn't evaporate, whether I was high or not. I had reached my bottom. I finally realized that nothing was going to change, or improve, until *I stopped*. I just wanted that whole cycle of addiction to end.

I knew, after years of steady addiction, that I would need to be hospitalized in order to get clean. I had never been detoxified before, and I was terrified by the prospect. But the fear of continuing to live the way I had been was greater than my fear of withdrawal. And so, for the first time in my life, I reached out for help.

I called a local drug agency, but there wasn't much aid available locally. Thirty-day programs did not yet exist, in my area, so the only alternative was a long-term program somewhere else, out-of-state. I knew that the farther from home I went, the better my chances of recovery. I called the contact given to me and went to detox just a few weeks later.

As soon as I saw the detox unit, I wanted to leave. It was such a depressing place. But there was nowhere else to go. The first ten days went smoothly. It seemed all too easy. I wondered why I had put this off so long. And then, in the second week of detox, I started to feel the withdrawal. It seemed as if every part of my body burned and itched. I was unable to sleep and experienced auditory and visual hallucinations. I reached a point where I felt I couldn't handle any more and would surely go insane. But the other addicts told me it would pass and that I would get high if I left.

I remained in detox for almost a month. A deep depression overwhelmed me. I remember thinking that I'd waited so long to finally give up the drugs and alcohol, but now withdrawal was causing me unbearable physical discomfort. I wanted immediate relief.

After I was released from the detox, I went into a treatment center for approximately the next six months. Around my second week at the center, I experienced one of the worst depressions of my life. It was as if, for the first time, I could clearly see what a disaster I had made of my life. I felt I was a complete failure. This time, there was nothing to blot out those feelings. I also feared that I wasn't making any progress and withdrawal would never end. Each day, I told myself that I would leave "tomorrow," but I never did.

That therapeutic community was the beginning of my physical recovery, but I credit the Twelve-Step fellowships for my entry into emotional recovery. During treatment, we didn't go to any meetings, but I had been to one Alcoholics Anonymous meeting, many years before, although I didn't remember much about it. I did, however, somehow keep in mind the name and location of the church where the meeting had been held. Remembering this meeting would soon become very important for me.

I left the treatment center prematurely because I knew, intuitively, that there had to be another way. After seven months, the only change I saw in myself was that I wasn't using. There had to be more to being clean than just existing and enduring life as I had done before. I was determined to start a new life, and it had to begin right back where I had fallen. When I called my family, however, I was given an ultimatum. I was to go back to treatment, or I couldn't return home.

With my little resources, I managed to get to the home of a woman who had been in treatment with me but had left after only a month. I needed some time to think and plan my next steps. That was a *very* slippery place. My friend's mother had a pill problem, and she offered me Valium when she saw how anxious I was. I did want those pills—very badly. But I didn't take them. A lot of pot smoking went on in that house, and I am sure that I inhaled enough to affect my mood when I was not even aware of it. There was also one occasion when I took a hit off the pipe, although I can't recollect that time very clearly, now. I was in a state of shock, at the time.

I left after two days. I experienced an enormous anxiety attack, on the bus ride home, and began to suffer recurring withdrawal symptoms. When we pulled into the station, I began to walk. About five o'clock in the evening, I arrived at the very church where I had attended an A.A. meeting, years before.

There was to be a meeting there, that night, and attending it marked the true beginning of my recovery program.

The people there were wonderful to me. A woman I had been watching during the meeting came to me afterwards and told me she was going to be my sponsor. Someone else said they would find me a place to stay, if I didn't have one. But I wanted to go to my mother's house, to try and mend our relationship.

When I arrived there, my mother was very angry and would not let me in. She had lost all trust in me, but she finally opened the door when she saw the sobriety and the spark in my eyes. I guess she began to have a glimmer of hope, too. I told her I would be going to A.A. meetings, and she said that I would have to attend the meetings regularly, if I wanted to stay.

I found, almost immediately, that I had to cut off all ties with any people who were using. Remarkably, this was very easy for me to do, because I was so desperate. It would be nice to say that from this point on everything went smoothly, but it didn't. I was still experiencing compulsions to use.

But they told me, in the A.A. meetings, that I could work it "one day at a time." I had never heard that concept before. The A.A. people told me to break it down into any block of time I had to. I would tell myself, for instance, that just for the period of time I was sitting in the meeting that night, I was not going to get high. And I would find I had made it through another day, free of drugs and alcohol.

The first three months that I was in the program, I primarily went to A.A. meetings, and then I found Narcotics Anonymous. I attended meetings of both groups, but I wasn't working the program the way it was suggested. I still had reservations and the old mentality of the quitter.

And I was terribly lonely. There weren't many people of my age in those meetings. I soon got into a relationship with someone I met in the fellowship. Although it turned out to be a very painful experience for me, today I am grateful, because I think that the pain is what boosted my participation in the program. While I was still in the relationship, I had a relapse because I was holding on to a resentment toward this man. For the first time, I realized that I had picked up a drink simply because of my inability to be honest about my emotional state. This became a clue to me about my whole life and its basic dishonesty.

Ashamed of my slip, I changed my sobriety date but found it difficult to talk about it in the meetings. Instead, I threw myself into the program's service work. I felt so *needed* by the fellowship. It gave me a reason to keep on going and to stay straight.

I kept very busy at this work, but there was still something wrong inside. I continued to harbor many of the old feelings, ideas, and attitudes. I knew that the Big Book of A.A. said that we had to let go of our old ideas, but they were all I had ever known. I didn't trust people. There was self-pity, jealousy, and resentment in my life. I began to understand that I wouldn't be able to stay straight for long if I didn't change.

At this time, God chose to put someone in my path who has been one of the most significant influences in my recovery. She showed me how to work the Steps. She was very patient and loving, yet firm with me and honest at the same time. She encouraged me to work on my relationship with God through prayer. I am so grateful to her for being in my life, as my sponsor, and for showing me the way to live an honest life.

As I began to work the Steps with her guidance, she told me that "surrender," in the Third Step, meant not only surrendering our drugs and alcohol, but the rest of our lives, as well. The Third Step was the most difficult part of the program for me. In order to begin the process of turning my life over to God, I had to change my concept of God.

I could not love or pray to the punishing God of my childhood. The longer I stayed in the program, however, the more I realized that I needed a Higher Power. Dependence on my fellows was not sufficient. I did see, however, that the love and caring I had found in the fellowship were manifestations of that Power. I know, today, that God works through people, and that is how I came to believe that there is a good and loving God.

For many years, I still attached some blame to my father for what I believed was his part in my addiction. I was never able to forgive him completely. But as a result of working the Steps, I recently had a wonderful healing experience. I was able to make my peace with him. I was filled with a genuine love and compassion for my father, and a true understanding of the situation he had been placed in during my addiction. Today I know that I can't hold on to anger and resentment, because they will destroy me and any relationship that I might have with God.

The painful process of looking within was taught to me by my sponsor. I have gone over several written inventories with her, and I have gained tremendous insight into myself and what needs to be done in the Seventh Step. I'm not working alone, and the Steps tell us that God can, and will, remove defects of character if He is asked.

Many wonderful things have happened to me in sobriety. I have a career, today, in the field of addictions. I have also worked in other organizations related to this field and have been placed in positions where I believe that I've been of service. I care about what I'm doing, for the first time. I'm interested in what happens with my life and other people's lives. That's a tremendous change for a self-centered person like me.

When I was clean for about six months, I attended my first Chemically Dependent Anonymous meeting. I was attracted to the people in the fellowship and found I could relate to many of them. There was also a very comfortable atmosphere, in the group, that I liked.

It was at that meeting that I met a gentleman who would later become my husband. Our relationship was the opposite of any I had experienced before. Neither of us was good at sharing our feelings, and there were many times when I didn't want to get to know another person or work on a relationship. But I learned in the program that anything worth having has to be nurtured. The bond deepened between us, and we married four years later.

Six months before we became engaged, I moved away from home to be with my fiancé. That meant that I had to change the meetings I had been attending, and I became resentful. I wanted to hide, many nights, and not go out to meetings. I was asked to take my "dis-ease" to the meeting when I was in that state. And that made sense to me.

After about a year of attending different programs, I still felt most accepted at the C.D.A. meetings. I thought I was being almost disloyal to my former fellowship, but I had to work through that and come to realize that it really didn't matter where I found my recovery, as long as it helped me treat my disease. The C.D.A. meetings were smaller in size, so I was able to get to know many of the members on a very deep level, and I have grown to love them. Because C.D.A. wasn't as well-established as N.A. or A.A., there was also a greater need for people to do service work. I always feel my program is incomplete when I am not involved, so I immersed myself in service to C.D.A. and developed a loyalty to its fellowship.

Things are going well for me, today. The second chance that I have been rewarded with was never promised to me, and I certainly didn't earn it. There are still those days when I feel that I don't deserve it, and I try to do something to ruin it. That's when I have to exercise faith in this program, remember how devastated my life was before, and realize that it is God's will that I remain free of drugs and alcohol.

I know that the only way I can repay God is by passing what I have received on to someone else. And my message is that there is hope, and a life, without drugs and alcohol. The compulsion to use leaves and the willingness to live does return. When I was new, on one of those bleak days when I was certain that I was going to leave the program, I read something in a book by Albert Camus: "Happiness, too, is inevitable." Somehow, I knew that it applied to me. And I decided that I would wait, just *one* more day, because it is true: If you work at this program, happiness, too, *is* inevitable.

Chapter 33
I COULDN'T KNOCK THE LOVE

My name is Sterling S., and I'm a chemical dependent. I'm going to try to tell some of my story, and what it was like for me, in terms of addiction to booze and other drugs (the chemicals), what happened to get me into recovery programs, and what it's like for me today. I guess the standard operating procedure is to start from the beginning, right?

My childhood was fine, I imagine what you could call normal. I liked toys, television, girls, my family, sports, and music. I was a pesky little sucker, very energetic. But when I hit that puberty period, I became directionless. Before then, I'd been involved with horses, and I liked the feelings that I got from showing horses and achieving little goals, riding and winning ribbons. But after a couple of years of that, around the age of twelve, I got bored with it and needed a challenge again, and a new pursuit.

Many of the guys in the neighborhood, those my age or a little older, were into other sports, and I soon got into the game of football. I also discovered the guitar and found that I had a knack for it and for singing. I picked it up pretty quickly, and soon my life became sports and music. It made me feel good to do well, to get all the accolades and trophies for sports and the applause for the music. My ego needed feeding. Looking back, I see that I needed to do good, good, good, and to have people tell me I was good. And I had to feel that I was good.

With music there seemed to come (maybe it just comes with age, and everybody goes through this) some attention, especially from girls, and I liked that. I liked to mix with them, but I was extremely shy. The girls liked the older guys, and I noticed that these fellows got a little loose if they had a beer. So I had a beer. But it really didn't do a whole lot for me. I guess I was a latent alcoholic, but I still got much more thrill out of the natural pursuits.

I was only sixteen when I got into one particular band whose members were really "older people," out of school already. Football was going O.K. for me, and I was making C-average grades in school. Let's face it, I liked to play, not work, but I didn't mind practicing for football or practicing music. This group of older musicians got lots of attention from our peers. So, to be like them, I got drunk a few times, not just drinking a beer or two. I was with this band for almost a year, and I remember a few nights when I got out-and-out drunk. I was just a silly child, and I thought it would help me get girls. Drinking made it easier to talk to them, but they were really not interested in such a wild little kid.

I got out of that group when I was a high school senior. I was still doing O.K. in football, but I got into another band. I also got drunk a few more times, but getting loaded wasn't the light of my life, at this time.

Then I went away to college, but I got homesick and came home to go to school. I got in with some of my musician friends who were also in school around my local area. I attended a community college, and we put a nice little band together. We did really well locally and then, when I was still only eighteen years old, we moved the band to a nearby big city. We had good chemistry, and a lot of energy, and we were superb. We were all on natural highs, just from the exhilaration of it all.

Within the next year, though, my father died. I suffered terribly. I loved my whole family, but my dad's death just rocked me. I felt I had lost my best friend. I had experimented with a little pot before, in addition to the booze. So I got stoned on the way to the airport to pick up my dad's mother for the funeral. I got stoned the next day, and I got stoned, again, for the funeral. My little chemical-dependent-and-addiction career really got started then, I believe, because I wanted to escape those feelings of pain.

After that, I started using something every day. I did speed, went back to college, played music, and did so well that I was earning the equivalent of $700 to $800 a week, in today's terms (this was during the Vietnam War era), in the city. It was a lot for a nineteen-year-old kid. I dropped out of school.

A year later, I was still getting loaded every day. Looking back, now, I can see that I began to let myself go around that time. My clothes started going from nice, elaborate outfits to just blue jeans and sandals and an old vest. But I got into another head change and decided that, even though I had been playing in the best club and making good money for quite a while, I needed something new. So I went back into athletics, again. I was now twenty years old.

I returned to school, this time to a small-town college out-of-state. I did very well, there, by taking plenty of Dexedrine, and amphetamine sulfate, and marijuana, and wine, and beer. I still trained, though, and ran, and stayed up late, studying hard. I wasn't in a band, now, and I was just exercising my body for sports, to be ready for the next year. I was at this little school for three years, during which time I became a walk-on in football the first year and did all right at it the next two years.

But, of course, I ended up finding all the other addicts, too. We wound up hanging together, the longhairs and I, even though I was a jock with *my* long hair hanging out of the back of my football helmet. I was a *little different* from all the locals and the up-North boys. I was the weird one from the big city. I even looked different, in all these wild clothes I had brought to school. I was still doing O.K. at school, in spite of the fact that I was getting loaded all the time. After a year at this college, I got married, and my wife moved to be there with me. By now, I was doing a lot of marijuana, and speed, and booze.

Then I had another head change and decided to leave that school, two years later, to come back to my home town so I could play music again while I finished school closer to home. In my senior year, I quit college altogether, only twenty credits short of graduation. But, I figured, what the heck did I need college for? I had inherited a business from my dad, and, obviously, I was going to be a rich and famous rock-and-roll star, right? Since I wanted to be one, naturally, everyone else who mattered in that kind of enterprise would want me to be one, too.

I thought I'd go back home, and play in bars, and get plenty of fringe benefits: perks like booze, and money, and attention. So I did that, and I got that. But I got another head change, too, and my wife and I split up. We were only twenty-one when we married, which is too young. She wanted me to get straightened out, to just do a regular gig. And she was probably right, but I couldn't. My head wasn't there. I wanted to rock-and-roll and do the night scene. And so we parted company.

I went back to the nightclubs and got into plenty more booze, and drugs, and women—the old wine, women, and song. I had about four years of wild times, from the time I was twenty-three until I was twenty-seven. There was pretty good money, and plenty of those fringe benefits. I felt good about myself, and I actually saw a bright future about to happen, right about the time I probably crossed over into real alcoholism. I also felt rocky, and I was starting to drink and drug most of the day. But lightly, of course.

My typical day went like this: I'd wake up and drink a little something left over from the night before on the night stand, maybe flick out whatever was in the glass and drink what was left. That was to get rid of the shakes from last night and to be able to get to the icebox to drink a couple of beers. Then I'd switch to something else, maybe soda pop, and lay off the booze, later in the afternoon.

Of course, I didn't even get up until about 2 p.m. But late in the afternoon, and into evening, I'd stop the beers and make the calls to get some speed, or psychedelics, LSD or mescaline, because they'd act like speed, and they got me wound up. I'd get to the club just flying, but not guzzling any booze. I'd drink ginger ales and cola drinks for the first three sets, from nine to midnight, and then it was *my* time. Now, I deserved it—my reward—and I'd switch to the hard stuff, just inhale it, for a nice, mellow last set.

Then I'd look for a party. And I always found one. I'd drink the hard stuff there, then smoke some PCP, then snort some more stuff and just get in somewhere, hopefully my apartment, before the sun came up. I used to hate the sounds of the birds, and the crickets, and the garbage men banging around! It was my duty, now, to get some good, solid sleep. So I'd pass out and come to around two o'clock in the afternoon, the next day, and just start in at the night stand, again.

My whole band was all messed up, too. Everybody was on something, switching around, trying to cut this out and cut that down. We knew we had problems, but we didn't know what to do about them. Deep inside, we knew we should stop all of it, but that was kind of ridiculous. Come on, now, everybody's got to be able to do a little something! Little did we understand, when one of us switched from one drug to another, and then to another, that he'd only stay with it until, after a few days, he got in a different frame of mind again, and then he'd end up back on his original drug of choice, hooked all over again. It was a vicious cycle. No one around my circle of friends knew, in the mid-seventies, what was really going on, as far as their drug use was concerned.

I changed bands and got out of that group of people for a while. I was going to play with a decent group of some renown in a major city. It just didn't work out, though, probably because they could spot me as an alcoholic. I came back home with the money I'd borrowed from my older brother as a grubstake, to get away with, still in my pocket. Since I had the money, and the time off, I drank way too much. I ran into about three girls in a row who were the same kind of drinkers, and we binged out every night. I don't know if I latched onto them, or the girls latched onto me, but I ended up broke.

There was nothing to stay straight for, anymore. I didn't have any shows to do. So I wound up in a stupor for several months. Then I got into a fight with my brother and got busted up pretty badly because I didn't really want to fight him. I just wanted to run my mouth, but he'd heard enough. I had to leave my apartment because he was living right down the hall. Since I had nowhere else to go, I went to live with my mother.

The fact that she had a gigantic liquor cabinet for entertaining her friends was probably what influenced me to move in with her for a while when my mother suggested it. Within a couple of months, I'd wiped out the entire contents of that liquor cabinet. She didn't realize it, at first, because she didn't even look. My mother didn't drink much, except to be sociable or when she went out, once in a while. But after a couple of months, she did begin to notice my drinking and smoking.

She also saw that I wasn't doing anything with my life. I was now twenty-nine years old, and I was getting nowhere, just sitting around, consuming everything, and getting fatter. She began to think I had a drug problem. I was always starting to cry, and I seemed to be feeling sorry for myself all the time. So she called Alcoholics Anonymous. I heard her call someone, but I wasn't sure whether she was calling the mental hospital or A.A. Thank God, it was A.A.!

My mother explained, over the phone, what she had been seeing. By this time, I was up to about two quarts of booze, one of my mother's and one of mine, or a case of beer and a quart of booze, per day. If you start early in the morning and go until you pass out at night, you can get rid of that much booze.

When my mother laid it all out for me, I had to listen to her because I really respected her. She wasn't like the rest of the people I hung around with who were all messed up. She added up the facts and said that maybe, if there were such a drug problem, and I had it, someone could give us some guidance on how to correct it or turn it around. It was hard to deny the facts, so I admitted that I might need help, because I wasn't doing such a good job on my own.

So Sandra F., from A.A., came over and got to the core of it, which was that I probably wanted to live more than I wanted to die. She assured me that people could die from continuing to live the way that I was. I believed that she had been in some of the same places I had been, the discouragement and the despair, and so I told her I could use some help. She said, "Let's go to an A.A. meeting," and I agreed, but I was afraid. She told me, "Don't drink for the rest of today, and I'll come back and get you, tonight."

That night, she brought me to a medical Inter-Group headquarters of Alcoholics Anonymous where they also held A.A. meetings. I was so scared, and I was withdrawing from alcohol because I hadn't had a drink all day. And I was sweating. It was hot. It seemed as hot as hell, and smoky, and I got this flash that somebody had handed out reports about my activities, and that these people knew all about me. It was a kind of conspiracy, and now they were laughing. But I wasn't.

I didn't understand what was going on there, but they didn't look the way I felt. I understand, now, that they were recovering, they weren't using, anymore. The stuff wasn't contaminating their bodies and spirits. But it had mine, and it had *me*, and I withdrew, all over the floor. I got sick, right on the steps I was sitting on.

A guy, Rick R., walked me out of there. Rick took me over and helped me. He was a contemporary, an artist. He took me outside and then helped clean up that mess—*my* mess. Oh, my God, he didn't even know me, and he did something like that, instead of letting me wallow around forever with it, or in it! He watched me continue to get sick for a couple more hours, and then he talked me into giving recovery a bigger shot. He said, "Hey, do yourself a favor and go to the hospital. Just go ahead and relax, get a shot, and warm yourself up inside. Go to sleep and, in a few days, come out of there feeling pretty chipper, and we'll see what happens then." He was a con man, he was.

He, Sandra, Stella D., my mother, and some other people got me into that hospital. They called my illness gastritis because the hospital refused to admit patients for alcoholism, in those days. I got my shot and some sleep. After a couple of days, I even got my appetite back (which was a miracle).

I was then told, "Do yourself a really big favor, now, and invest in your life. Take the big step. Take two weeks out of your busy life and go to a rehab." My attitude was that I couldn't see how the world out there could possibly get along without me in circulation for that long, and I really believed that. But I was told, "You can die from this disease or condition of yours. Why go through that? Take a couple of weeks and get some education, and some meals, and get back on your feet." So I said I would, reluctantly. Very reluctantly.

When I went to that rehab, I was afraid to go in; then, after I started to feel good, I was afraid to leave because they were taking care of everything. The world looked pretty scary when I got off the stuff. But I got off it all. And I came out believing that I had taken the first step by admitting that there was alcohol in my life, and that the reason I probably drank so much was because of all the drugs that I took. I got out of there convinced that I didn't want to do *any* of it, anymore, and I went to some more A.A. meetings.

But, somehow, I just didn't get the picture. I still had a lot of denial about letting other people help me, too much false pride. I thought I could deal with my problem on my own. I went to the meetings, and when people talked about alcohol, I wondered why. If we were trying to stay away from drinking it, why did we go there and talk about it so much? I asked my mother that question, too. Since she was my best friend, and she thought that I made some sense, she didn't push me. So I didn't go to any more meetings.

I went for a "geographical" cure by moving from one side of town to another, where I moved in with some guys who worked at a boat yard. I thought a change of career would help, so I started working there with them. It was nice, decent exercise and some cash, and I could lay low. It turned out that these guys drugged, though. One Friday, after I had gone a couple of weeks without drinking, I had a beer. I wasn't going to meetings, so the next Friday came, and I had another beer. The Friday after that, I had two beers, then three beers, and I was off and running.

I'd binge out somewhere, and then I'd straighten up and wouldn't do anything, all on my own, no drinks or drugs, for a week or two. Then I'd have, maybe, a little pot, and then a little more pot, and then a beer, and then a few more beers. Or, maybe it would be just PCP or Crystal Meth. I'd do one of everything I had ever done before, and it would eventually turn into two. Then I'd get thirsty, so I'd end up on a binge, again. I would go on in this kind of cycle, then I'd straighten out, and then I'd do the same thing again.

Ten years ago, I had my last beer. It was eleven months from the rehab to my last drink. During that time, I still didn't understand what was wrong, that I was an addict, and an alcoholic, all of that together, which is a chemical dependent. Then, one day, I just looked at my hand. It had a can in it. I was trying to get a job in a band, again, and I wound up at one rehearsal where I couldn't play three notes in a row, no matter how much I wanted to. "Do, re, mi." Anybody can do that, right?

But I couldn't. With all my years of playing the guitar, I couldn't play, now, because of this stuff in my hand. I finally realized and admitted, right there, that I was powerless over the stuff. That's when I picked up the phone and asked for help. I finished the last six-pack I had there first, of course. Actually, I drove around a little while, thinking about it, too, before I phoned. But I knew that that was it, and I had a kind of sadness in me because I knew I was actually going to let it go. I knew what I had to do. I was going back to that outfit, A.A.

Then I went to see a guy I didn't really know. When I'd stopped at the body shop where he worked to get my car fixed, during that year of my own "program," I had noticed an "Easy Does It" sticker on his desk. And I remembered that now. It had haunted me. I didn't even like to drive by that place, after that, because he might see me. I suspected he was in a fellowship. But now I went there, drunk, and asked him what the sticker meant.

He talked to me for about an hour, just shut his door and refused to take any business during that time, and he listened and gave me hope. He said, "Go ahead and call your buddy, Rick. He'll come help you." So I went home and did that and finished that last beer while I talked to Elin R., who said Rick would be over as soon as he came home from work. When he arrived, he laughed because he had told me, a long time ago, what would happen. Then he said that it was all over, if I wanted it to be. I could do anything I wanted to do with my life. Anything was possible, now, if I'd let go and just follow along, follow these Steps that we're all taking, today. I would have a spiritual life now, a spiritual program.

That made me feel good, and kind of relieved, because I always knew there was a God. Even in the barrooms, I felt a spiritual bond with all the people in there, somehow or another. We were not communicating, just kind of bouncing off each other, but we were all in there, lonely, looking for love in whichever kind of way we could get it, or had gotten used to having it. But we had this wall between us and our Creator which kept us from knowing how to communicate love to each other in a healthy sense.

I'd seen, through the love demonstrated to me by the A.A. people, and by the fact that these total strangers did things for me and did not ask for anything in return, on the few occasions when I'd met them, that they understood real love. That was what attracted me. They wanted nothing, but they offered me a way out of the hell I was in. I couldn't knock that love. And so I started going to meetings, and started to live, and began to do my own thing, to get music jobs, again. I worked in bars, but now I did it cold sober.

I've been in the music business since then, off and on, and played at bars, and I've found out (and this is important) that you *can* do whatever you want to do. I want to play and, even though there's booze and all those other elements in the bars, if I want to go do my work, I can. If you've got business being in one of those places, it's O.K., as long as you make sure you're talking to your sponsors and other people in meetings about the chemicals. I go in and play, and enjoy it because I'm always plugged in to my universe with my music. It's super, like I am a kid in my teens, feeling good about doing things, sounding good, performing well, having fun playing, again. And it's all right. But I have to go to meetings, and pray, and not use the things we all hear about in this program, at the same time.

And I can do other things, too, besides music. I had had a lot of false pride about not wanting to take day jobs. That attitude kept me on a cheap-beer budget for quite a while, but I found out that there were other things I could do to earn a living. And I have done them.

About a year after my reentry into A.A., a few of us who were members, and who used more than one substance, created a sort of catch-all program for ourselves and others like us. We knew what our problem was—we were addicted to chemicals. We called ourselves Chemically Dependent Anonymous, and in the ten years since the fellowship's founding, our growth has been phenomenal. My recovery was strengthened as C.D.A.'s program brought me to realize how my use of chemicals had blocked my own growth.

Today, I feel at peace with myself, in my recovery, with my recovery tools. I know what to do to stay clean and sober. In my ongoing adventures, I have many peaks and valleys. But I know that anything is possible. There are many things I still want in life; there are also things I have to keep working on. I want to grow in my music career. I've peaked and valleyed with that, and with finances, too, but right now, I'm fine. I have to work, though, so I've started a little courier company. Last year, I got married, and I also bought a house.

I've done some recordings, and I'm still trying to make contacts to help that area of my music grow into something more fulfilling. I really feel that I've outgrown working in bars, on a nightly basis, to generate income and expression. I can't see playing for five hours a night, five days a week, forever. That's behind me. I'd also like to get into concert work, something else I'm constantly working on. I've got to get going and keep growing.

There are plenty of tools and people, here, to help me: my beautiful wife, my wonderful friends, all the co-founders of C.D.A., all the new people, and Phil C., my sponsor in A.A., who keeps it simple for me. I've learned to let out my emotions, and they get more intense as time goes by. I guess I'm peeling the onion, getting down to more raw nerves. I'm taking more chances, so I'm feeling more rejections—but more triumphs, as well. And that makes for a good life.

Each of us has to keep doing the same things, using the tools. We have so many *other* "things" to do in our lives, sometimes, that living the program seems more difficult than it used to. But we have to keep increasing our efforts. We're living more, now, experiencing more, and we have much less time, all of us who have grown up together in these programs. Often, it seems we tend to take too much for granted. It seems to be more of an effort to say the prayers, to go to the meetings, to listen to the newcomer on the phone. But we do it, we follow through, because the root of it all *is* the program. We have to be willing to work, to not let it get stale for us.

I hope anyone who is exposed to my story will be helped by it, whether you're a drug addict, an alcoholic, or a chemical dependent. I'm sure you will, because it comes from the heart. I thank all those who have come before me to pave the way. I consider them the wisest people I know, and all the newcomers the luckiest people I know to have reached this point, to be reading this material. I wish us all, in C.D.A. and in all of the world, good luck and Godspeed.

Chapter 34
A MEDICAL MIRACLE

I was raised in an alcoholic family. My father was an alcoholic, but I didn't actually know that until I came into the program. I knew that he drank a lot and that he slept much of the time. My sister and I were very afraid of him because, when he was drinking, he had such severe mood swings. When he'd first start drinking, he'd be really nice; then he'd pass out for a little while, and as soon as he woke up, we learned to try to stay as far away from him as we could.

When I was eleven, my mother died. I think that's the most devastating thing that has ever happened to me in my entire life. The day of her funeral was the day I took my first drink. I heard somebody tell my father, "Here, have another drink; that will make you feel better." I needed to feel better, too. I hurt a lot. So I sneaked into the kitchen, poured myself a small glass of whiskey, and drank it straight down.

I remember that it tasted terrible, and I thought it wasn't going to stay down. But after it did, I got a warm sensation inside. It made things seem different. I wasn't any happier, or any better, but it made me almost numb about the situation. So right from the very beginning, I always drank to make things feel better, to make *me* feel better.

When I was twelve, I was hospitalized with stomach pains. Doctors couldn't find any reason for these pains, so I started seeing a psychiatrist. The doctors eventually gave me some kind of a drug, belladonna, to slow my stomach muscles down, but I continued seeing the psychiatrist, too. He, in turn, started me on mild tranquilizers.

I couldn't seem to cope with anything, once my mother died. I couldn't handle school. I'd get through one or two classes, then I'd tell the teachers that I was sick. I had this panic that came over me, a fear that I was going to die, and I had to get out of there. Sometimes, the teachers would not let me go home, and all I would do for the rest of the day was put my head on my desk and cry. I just wanted to be in my bedroom at home, to be left alone. And that's the way I always wanted to go through life. I could only be around people for a short period of time; then, after a while, I just wanted to be by myself and have everybody go away.

Early in high school, I started sneaking alcohol from my father. I would take some out of his bottle and fill it back up with water, dilute the alcohol so he wouldn't notice I had taken any. I would go up to my room, or I would go outside, and I'd drink. The more I did it, the more the alcohol made me feel better. It made me happy.

It also helped me to get along with people. I was so afraid of the way I acted around my family, ever since I'd started going to see the psychiatrist, because I thought that if I didn't behave perfectly around them, they were going to put me back in the hospital. I always had to pretend I felt fine, and the alcohol helped me to do that. When I got home from school, before my father got home from work, I would drink, almost on a daily basis.

I started hanging around with older kids, mostly guys who had dropped out of school and who didn't have very good reputations. They always had booze, and I just wanted to drink. I started getting into some trouble. I used to "hook" from school quite a lot. I would walk to school, where the guys would pick me up, and we'd go off to the beach or just hang out at somebody's house where we could drink all day long.

It seemed that I always got caught, but I would use the excuse that my father was a drunk, my mother had died, and I was so confused. I turned on the tears, and everybody would look at me and say, "Poor Cathy." That is how I used to get out of trouble. When I was called in to the police station a few times, I gave them the same story, and they felt sorry for me, too.

By the time I was a senior in high school, I had to get out of my father's house; his drinking was much worse. He had hit me when I was younger, but I soon found that, with a little more alcohol inside me, I could hit back. So we had some pretty serious fights. I used to run away from home. He'd call the state police, and they'd come looking for me. It was just a Godawful, ugly scene, all the time. I started hanging around with one particular guy, and I really fell in love with him. Before graduation, I was married.

I married another alcoholic, someone who drank and treated me exactly the way my father had. But I let him do it. I didn't want to be alone, and I didn't want to have to go back to my father. I figured marriage was the lesser of two evils.

I did graduate from high school that year, but I don't know how. I spent more time out of school than in it. My marriage only lasted three months. After too many drunken fights, and my husband's extramarital affairs, someone from where I worked started paying attention to me. He was much older than I was, but I didn't mind. I just felt that, finally, somebody cared. After work on Fridays, we used to hop in the car and drive to out-of-state bars, where we would drink all night. Once again, I was hung up with an alcoholic.

A few months after that, I met my second husband. Our relationship was a turning point in my life. I had never tried drugs before; I had only drunk alcohol. But this guy introduced me to all sorts of drugs: marijuana, cocaine, LSD. They were wonderful. I didn't have hangovers in the morning when I used them. I didn't get into fights. I didn't get into a lot of the trouble, at first, that the alcohol had gotten me into. This man not only had drugs, he was very wealthy. I knew I didn't really love him; I didn't have the feelings that you should have to marry someone, but he had what I wanted most in the world. He had something that let me escape.

I don't think there had been too many days, since I was a young child, when I hadn't taken a drink. But now I had something more wonderful, I thought, than I had ever experienced in my whole life. I can't explain it, but drugs of any kind made me feel, for the first time, that I had control, that I knew what I was going to do. I was going to do such marvelous, magnificent things. I was just sitting on top of the world.

My husband's family owned a glass factory. We first met when they opened up a new factory in my home town and I went to work there. After my husband and I married, we went out West to open up a new plant. He trained the men, and I took care of the women. I thought that was a perfect arrangement. I had a management job, and I felt like somebody. But after work, and on all our weekends, we were getting high. There wasn't much else to do in that town.

After we were there about five or six months, I became pregnant. When my husband's family heard about it, they said that no daughter-in-law of theirs was going to work. I was sent back East to set up housekeeping for my new family. I really hated it, right from the start. I didn't like the idea of living next door to my in-laws. I felt I could never live up to the expectations of such a very wealthy family. They immediately tried to teach me everything I needed to know. It was almost like *My Fair Lady*. They wanted to turn me into something that I wasn't. They taught me the proper way to set a table. I was even given Amy Vanderbilt's book on etiquette.

While I was pregnant with my son, I was really afraid that something was going to be wrong with him, so I stopped using cocaine. I just drank a little bit and smoked pot. After he was born, it was a relief to find that he was all right. And I was finally free to go back to using my preferred drug, cocaine.

I used to justify my use of this drug by telling myself that it made me a better mother. When I wasn't getting high on coke, I felt tired all the time, and I would often doze off when I knew I needed to be awake, taking care of my son. So I'd snort a couple of lines of cocaine, and then I felt like Supermom. I not only could care for my son and have time to read to him and play with him, but I could also keep my house clean.

That was very important to my husband. He insisted on a clean house. Some days, when I was tired and had had a bad day with my son, my husband would come home and say, "What have you done all day?" I always felt under pressure to be perfect. I had to look great, my son had to be bathed, and the house had to be immaculate. Dinner had to be on the table. With the help of cocaine, I could do it all.

When my son was just under a year old, our marriage began to go sour. I thought another child would make it better, so I got pregnant. We had our second child, a little girl, before my son was quite two years of age. Our daughter came six weeks early; to this day, I think it's because I used drugs a lot more heavily when I was pregnant with her. Since my son had been all right, I felt that this child would be, too. Still, I did cut down on my use of drugs, although I drank a little more than in my first pregnancy. I smoked much more pot, and I did cocaine, off and on, the whole time, too. My daughter was born not only premature, but also underweight, at five pounds, and she was very jaundiced at birth.

That really scared me. I prayed to God that everything was going to be all right with her, and I promised that, if He answered my prayer, I wouldn't use drugs anymore. But, of course, once she came home from the hospital, started putting on weight, and wasn't as yellow as she had been, I felt that I could celebrate. I pulled out my stash and got high.

Now that I had two children, I had to do more cocaine. There was so much more work to be done each day. So I just started snorting cocaine all day long. I began to have some physical problems which led to my needing a partial hysterectomy. I found that I enjoyed being in the hospital, having somebody else take care of my children, my husband, and my house. I didn't have to do anything except rest and get pain medication every four hours. I was in the hospital for about a week. When I got home, my husband had hired somebody to take care of the children until I could recuperate. I could now stay in bed all day, take my pain medication, snort some coke, watch television, and not have any responsibilities at all. That was wonderful.

About six months after my operation, I had some problems with my back. I had had back pain, off and on, when I was growing up, but this seemed a lot worse. I went to my general physician, and he said that I had a disc problem and put me on Valium. After I had taken the first few of them, I felt I was in heaven. I had no pain. I felt as calm and as cool as a cucumber. When I did my coke, it was completely different than when I did it without the Valium. Using the two, together, gave me a new kind of high. I stayed on the Valium for five years. By the end of that time, I was getting it from three different doctors.

About six months after my back problems, I became very depressed. I called my gynecologist because someone told me it probably had something to do with my hysterectomy. The doctor put me on antidepressants. Between these pills and the Valium, along with the coke, the pot, and the booze, I never seemed to touch down. I went into the hospital two more times, for my back and for migraine headaches. I was falling apart, physically. But I enjoyed going into the hospital because, again, I didn't have to handle any responsibilities when I was sick.

I then found a really good drug connection—my hairdresser. When I went to get my hair done, he'd have something waiting for me, and I'd go into the bathroom and snort a couple of lines, or try this pill or that drug. I'd sit in his chair, while he was doing my hair, and be just flying! When I told him I was really having some trouble coming down off the coke, he said that he knew an out-of-town doctor who would give me a prescription for Quaaludes, as long as we got it filled at his brother-in-law's pharmacy across the street. So, twice a week, we'd take a trip to get our 'ludes.

I was still very unhappy in my marriage, so I thought that my problems were largely due to my marital difficulties. If I ended the marriage, everything else would be fine. One day, I called a lawyer, made an appointment, and told him I wanted to get a divorce, without ever discussing anything with my husband. Only two weeks later, I left with the children to go back to my home town. During the five years of my marriage, I had pictured all my friends still back home, partying, getting high, and doing all the same old things. I had wanted to be a part of that, and now was my chance.

I was so sick by the time I got home that I didn't want to be alone, and I had no connections there. So I hooked up with my first husband again, forgetting all about the problems we had had before. By that time, he had been in a fellowship, but he hadn't been able to stay sober. It just seemed that the two of us were meant to be together; we were two really sick people. He connected me with a drug dealer, and I still had plenty of money from my divorce settlement, so I was able to get my drugs again. To this day, I still can't believe I subjected my children to all that. I had taken them away from their father and immediately moved in with someone who was a complete stranger to them, another addict.

About two weeks later, I woke up one morning and knew that I had to get away. I called my second husband and asked him to please come and pick up the children. I was going to go away for a while. Within two hours, I was on my way to the opposite coast, to a place I had never been to before. I do not know what prompted me to do that. I bought a first-class ticket to get there because I knew you were allowed to drink all you wanted to, without paying, in first-class.

I can't really tell you very much about the trip, because I was in a fog the whole time. I know I got back with my first husband out there, and we ended up in another great big fight. He knocked me out, right into the bathtub. At that point, a light came on, and I realized that something wasn't right. I was back into the same physical abuse, again. I had sent my children away, and I was in a part of the world that I didn't even know.

I returned to my home town and made an appointment to see a drug-and-alcohol counselor I had seen as a teen-ager, when I got my first DWI. He told me he had known, then, that I had a problem. He offered to get help for me and sent me to a state hospital. I really believed that I was crazy, by now, and that the reasons for my insanity were people, places, and things. I never once thought the drugs or alcohol might be responsible. I stayed in the institution for ten days, locked up in a cell. I was later told that I had had about nine seizures in the hospital, but I don't remember any of it. I had almost been arrested, too, because I was holding speed when I went into the institution. I was one pretty sick cookie when I went in there.

When my head started clearing a little, I realized that what I had been doing wasn't good for my children or for me. I talked to my counselor, and we discussed my going into a rehabilitation center. I agreed, and he entered me into a twenty-eight-day program. I was scared to death. I knew that I wanted to feel better, but I hadn't thought about quitting drugs, yet. That was the farthest thing from my mind. I think what I probably wanted was to feel better only so I could go back out and use again.

But I learned a lot in rehab. I began to feel better, physically. I started to eat, something I had been doing very little of, lately. I had probably weighed about ninety pounds when I entered. I was advised not to go back to my home town when I got out. And I finally found the courage to break off with my first husband.

The rehab people had recommended that I try to go to ninety meetings in ninety days, but I thought I could recover on my own. I had never tried to do it alone, before, and I really wanted to try. My first week out of rehab, I applied for three jobs, and I was chosen for all three. I made a decision between them and started to work. When I got my first paycheck at the end of the week, without even thinking, I stopped at a liquor store and bought myself a six-pack of beer, to celebrate. I had forgotten all about the rehab; I had forgotten all that I had been through.

A week later, my second husband brought the children back to me. I was now living with a man I had met at rehab. Not too long after, we began getting high together. Then he decided that he really wanted to get straight, so he left me and moved in with his parents. I was just devastated.

A few nights after he moved out, I made up my mind that I was going to see what this Alcoholics Anonymous was all about. Chemically Dependent Anonymous hadn't been formed, yet, so A.A. was the only organization I had heard about when I started going to meetings. I heard the people say, "It gets better." I heard, "Day at a time. Don't drink, a day at a time." I heard so many things that stuck in my mind. The people there planted a seed. They also reminded me of a lot of things I had been taught in rehab.

I went to some more meetings. I stopped drinking, but I still continued to smoke pot. I figured that was O.K. I hadn't heard much about other drugs, around the rooms, only that I shouldn't drink. My boyfriend moved back in with me, and we began going to meetings together. I also met some other people, including a couple who were trying to start a new fellowship, called Chemically Dependent Anonymous, and I was asked to help. About five or six of us would go out to the founders' house, once or twice a week, sit around their living room, and talk about why we were forming this new group. We tried to write some literature about it.

You know, when I look back on it today, God was

really acting in my life when He helped me find these people. Who would ever have believed that anyone as sick as I was, at that time, would become part of something so beautiful, an organization that has helped so many people? Since I have been straight, I have seen people come into the rooms feeling so hopeless, and so sick, just as I once did. But the happiness and the caring that they experience is truly a miracle. Every one of us is a miracle.

We started holding C.D.A. meetings at Rick and Elin R.'s house, and then the big night came when we finally got a church, and we had our first official C.D.A. meeting. There were about six or seven people there, and the man I was living with, then, chaired the first meeting. He had been clean about six months, by now. It was a really special night, in that small room which we called "The Dungeon." That was how it all started.

After the C.D.A. meetings began, I heard, from this new group, that anything that affects me from the neck up also affects my stability and cuts off communication between me and my God. I realized that I couldn't even use pot. It was rough trying to come off everything. I had never realized how addictive pot was until I tried to quit. But I managed to do it. I stayed clean for about three months, and then my boyfriend moved out again. I didn't want to feel the pain, so I went back out from the fellowships.

Before getting high, one night, I gave my children $2 each. I was feeling guilty because I knew what I was about to do. My children had been really proud of me, watching me get a one-month chip, a two-month chip, and then my three-month chip. They knew why I got those awards, that they meant mommy had not taken a drug for three months. But this night, I went out to see a girl I was working with, and she gave me some pot and some Quaaludes. I came home again, sat the children in front of the TV, went into the bathroom, and commenced to get high.

A friend of mine from A.A. came over that evening and saw that I was on pot. She told me that as long as I didn't take a drink, I could still go back to A.A. and keep my sobriety date. Thanks to C.D.A., I knew she was wrong. I was high, and I knew it didn't matter what I used, whether in liquid form, pill form, or whatever form. I was being affected. I was using a mood-changing and mind-altering chemical. They were all the same.

But I had no idea how that night would change my life, how nothing would ever be the same again. When my six-year-old son saw the condition I was in, he was heartbroken. He packed up his suitcase and put his coat on. Then he took the $2 I had given him and ripped the bills up and threw them at me, saying, "Mommy, I hate you! You're a drunk!" I couldn't even look him in the face. He was right. He was looking at me the same way I had looked at my father when I was younger. I was ashamed and deeply embarrassed.

A girlfriend took the children to spend the night with her. Then, when I was all alone, I talked to God for the first time since my mother had died. From the time I was eleven years old, I had hated God. He had taken my mother away from me and left me with a father who was a drunk. I said all these things to Him now. I let out all the anger and told Him about all the unfairness that I thought was His fault. I talked to Him for most of the night.

Finally, I believe, He answered me. It became clear to me what I had to do. I had to get better. I didn't hate God; I just hated my life. I hated what I was putting my children through. It had to change. At that point, I realized that drugs were my problem. All the denial was gone, all the blaming of people, places, and things. I turned my life over to God and to the members of C.D.A. I was going to listen, I was going to take suggestions, and I was going to try to stop hurting.

I went back into the rooms the next day and told everybody what had happened. I said that I now had an honest desire to be a part of the fellowship. I wanted to get better. That was seven years ago. My first year in the program was very hard. I had to learn everything all over again. Just functioning on a day-to-day basis, without any chemicals, seemed almost impossible. But it slowly started getting easier.

My third year was the real test. I had to have major back surgery and needed to have pain medication. I was very frightened. I didn't know what it would be like to be back on drugs. And I really didn't know if, once I got on them, I would be able to stop. But thank God for the fellowship. I don't think I would have been able to come off the drugs as I did, if it hadn't been for the people. Every day, somebody from the program came to offer support. They even brought meetings to my house so I could attend.

I had to have another back operation thirteen weeks after the first one. I was sure I would not be able to stop taking the drugs if I had to start taking them again. I had been on them for quite a while, the first time. But I never abused the medications I was on, and I managed to use them just as the doctor prescribed. Again, thanks to the people of C.D.A., and to the program, I made it!

I hope that my experience will give hope to others in the fellowship who might have to undergo surgery, someday. I think there will come a time in most people's lives when they will legitimately need some kind of medication, for one reason or another. But if they have a firm foundation in the program, I know they can get through it. You can get through anything, just as I did. And you'll never have to do any of it alone.

When I came off the medication the second time, I experienced another miracle. For the first time in the three years that I had been in the program, I found that I would rather be straight than loaded. I had gained unbelievable control over my feelings and emotions, so that I hadn't become addicted again when I was on the drugs. Now I preferred the way my head felt, straight, to the effects of the medicine.

It's really hard for me to list all the other miracles that have taken place in my life since then. My children are still with their father, and I know that this is probably God's will. I have been able to accept that. But I have a wonderful relationship, today, better than I could ever have imagined. For five years, I've been married to a remarkable man who is also in the program. He has given me so much help and support. And I have a faith in a Higher Power, now, that is incredible. God has always been there for me. It just took this fellowship for me to find Him. I don't need to look for happiness, now, through a bottle, or pills, or snorting something up my nose. It comes from working the Steps of C.D.A. The miracle has happened in my life, and it continues happening, a day at a time. I hope those who read my story will let miracles happen to them, too.

Chapter 35
NO MORE EXCUSES

A lot of my excuses, and the things I used for excuses to keep me out there drinking and drugging for as long as I did, began right at birth. One of the big ones was that my natural mother left me in the hospital and never came back for me. As a result, for years, in all my relationships, I always thought I was going to be abandoned.

The medical staff in the hospital discovered, soon after my birth, that I wasn't normal. I didn't respond to light or to sound like other kids. I didn't even cry right. They thought I was going to have all kinds of problems. I wouldn't be able to see, or hear, or talk. Doctors started performing operations. So one of my main excuses for feeling sorry for myself used to be that I had a right to get on the "pity pot" about my handicap. After all, I was different from other kids.

My behavior patterns began to form at a very early age. The operations started when I was less than four months old. Between that time and my fifteenth birthday, I had forty-nine operations: on my eyes, my ears, my throat, my feet, everywhere. One thing I learned from being in the hospital (and I was a long-term hospital patient) was that I could push a button and a nurse would come in and give me a shot for the pain. I loved that. A nurse would come and shoot me with a needle, and I could feel the drugs going up through my body and making me feel good. Using drugs to relieve pain was the behavior I learned as a child.

Before I start making everything sound as if my whole life was total misery, though, let me back up one second and mention something really positive that happened to me at a very young age: The man who is now my father adopted me. When he decided to adopt, he had every opportunity to choose a perfectly normal child, but he took me, the one with the disabilities, the one he knew would have a physical handicap, the one he knew would have to have many operations. I was the one he chose to bring into his life and to love.

I understand, now, how difficult that must have been for him. And I also realize what my father did for me, what he did for my life. He played a big part in my development, in enabling me to be the person I have become. Even though I could not have recognized it for what it was, at the time, I know, now, that his adopting me was one of the circumstances that led to my being in Chemically Dependent Anonymous today. My father has been one of the major influences in my life, especially as an example for my recovery.

I had some problems fitting in with my new family. I felt so out of place. My father and a neighbor used to sit out at a picnic table and drink beer, and I liked to sit there with them. I was just a little kid, and they were the big men, and I looked up to them. Often, when I sat with them, they would let me have some of their beer. That made me feel I belonged. It was such a big deal to me, to be allowed to be with them there. And so another behavioral trait that I acquired, very early, was equating alcohol with companionship.

My belief that I was always being abandoned by

women also made me feel I was not normal. It was not just that my mother had left me in the hospital. I became close to a grandmother, and she died. A sister I cared about left to get married. My adoptive mother also left, and she created another family, without me. These abandonments made me think that I was fated always to be a loser in relationships. So I approached most of them with the attitude that they wouldn't last.

I also had problems with the educational system, from the very beginning. When I went to kindergarten, I didn't fit in. I was kind of an obnoxious kid. The teacher used to write things on the board and ask me what they were. Since I couldn't see what she wrote, I made things up.

After a year of that, the county said that I wasn't able to function in public school with normal children, so they sent me to a school for the retarded for two years. I'm not sure how I ever got out of there. I told the school counselors all sorts of fantastic stories about my life. None of my tales were true, but they were my way of surviving in that environment.

I didn't feel that I fit in anywhere: not at that school and not with the kids in my neighborhood. I didn't attend the same school as everyone else did, and I was ashamed to admit where I had to go. That made for a very uncomfortable life. I went around with a chip on my shoulder. I thought people picked on me because I couldn't see. After a while, I felt that I had fought every single kid in elementary school.

When I got to an age where it seemed very important to have friends, to go to parties, and to be able to associate with and talk with girls, I didn't know what to do. But then I discovered that drinking and pot were the "in" things. If I had some pot, the other kids would befriend me, and the girls would talk with me. So I always had pot. And all through junior high and high school, I was a popular kid. Still, I never really got into marijuana or the other street drugs, myself.

I turned thirteen when I was in the fifth grade. At that point, I was sent to a private school where I was given an aptitude test. As a result, I was moved up a grade. I had to struggle for a while, but I started having some enthusiasm about getting an education, now, because of the encouragement I received. I began to study much more, on my own. I also got involved with the wrestling team at school and the track team, and I began to be enthusiastic about these activities, too.

When I started using drugs, all of that went out the window. Suddenly, the only thing that was important seemed to be the partying. High school, for me, became one big party. It was a wild time. I did everything under the sun. I was so reckless that I should have been killed.

On my eighteenth birthday, some friends and I, drunk as hell, took a ride on top of a station wagon, acting as if it were a surfboard, on a rough country road. Later that night, as I was leaving my party, I walked out onto a porch landing that was twelve feet above the ground. I figured that I would walk to the edge of the porch and follow the railing to the stairs. When I came to the edge, I found there was no railing, so I thought that I was at the steps. Then I took my first step, and I realized that it was much steeper than I had expected. I did a complete flip and ended up on the ground, on my back. I just bounced up on my feet and staggered around, laughing about it. Everyone who saw this little episode found it quite amusing. Something must have been watching out for me that night, or I would surely never have survived it.

But I thought I had my drinking and drugging under control. In high school, I was able to party in the morning and then stop. In college, I cut all of that out. My first two years, I only partied on weekends. I stayed straight during the school week, took a lot of courses, and really studied.

I always had a plan for the weekend, though. I had a good drinking buddy, and I would get in touch with him, about the middle of the week, and set it up so he came over to my house at the end of the day, on Friday, with a case of my favorite brew. My part was to provide the pot. And that's how we began our weekends. I would live it up until Monday, when I would return to my rigid routine.

All week, I would get up early in the morning, start studying, have a heavy schedule of classes, come home and eat dinner, go to bed, and then get up early to study again. I was very obsessive about this routine, and I got through junior college doing very well. I even received high honors.

But something happened at that point. I'm not sure exactly why, but I started acting the way I had in high school all over again. I was partying every day. After a couple of weeks of this, I was ready to go back home. I enrolled in a guide-dog school near my home and met lots of people there who really liked to party, too.

Once, we decided to go on a camping trip. A bunch of us were going to get back to nature—live in the woods for a while and act like men. We practically died. When we were preparing to go, we made sure we had plenty of bottles of beer, and found the pot, and had everything we needed. Except we somehow forgot to bring the food. I forgot my sleeping bag, too, but it was August. It should be warm in August, right? I almost froze my butt off.

I tried to get back into college, but I couldn't get it together, right then, and I couldn't face a single day without starting it with a drink. I couldn't remember things, anymore, so college just didn't work out. Finally, I went to a rehab to learn vocational training, because I'd decided that college was not for me. I would just acquire some skills and get a job. They trained me very well, there.

When I got out, I figured that the best way to get a job was to go somewhere and prove to an employer that I could do the work. I found a place that would take me, and I worked for them for nine weeks without pay. I thought that would be the best investment I could make to get a permanent position. But at the end of the nine weeks, they told me they didn't have anything for me.

It got to a point where I decided I would have to go back to college. I'd take one class. I should be able to handle that. Anybody could take one class a week. I borrowed money from my father to pay for the class. I went once. I couldn't handle it.

By the time I was ready to come into the program, I was someone I didn't like very much. I was depressed about myself because I was a blind bum. I was living off my father and collecting welfare checks, or their equivalent. I wasn't working. I wasn't going to school. And I wasn't nice to people, most of the time.

That's where I was when, all of a sudden, the drugs stopped working for me. A typical example of what I was doing at the time was drinking shots and chasing them with beer, as well as doing bongs. I remember this particular night, I'd had about seven shots, and I was just starting to get a buzz from the pot, when it was exactly like a switch being turned off—that quick. Nothing! The next day, there I was at home, with a hangover, feeling miserable. But I'd had none of the enjoyment from the drinking or drugging. It was all gone. I had just blacked out, and that was it.

And on top of that, I was very depressed. While I was in this state, depressed and broke, and therefore unable to get my drug of choice (which was pot, used on an almost-daily basis), an old friend of mine dropped over. He was a couple of years older, an old drinking buddy. He had been out of town for a while, and I thought he might have brought back some good drugs.

But he said, "No, I don't have any drugs." And he started talking about how great his life was, how well things had been going for him. He ran down to the new truck he had just bought and brought back a book. Then he began to read out of it, and he started telling me about these meetings that he'd been attending.

So I asked him a couple of dumb questions. First, I asked, "How often do you go to these meetings?" And he said that he went every night. Then I asked him an even more stupid question: "Are you going to one tonight?" He replied, "Yeah. Do you want to go?" And I said that I did. To this day, I don't know why. I kind of surprised myself.

My buddy was on his way to his father's house. He told me, "You get a shower, because you need one, and I'll be back to get you." He was a little late, and when he didn't return at the time he'd told me to expect him, I thought, "Good. Maybe he won't show up. What do I want to go along to this meeting for, anyhow?" But he did show up.

Another important influence on my decision to go with my buddy, just at this point, was my father's example. He had been in the program for quite a while, and that had also started me thinking. He went out to a meeting every night. He would tell me, before he left, "Hey, I'm going to such-and-such place to a meeting," and I would think to myself, "Now, isn't this weird? Here I am, in my early twenties, sitting alone in this house; and there he is, in his early sixties, going out every night with his friends. There's something wrong, here."

So I was proud when I could tell him that I was going to a meeting, too, with *my* friends. I don't remember much at all about that meeting. But I told my old drinking buddy I would follow it up and go again the next night. The only thing I do recall is getting home, calling my girlfriend, and telling her where I had gone.

The following night, before someone came to take me to the meeting, another friend dropped by with some drugs. He asked me if I wanted to get high. I said, "Yes. But first, I'm supposed to go to this meeting with someone." So I talked my druggie friend into attending the meeting with me. After we had sat through it, the guy with the drugs walked up to me and asked, "Do you want to go out and get high with me, or do you want to stay here with these people?" And I told him I wanted to stay. That was a major step for me because I had seldom, if ever, turned down drugs before that night. I hadn't had a drink or a drug for two days, at the time. I haven't had a drink or a drug since then.

Many other changes have taken place in my life since that night. At first, it was a struggle to get up every day and to start doing something positive, not just doing without the drinks or drugs. For the first few months, I smoked a lot of pipe tobacco and cigarettes. Then I started becoming more active. It was hard, after sitting at home for so long. I had to work myself up just to get up and do some simple things, maybe wash the dishes, or fold some laundry, or help my father in some way around the house, anything to get myself motivated and moving. Most days, my greatest accomplishment was to take a shower and get dressed so I would be ready for someone to take me to a meeting.

Because I wasn't able to drive, people from the program literally carried me to my first meetings. They made sure I got there every day, and I needed that. Still, my biggest problem was wondering if I really wanted to do all of this. I said, "Yeah, I feel miserable. Yeah, I think that this pot has been making me lazy. But give it up for life? That's outrageous!" So the people told me, "Don't worry about that. Just think that you want to give it up today. You want to stay clean and sober today."

That's how I had to start living. For a while, I had to think, "One hour at a time." After about a month, I realized that smoking cigarettes and pipe tobacco was just an extension of my compulsive, addictive behavior. In kind of an angry mood, I threw away my pipe and said, "I'm going to have to stop." I knew I was doing the same type of thing, sitting back and smoking, that I used to do with pot.

Then I went through a stage of depression for a while, where I felt very sorry for "poor me." I thought that I wanted to die. If I weren't blind, I knew I could find a job anywhere: at a gas station, or waiting on tables, what have you. I wouldn't need a job that I was specifically trained for, either. If there hadn't been someone in the program to tell me that it was probably God's will that I didn't have a job right then, that I had to be patient, I don't know what would have happened to me. They told me to pray about it.

Eventually, I got the good job which I still have, today. That is a miracle because, when I was still using, I thought that I would never be able to handle getting up in the morning and going to work every day. I didn't want that kind of responsibility in my life.

One night, a friend who had promised to take me to a meeting didn't show up. That was a turning point in my sobriety because it proved to me how much I really did want to go. I called people I knew were going to be there, and I even called a hot line, but I just couldn't find a ride. Finally, I got an old friend of mine, a guy I had once drunk with, to take me to the meeting place. I was really determined to get there, that night. I arrived at the location for the meeting and realized I couldn't figure out how to get in. There was snow on the ground, and my dog and I were wandering around in the snow, wondering how we would ever find the door and the meeting room. Somebody finally saw me out there and yelled out the door, giving me directions. That incident convinced me that I really did want the program. I wanted to stay clean and sober.

After that night, I got a sponsor. I also started to consider working the Steps. Up to that point, when I had heard people talk about the Fourth Step, I would think to myself, "Writing a personal inventory? No way. Not for me!" But I learned that I must do these kinds of things. I began to get more involved in the program, too. It was around this time that I started going to C.D.A. meetings, as well as to Alcoholics Anonymous.

There are all kinds of very exciting things that have happened, since then. What has really changed for me, today, is my whole outlook on sobriety, especially where spirituality is concerned. Before coming into the program, my attitude was that I kind of admitted I was an alcoholic and a drug addict, but it didn't really matter. Today, I care very much that I stay sober. I did not have any faith that a Higher Power, God, was needed in my life, and I totally resented that type of thinking, that type of principle. But I was miserable because I thought that I had all the answers. If everyone would just leave me alone, I would be O.K. Today, I know that I need to get on my knees and pray. I also read a little spiritual literature every day. Now that I am able to work the program by using the Steps and by trying to keep an open mind—I'm kind of a hardheaded, stubborn type—life is immensely better.

Since relationships have always been tough for me to handle, the really good relationship that I have with my father, today, is very important. I'm able to appreciate so many things about him, now. When I was as young as fourteen, he had tried to get me to go to meetings because he thought I had a problem. I didn't agree, then, so there was a lot of conflict between us. That was when he was trying to get sober and I was just beginning to use. Now, we don't have any need to fight. In fact, I don't think we've had any serious arguments since I've been in the fellowship. That's miraculous. Also, today, I have a relationship with a lady which has lasted, a big change in my life.

One of my most important improvements is that I'm able to feel much better about myself, these days. I not only have some self-esteem, but I'm even able to get up and talk in front of people and feel comfortable about that. Speaking at meetings has gone a long way toward making me realize that I belong in a world where I once thought I'd never fit in. I can deal with my problems. I don't need excuses, anymore.

What I pray for is that something in my message will be an inspiration to you, just as the things I heard, when I first came in, were an inspiration to me: to stay in the program, to keep coming back and associating with some of the winners here. It is the people who—when they set examples for me to follow, when they gave me advice—helped me to become clean and sober, as I am today. Most of what I've heard in these meetings I've been able to apply in my everyday life, and that has made it so much easier. A very important part of C.D.A. is in the fellowship, the caring among the people.

Thank you for this opportunity to share with you the things that have given me my strength, my faith, and my hope.

Chapter 36
KEEP AN OPEN MIND: SOMETHING MAY FALL IN

I love the memories of my childhood. It was a healthy one. My parents loved me, and, as the first son after two daughters, I may have been a bit spoiled. But I was a basically good kid who learned right from wrong and didn't make trouble. Other kids, I assume, thought I was intelligent; girls thought I was handsome. I had respect from my peers. At least, that is the way I think people saw me then. I was small for my age, and not really physically fit, but I tried hard in the inner-city Catholic school I attended, and I received good grades.

When I was eight years old, I started smoking cigarettes. The association between smoking tobacco and cancer was just beginning to be made by the medical profession. But fear of cancer couldn't stop me. I wanted to be cool. So I secretly smoked with a friend who was nine and also wanted to be cool.

Being small for my age was no fun. Throughout grammar school, and into high school, most kids I knew always seemed to be a head taller. I put up with this because I had no choice. But I always wondered, "What if I hadn't started smoking so young?" I attended an all-boy's high school, where I refused leadership opportunities and became introverted and shy. Yet life still seemed nice and secure through those years.

But all was not well in our family. I had three sisters, each quite different from the others. My oldest sister married an alcoholic who is now recovering. My second sister has been married twice and is chemically dependent. Only my youngest sister seems to have escaped unscathed. She has a master's degree in sociology and works in the field of addiction. And then there was me.

My parents, who have never had problems with substance abuse, are extraordinary. No matter how much I messed up, or how much they were disappointed by my arrests, my need for the help of institutions, my failure at jobs, and my lack of love relationships and friendships with others, they always eventually adjusted, forgave me, and went on with their lives. I truly believe that my parents did the best they could. God knows that, when I got through with me, I didn't leave myself, or anyone else, too much to work with.

My college years are when I really began to get out of control. After attending a community college for two years, I went away to a university for a lot of good reasons: It was time to be on my own. I would be able to make more friends where I didn't have my family to depend on. I could escape the service, and the risk of being killed, since the U.S. was involved in Vietnam at the time. Finally, my first relationship had turned out badly, and I wanted some kind of escape from that rejection.

I turned to drugs and booze with reckless abandon. My mother's father had been an alcoholic for over fifty years. It now seemed that I was going to follow in his footsteps. Classes had not even started yet when, on my second night away from home, I decided to get drunk. I had never been drunk before. But I decided to loosen up, to try it, to really live. I was with some more-experienced guys, seniors. They would show me which end was up, and how to drink, I thought.

But that's not exactly how it went. I started drinking beer at six o'clock in the evening and didn't stop until close to three the following morning. It was difficult, but I was still standing. I had kept up with the best drinker in the house. He finally admitted that he couldn't outdrink me, and we both set out for our rooms. That's the last thing I can remember clearly. I was in and out of a blackout the rest of that night.

The next day, I felt that I had competed with the best senior and had not been beaten; I had done well and had won his respect; I had been able to articulate my views and opinions. I felt that I belonged, and that I was important. I had found courage, knowledge, and euphoria. I knew that I had found the answer. Alcohol worked for me.

The truth was that I was in trouble the first time I got drunk, blacking out, vomiting, and having diarrhea for three days. But the blackouts were a price I was willing to pay. I was having fun, it seemed, for the very first time. I knew I would be getting drunk a lot from now on, as a way to relax. I relaxed my way right out of school, out of friendships, out of jobs, and out of my mind.

Drugs were given the same priority. I liked getting high. It was cool. Being high was my act of rebellion against authority. I had the same reasons for drugging as I did for drinking. And if I could do both, I was a double winner.

The result of this attitude was an overdose. I ate four grams of hash while I was drunk and became mentally ill, paranoid and psychotic. I had to be hospitalized for over three months. And I never really recovered from being in the hospital. Ten years elapsed, and the same behaviors, using and abusing drugs and alcohol, were still present. I did want to be well. I just didn't want to consider the obvious fact that drugs and alcohol were the problem, not the solution. I had a disease whose major symptom was that I thought that it was okay to use the problem *as* the solution.

Let me tell you about being hospitalized. There are many words to describe psychiatric units, and they are not usually kind or flattering terms. The one I like best is "nuthouse." It implies the lack of therapeutic values to be found there. People with mental problems are simply put into the nuthouse. You might be a sociopath, or merely a maladjusted neurotic. No matter what your degree of trauma, you can be almost certain that you won't be attended to or categorized according to your real problem. A molester might well be placed in with the molested. Catatonics might be housed with the extremely anxious. There will be no cure in the nuthouse. Survival is the name of the game.

Inhabitants of the nuthouse learn to adapt. They put their time in, warehoused, hoping to survive long enough to be discharged. Patients become conditioned to this lifestyle and then simply revert to the type of behavior that got them placed in the nuthouse, in the first place, when they are finally released. They repeat this process over and over—sometimes, unfortunately, for the rest of their lives.

My first hospitalization took a lot out of me. When I was discharged, I was not really ready to leave. Just before my release, one of the aides I respected and had become friends with said to me, "You'll be all right. Just don't drink or use drugs." And I didn't, but I let that fact fool me, and I began to rationalize that my ability to abstain proved that I wasn't an alcoholic. I could stop when I wanted to. (Of course, I also started up, again, when I wanted to.) After discharge, college seemed out of the question. Employment was something I was becoming fearful of. What was I going to do now?

Not knowing what else to do, I signed up for group therapy. There were two whiz kids leading the group. One was a semi-attractive social worker in her middle twenties and the reason I had signed up for the therapy. I might best describe her as a liberated woman, a hippie with a job. The psychiatrist, the other half of the team, was not yet thirty years old. He had shoulder-length hair. He also had indefatigable energy. His drive came not from within himself, however, but from the pharmacy downstairs.

It was pop psychology time, and I didn't have the foggiest notion of what was going on. I was dazed and confused, a walking contradiction—"partly truth and partly fiction," as I think a songwriter once wrote. My skilled team, and the group, couldn't crack me. I was already cracked. I refused to open up and talk about my feelings. During the two-and-a-half years that the group existed, various members came and went. There were four of us clients, however, who stuck with our therapy religiously for most of that time.

One was a woman of about twenty-five, not especially good-looking, who had been in medical school. I felt closest to her, and we dated a few times. I opened up to her more than to anyone else, which was not very much, even at that. But I could make her laugh. I felt at ease with her, and she with me, to some slight degree. Knowing her brought me out of myself a little.

While we were still in group, she had to be put back into the psycho ward, the same one we had both been in only eighteen months before. We had both talked about suicide, but even though I was always worried and was in deep despair, I somehow knew that she was sicker than I was. It was when her roommate attempted to take her own life that my friend had to be hospitalized again. I started visiting her and was able to make her laugh, even in the hospital. I would make fun of the older generation and of our own age group. Being cynical and sarcastic seemed to come naturally to me. It was easier to tear things down than to build them up. She liked that attitude, too. It was our escape.

I even made fun of myself. My friend thought it was hysterical when I gave her my theory about why I had gone crazy and had to attend group therapy. I told her that I couldn't deal with the phase I was going through in my life, the crisis state I was in. Coping with the fact that, at age twenty, I was going through menopause was too much for me to bear. No wonder I had lost my mind. Anyone would. She laughed long and hard at my absurdity, which was difficult for her to do, especially since she was on so much medication that repressed her emotions. My only good times were when I was visiting her.

Another faithful member of our therapy group was a young black woman whose estranged husband was in jail for most of the time that she was in therapy. I found her most attractive, and she liked me. When I had a car, I would sometimes give her rides to group meetings. But at this point in my life, in my early twenties, the female members of the group didn't have to worry about my acting out sexually. I had been badly burnt in my first try at love and was scared to death to have any kind of relationship. I avoided letting anyone get close enough to talk about intimate feelings. I tried not to feel.

These members of the group, and its leaders, were very special in my life. I still think of them fondly. But, therapeutically, I don't think any of us were very great, or got any revelations from our group experience. We were merely trying to tread water in the sea of our emotions. I know I had very few insights. I did develop some good self-pity skills, though. About two years after therapy, I was still contemplating suicide constantly. But the group did keep me out of the psycho ward for thirty months.

When the group disbanded, the freaky young psychiatrist made an interesting suggestion to me. Never had there been any mention of anyone in group having drug or alcohol problems, throughout the entire therapy. We were all getting high, all that time, except the black woman, and it was never even considered an issue. My problem concerning drugs and alcohol, I thought, was that I was not getting enough. But my group leader told me that I needed additional therapy and further help.

He was right. Within a year after the group dispersed, I found myself spending the night in the city jail because of my disruptive behavior. I had been living in the big city, alone, for about three months, drinking bourbon and smoking reefer every day, and working at a clerical job at a downtown freight-forwarding office. I had worked my way up from messenger to making lots of important decisions, concerning thousands of dollars, daily. I took all my responsibilities very seriously. I worked there nine months, altogether. For the last month, I ran the office, along with another employee, while the boss went on vacation.

During that month, I started acting out more, in every way. I became more dedicated to work, but also more dedicated to drugs and alcohol, and more sexually active—in the red-light district and also with a woman I had met in connection with my work. The candle was definitely burning at both ends. I was twenty-three, now, ego gone amuck. I thought I was invincible.

When the boss returned from his vacation, he gave me a big raise. I certainly deserved the monetary reward. The work had been done, there had been no complaints from the main office, and the customers were satisfied. But the angry young clerk who greeted him on his return had turned into a hungry, broken, vicious psycho case. I was a wild man, full of paranoia. I had been starving myself so I could spend all my money on sex, drugs, and rock-and-roll. I quit my job.

Realizing that I was once again in trouble emotionally, I put myself back into the hospital. But there was nothing the hospital could do for me. I didn't go to the emergency room; I went directly to my old psycho ward. Breaking procedure like that is forbidden, and I was arrested. It took half-a-dozen men to restrain me. The police directed me to another psychiatric hospital across town. I was so completely paranoid that I had to be put in a straitjacket. The hospital staff tried talking me down for many hours, off and on. I refused sedation.

Then a kind male nurse approached me, and I physically resisted him when he tried to coax me into taking some liquid Thorazine. I finally picked him up and threw him across the room. As a result, I spent the night in jail and was then transferred to a locked ward, in the same quarters as the criminally insane. I was charged with assault. I spent three months in hell, in cramped quarters with a bunch of crazies.

I celebrated my twenty-fourth birthday in that locked ward for the criminally maladjusted. Everyone in there was up on some kind of charge. Everyone was probably as guilty as sin, but we were all feeling persecuted: mistreated, unwanted, unloved. However, because of the medications we were being given, we were unable to feel anything more. And I was grateful for that. I was tired of suffering, and I didn't want to have to face what was happening to me.

The first time I had been in a locked ward, I had been unfeeling due to the tranquilizer, Thorazine, which I had been given. This nuthouse, however, prescribed Stelazine. They juiced me up pretty well. There were times when I was so medicated that I was completely at anyone's mercy. There was a guy there who liked my shoulder-length-shag haircut a little too much, and in the wrong way. He was fifty pounds heavier than I was. Many nights, after being medicated, I had to fight off his advances. I acted out a lot, yelling and hitting him, because I was afraid of being raped.

As a result, I spent a good deal of time in seclusion. This solitary confinement could last for hours or days. It all depended on your attitude. I was in there quite a bit. But that wasn't as bad, I thought, as having a boyfriend. Even though living in reality was not my strong point, being victimized was a real fear. My big accomplishment, in that locked ward, was not being attacked by Dr. Strangelove.

When the male nurse I had assaulted dropped the charges, a few months later, I was put on a nicer, less-restricted ward that was not so crowded. Some of the patients there were even voluntary ones. After a month on that unit, I was given ground privileges. I got a girlfriend, someone from another building.

But this institution left me emotionally scarred. After I took leave of it, I went into a severe depression that seemed never-ending, although, actually, it lasted two years. I retired from society, for the most part, and went into isolation at my parents' home. I really wanted to die. And it was many years before I wanted to live again.

Even though I had learned how to survive in the nuthouse, I had never learned how to survive outside. I reverted to my old ways when I was discharged, and I repeated the process of going in and out of hospitals ten times in ten years. It was all pretty disgusting. I was hopeless, and helpless, unable to realize that I could change, that I just needed to surrender to the fact that I could not use safely. If I had only been willing to change my lifestyle, I could have had a life worth living so much sooner.

Denial was my biggest obstacle. Something had to happen, and when it did, recovery also started to take place. Now, every day that I don't put chemicals into my body to alter my mood, since "it" happened, I've been recovering. And it keeps on happening, with every day of continuous abstinence.

So what did happen? It's very simple. My last drunk lasted for five days and occurred after a two-year binge. I had taken only four drinks of alcohol. I wasn't even using pot. But on this occasion I found myself, a naked vagrant, in a police station two hundred miles from home, babbling incoherently. My disease had progressed to the point where I had to suffer D.T.'s and hospitalization, again.

This time, however, I was willing to want something different. And I was given a second chance by something greater than myself, something greater than any nuthouse. I like to think that God intervened in my life, at that point, to help me become aware that I was going nowhere, but that I could matter in this world. All I had to do was to want change and ask for help. If I did, love, in the person of mankind, could also intervene.

Thus I was given hope. And when I'm doing the legwork, doing whatever it takes to abstain, today, I realize that I am still receiving the miracle that I did back then. It was a miracle for someone as sick as I was to become so willing to abstain. But such willingness begets change, and change begets learning. Learning begets growth, and growth, in turn, begets recovery. And there is no end to recovery. Yet it all starts with the simple task of not using on a daily, continuous basis.

My recovery was not easy, at the start. Being in jail, and withdrawing from alcohol there, was a horrendous experience. I suffered extreme delusionary thinking, running the gamut from believing that I was the savior of the world to knowing that I was the antichrist. I saw imaginary rats coming out of the ceiling, and I shot them dead with a just-as-imaginary gun in my hand. After explaining to my jailers, all night long, that I was crazy and an alcoholic (I had admitted my craziness before, but never the alcoholism), they began to believe me about the insanity, but didn't seem to care very much about my other problem.

They transferred me to a state hospital, my tenth institution in ten years. I was used to the routine, by now. You wake up, or rather, get up (I was never getting much sleep when I was in this kind of altered state), roam around the day room, and mix with the other patients until breakfast. Meals are the big event each day. I thought to myself, "Nothing has changed. I'm in another institution where the only things to look forward to, eating and medication, involve waiting in lines." It was the same old procedure that had always occurred before, that of being warehoused until I was stabilized and could then be released.

Although the routine never changed, the situation and the environment had gotten progressively worse. I was severely beaten one day, two weeks into my stay. I had conned my way into the day room. A drunken aide was there, harassing a patient who was a former professional middleweight boxer. The aide was very big, about 225 pounds, and very drunk. The patient wanted no trouble and just took the verbal and physical abuse without fighting back. I was very hyperactive, normal for me whenever I quit drinking. I was jumpy and anxiety-ridden, my mind going a thousand miles per hour. I was in a bad way.

But my insanity told me to protect this poor patient, and I asked the aide, "Why don't you pick on someone your own size?" (By this, I did not mean me.) The aide and I started to fight. He hit me very hard, all over my body, but mostly in the ribs and stomach. And I fought back with all the psychotic viciousness I could muster. Somehow, I caught him flush on the jaw, and he went down like a dead tree.

Other aides, watching us the entire time, were not expecting a patient to get the upper hand. But I was not about to observe the Marquess of Queensbury rules of boxing, at this point. I wanted blood. So I started racing toward the aide as if I were a kicker in a football game. I had decided to tee off on his head. I was not a nice person. I was not only very mean, but very sick.

A couple of aides intervened, fortunately. I don't doubt that I would have tried to kill that drunken aide if they hadn't stopped me. They threw me to the ground. Many other aides then came to help, and I was held down and struck repeatedly for what seemed to be an eternity. I was shaken up pretty badly and was afraid that I was bleeding internally.

This experience was the beginning of my spiritual awakening. I finally became ready to start admitting that I had a problem with alcohol and drugs, and I made a vow to God that, if I got out of that hospital, I would seek help through Alcoholics Anonymous. I called my father and told him what had happened. He raised a lot of Cain with the hospital, and I was released two weeks later.

About eight months after I joined A.A., Chemically

Dependent Anonymous was founded. I became aware of it because I knew its founders. I respected them, and so I went to their meetings, but only occasionally, since I was very active in A.A. by then. But the members of this new fellowship impressed me as sincere in their efforts to make C.D.A. grow.

My problem was that I didn't have the same goal for myself. I went to C.D.A. mostly to share my experience, my strength, and my hope, as a speaker. I went, usually, only when invited to chair a meeting, and I liked the fellowship only to the extent that it gave me a platform from which to talk about my sobriety. I wasn't a member; I was a guest lecturer! I was totally ignorant of C.D.A.'s ability to enhance my clean time. I felt, rather, that I could enhance the credibility of the group.

I lived in this unenlightened state for some time. Finally, the hard work of the members paid off. I realized that Chemically Dependent Anonymous was not merely an extension of Alcoholics Anonymous. C.D.A. began to achieve the status, in my mind, of a support group which could really increase my quality of living. People were staying clean in this fellowship because they were involved, not in spite of their involvement. My devotion to A.A., and my ignorance, had blinded me to these facts, up until now. After four years of recovery, I started using the three fellowships, Alcoholics Anonymous, Narcotics Anonymous, and Chemically Dependent Anonymous, much more in unison.

I was now working in a treatment center for alcoholics and addicts, and I played a part in getting C.D.A. and the center to hold a meeting of the fellowship there. Both sides agreed on an open-group format. It has since become a useful meeting not only for patients, but for other substance abusers, as well.

By the time I was five years into recovery, I was

utilizing all three support groups as a way to stay clean. A.A. and N.A. gave me the exposure to quality and quantity experience. But in C.D.A., I found both quality and camaraderie. The love and enthusiasm of its members broke through my denial and my ignorance of the program's God-given effectiveness, and I started involving myself, more and more. I got a Home Group and a sponsor, and I became active.

"C.D.A. is not my life," as the saying goes, "but it [certainly] *gives* me life." It has shown me a dimension of recovery that I had been lacking: love and forgiveness of myself. I have healed greatly because of the love I have found in C.D.A.'s rooms. I am very grateful to be a member in good standing today. The fellowship helps to keep that sick, nuthouse patient, the person I used to be, away.

I still work in a drug-and-alcohol treatment center, but in another state, now. We have C.D.A. here, too, and a Step Group has been started. The fellowship is so small that it meets only in my apartment. But I feel it enhances the quality of my own recovery, and so I'm committed to being a part of C.D.A., wherever I am. I know it helps others, also. I understand, only too well, about those feelings of denial and ignorance. Higher Power willing, C.D.A. will survive and flourish in this new state. I feel confident that the fellowship will grow. Its members are too positive for it not to succeed.

Today, a state trooper gave me a speeding ticket. I arrived late at my job. But I did a good day's work and had dinner with a wonderful woman who cooked a delicious meal for us. We took a walk, on this cold winter night, and talked. Part of our conversation was about dreams coming true. During active addiction, my dreams had never included trying to recover, establishing friendships, caring about people, not allowing myself to be hopeless and helpless.

Today, I got a ticket. If it had been the old days, and I were still using, such an occurrence might have set me off like a stick of TNT. Instead, I talked out my frustration and anger with some friends. I was able to laugh about what had happened. I thanked God for another day of not using chemicals to control myself. Talk about dreams coming true! I've come to love life, and to face it daily, however difficult, non-chemically. Isn't that great?

Chapter 37
A LOVE STORY

What I want to share with you is my experience, my story, and my own particular opinions. Mine is a love story, not a tale of horror, because what I have experienced through Alcoholics Anonymous, and Chemically Dependent Anonymous, and all these Twelve-Step programs, is a new love of life and the discovery of the meaning of love. Once, I knew nothing about love. I'm certainly not, even now, speaking as an expert. I'm more an explorer of love. I'm new at it, but I think this is the most exciting adventure I've ever been on.

There isn't just a spiritual *part* of the program of C.D.A., as far as I am concerned. The program *is* a spiritual one. And the major discovery I have made, since coming into the fellowship, is learning how to get close to, and become comfortable with, the God of my understanding.

Here is a story relating to that God which took place a couple of thousand years ago, when He sent down what I believe to be the most positive example Who has ever walked on this earth. This Man was performing many miracles. And one day, He came upon a blind man, standing at a gate, who really wanted to be healed, to be able to see again. The blind man called out, "Lord, help me!" And all His disciples said, "Leave Him alone. He's busy." But the blind man called out one more time, "Please, Lord!" And He walked over to the blind man and asked him, "What can I do for you?" The blind man replied, "I'd like to be able to see." So He leaned down and spat in the dirt. He picked up the mud He had just made from the dirt and put it on the blind man's eyes. And he was able to see.

This story explains exactly how I was when I first came into these rooms. I was completely blind to life and had no idea what it was all about. I had no principles, no values. But you people loved me until I was able to establish some principles and values to use in everyday living.

What kept me sober for my first six months in the program, besides your love, was the fact that I couldn't wait to get up there and tell you what a bad-ass I was: how much alcohol and how many drugs I had used. I was really going to impress everybody with my story. But when the time finally came, and I got the opportunity and threw some of my worst horror stories at you, nobody blinked an eye. So I thought, "If I can't impress these people with how bad I am, maybe if I take all that energy and try to use it in a positive way, try to do good and work this program the right way, that will impress them. Maybe I'll get them to love me, that way." What happened, instead, is that after a few months of doing what I was supposed to do, and following directions, I was able to love you. And I was able to love myself.

I am no longer so proud of all my drug stories, today. But, as the program asks us to do, I want to share some of the way it was with you. The first thing I must say is that I honestly don't remember the pain, now. My life is not about pain, anymore. It's about challenges, not problems. Hearing that statement is one of the reasons

I got into the program. I went up to a guy at a Step Meeting, one night, and said, "I've got a lot of other problems besides drinking and drugs." And he told me, "Ronnie, so did I. But when I came into these programs, my problems turned into challenges." And that was an attractive concept.

I grew up in an alcoholic family. I swore I would never drink because I didn't want to be like my father. The first time I did drink, it was because of peer influence, and I had a blackout. It was on a Christmas Eve, many years ago. I vomited in my family's living room, passed out, and knocked over the Christmas tree. Then it was off to the races, from that very first drink. I had had a promising athletic career, but I flushed that right down the toilet. As soon as I found that magic in alcohol, it became the number one item in my life.

The reason alcohol was so magical for me was not in the taste. I never liked that, from the first time I drank until the day when (I hope) I took my last drink. Alcohol's magic was that it enabled me to tell people I loved them. It gave me courage to tell people I was angry at them. I was able, for the first time in my life, to express what I wanted to say. It made everything so much easier.

At first, I just drank on weekends, and then daily, through my high school years. In college, I got into the love-peace-hippie movement and grew long hair. I also went to work as a bouncer at a nightclub. But in order to get to work, I'd have to drink: half-pints of vodka, straight. Then I'd go in to the club and drink beer all night. I started hanging around with the band. I'd always had this terrible need to be in with the "in" crowd.

One night, a whole bunch of girls, and a few guys, came into the club. One of the guys came up to me and said, "Look, if you want to be able to stay up all night and party, and the odds look good that you will be doing that, you don't want to be falling asleep." I told him I felt fine, but he insisted: "Here. Try one of these," and opened up his suitcase. In it, he had literally thousands of Dexedrine pills. I told him I didn't want to become a dope user. I liked my beer. But he persuaded me to try "just a couple." I tried them, and they made me feel like Superman. I couldn't quit talking. Eight days later, I still hadn't slept, and I was taking sixteen pills a day.

That says a lot about this disease. The first time, I wasn't willing to take two. But eight days later, I was up to sixteen. Nothing compulsive about that! By the eighth day, I not only hadn't slept, but I was hallucinating, too, seeing fights in the bar that weren't really happening. I was told not to come back to work.

I was frightened enough to swear off the drugs and leave town. I met a teen-aged girl (I was only twenty-one at the time), and we got together. I was soon back on drugs, again, and I upset her life, as I did everyone's while I was using. Eventually, she became pregnant, and my drug use progressed even more after that.

We agreed that she would give the baby up for adoption. But once she started to feel life, she got all excited and wanted me to feel the baby kicking. I refused to do it. I didn't want to get attached to that baby. Deep down, I suspected that she was never going to be able to give it up, and, after the seventh month, she admitted it. So I left her. I couldn't handle the responsibility.

I started taking LSD, the first time I'd tried that drug. But I don't want to de-emphasize the importance of my alcoholism, because I was blitzed all day, every day, too. I considered that just a normal part of everyday living. I decided, while on a hit of LSD, that I should do the right thing and go back, get a job, and raise my child. But it wasn't until three months later, after the baby was born, that I finally got around to doing that. In the meantime, I partied until I got a call from the hospital. I hurried there and sat in a waiting room for three days, awaiting the arrival of my son.

For the next three-and-a-half years, I tried to live with my girlfriend and be the best at what I thought a father should be. The only problem was that I didn't want to get married. I never wanted to hold my son. I never changed his diapers. I could never tell him I loved him. Other people who came to see him told me how great he was, and I would agree. But he was more like a big bother to me, an accident in my life. That's not easy to admit, today, but I am trying to be honest about it.

I used to watch television, and I'd see all those family shows and wonder, "Why isn't my family like that, all happy and everything?" I know why, now. There was some part of me that didn't want to be there—a disease inside me that made me unable to handle the responsibility, that just wanted to chase that buzz all the time. The mother of my son finally left me. And, at the time, I was glad. I set about, for the next eight years, doing exactly what I wanted to do. And that was making money off other people's weaknesses, dealing drugs, and just running, and ripping, and drinking.

Eventually I got busted for possession of a couple of hundred pounds of pot and all kinds of pills, and I went to court. But I had a good lawyer, and he got me off. That episode taught me nothing. I was afraid, so I stayed high, up through the day of my court appearance. When I escaped being convicted, I just thought, "Well, I'll always get off."

Shortly thereafter, I got into another relationship, this time with a girl who had a six-month-old baby, and I completely upset *her* life for five years. Usually, we sent her little girl to day care every day, even though neither of us had jobs. But eventually my girlfriend got a job. (By this time, her little girl was in kindergarten.) One day, my girlfriend asked me to babysit with her daughter. It was the only time she had ever done that. She went off to work, and I rolled a couple of joints of PCP and smoked it. When my girlfriend arrived home from work, she found me hiding behind the refrigerator, naked, in a fetal position. Her daughter was just standing there, staring at me, horrified.

I spent eight years under the influence of PCP on a daily basis, convulsing every time. I took sets (uppers and downers together) on a regular basis for fifteen years, often forgetting how many of each I had taken. Then I would O.D. on them.

After the babysitting incident, I moved out-of-state, trying to start a new way of life. I also needed to get away from the mess I had gotten into. I had been busted, again, for manufacturing PCP, possession, and dealing. But the move didn't work out, either. My brother owned a bar, and I stayed stone drunk for a year, drinking every day and, every night, passing out on the bar in his restaurant.

So I went back home and stayed there for the next two years. At one time, I even had a nice house, two cars, a good stereo—all as a result of dealing dope. But I eventually ended up on welfare and food stamps because I had to feed my habit, too.

One day, I looked in the mirror. I was, by now, thirty years old, and I wondered, "What is the matter with me? How come everybody else is getting it together, and I am such a loser? Am I retarded? Is this the result of all the drugs and alcohol I've put in my body? Where did I get these circles under my eyes? How did I get up to 205 pounds? What the hell has gone wrong?" I was afraid, but I had no one to share my fear with. I didn't know anyone who really cared. I had never dared to confess to the people I was running around with that I was weak, that I was hurting, that I had any feelings at all.

Finally, I started shooting drugs intravenously. There is such a feeling of desperation and disgust when you wake up and your arms look like hamburger. You don't have the courage to kill yourself, but you really don't care whether you live or not. I felt that way a lot of the time, by now.

Then I got a phone call. Someone said that I'd better get to the hospital because my father had been brought in, and he wasn't going to make it through the night. I took a handful of Percodans and went to see him. I was horrified. I saw a man dying of the same disease that I had. I realized that there was very little difference between us—I was dead, inside, already. It just cut right through the denial.

Something else that was strange occurred that night. One of my brothers was there, one I'd not been particularly close to, over the years. But as my father was dying, he put his hand out, and we all said the Lord's Prayer together. I was deeply moved by that experience. I couldn't remember the words very well, but it didn't matter. We came together at that moment. Afterwards, my brother and I started to talk, and I found out that he was in a program and hadn't taken a drink in six months. I thought, "Man, that's pretty good. How do you *do* that?"

Not too long after my father's death, I found myself in a church. I was going to light a candle and say some prayers for him. But I found myself lighting two candles—one for him, and one for me. I'd finally reached my bottom. I was being subpoenaed by the grand jury for manufacturing drugs. I had been thrown off welfare, which I have to admit is the best thing that ever happened to me. I just didn't know what to do. So I asked, "God, please give me some direction. What can I do?" I wish I could tell you that, from that moment on, I was saved, and I never found it necessary to take a drink or a drug again. But that was not the case. I went right back out and used, again, for quite a while.

Then, all of a sudden, the drugs just quit working. The alcohol didn't give me the buzz, anymore. And I found myself alone in a room with a hypodermic needle, and the alcohol, and the drugs, and I couldn't get high. The hardest thing I've ever done was to pick up that telephone and call my brother. But I did. I told him that I needed some help. And he put me in touch with people from A.A.

I was living in a downtown area of a major city at the time I called my brother. I had a car, but I was incapable of following directions. It was all just too overwhelming, even when people tried to tell me how to get to the meetings. But the subway wasn't too far from the house, and I managed to get there. People from the fellowship would meet me at the other end, every night, and take me to the meetings. They welcomed me, but I couldn't look them in the eyes when I first got there, because of my lack of self-esteem. I *knew* there was nothing honest about me. I had been out there for seventeen years, beating myself, lying, and cheating.

When I got into the program, it was not what I didn't know that hurt. It was what I "knew" that just wasn't so. I was completely confused. There was one thing I did know, however. When people were at the meetings, they were laughing from their hearts. I liked that. They gave me their phone numbers and told me to keep coming back. They were talking about positive things, so I kept showing up.

The first year, I went to four house meetings. But I

had a few little slips in the first year because I had something called a habit. That's something I don't hear much talk about in the rooms. I had a habit of drinking and drugging when I came into A.A. I wanted to stay straight, but I wanted, even more, to stay straight and still be allowed to use, once in a while.

In the beginning, I came to meetings every day, but I had a slip after seven days, and then after nineteen days, and again after thirty-one days. I'll never forget the last time I used. I had met a girl at my sister's wedding. I called her up and said, "I don't know what I'm going to do. I'm getting tired of coming into these meetings and telling the people that I have been slipping." She replied, "I think you've got to make up your mind. Do you want to get loaded, or do you really want to get straight?" Her question was the big crossroad for me.

I moved out of my house in town and knocked on the door of an elderly aunt. I told her I was a drug addict, but she couldn't accept that. I said, "Believe what I tell you. I have a lot of credentials, a lot of history. I just happen to be *sharing* it with you." She said, "Why don't you go upstairs and take a nap, and then you'll be all right."

When I came back down two days later, I think my aunt began to believe me. Anybody who can sleep for two days must have some sort of problem. But she was good to me. She helped me. She let me stay there, and she did my laundry. So I tried. I got a job.

For the first year in A.A., all I did was come to meetings and not use drugs. I left the rooms when people began talking about their particular God. I didn't want to hear anything about the spiritual program. All I wanted was to stay straight. That was good enough for me. And I made it!

I had some time to fill when I was straight for about

six months. I had heard that you should try to do things, in sobriety, that you had always wanted to do when you were using but had never had time for. So, when I was thirty-four years old, I wrote my first letter. It was to a guy in prison, someone I had dealt drugs with. I was all excited about being straight, and I enclosed that "Acceptance" pamphlet—the one with the dove on it—with my letter. I wrote, "Man, I haven't used drugs for one hundred and eighty days. I've got a new way of life, and I want to share that with you." I'm sure he was thrilled to hear my news, sitting in the penitentiary while he served five years.

But four years later, I got a phone call from that guy. He was once called the biggest PCP manufacturer in the United States, but this year, he'll be celebrating two years in the fellowship. As a matter of fact, he now goes back to the penitentiary to give the program away to others. That's the way it works.

I was looking for more things to do, in sobriety, so I called the mother of my son, on Mother's Day, that same year. By this time, my son was thirteen years old, and he had been legally adopted by his mother's husband. The only times I had been allowed to see my boy were on Christmas and his birthday, up until then. And I had always been loaded when I arrived to visit him and give him his presents. I had to be loaded to get up the courage to show up at all.

I told my son's mother that I was straight, and she said that he had been asking questions about me. She had recently separated from her husband and wondered if I would like to take our boy for the weekend. She had heard I was in a recovery program. I couldn't believe my ears. That was one part of my past that I had never thought I'd be able to make up for. I'd never dreamed that I might be able to have a real relationship with my son.

He and I spent the weekend together. It was tough, because I still didn't know how to be a father. I had no idea how to give him love; I didn't know what to do with him. So I just prayed and went with my heart. When I first sat down with my son, I said, "Look, I haven't been here in a long time. I've been sick, but I'm getting better now. I hope that I'll be able to put back into your life some of the things that I wasn't able to give you before." Eventually, the walls between us came tumbling down. We went sailing, and he was a controller, and so was I. We had problems deciding which way we were going to go. But I'm here to tell you we didn't sink.

I thought maybe my son would like to go to camp, since I had enjoyed that when I was young. I took him to the same one I had gone to. He was all excited, and also a little bit scared, when it came time for me to leave, but I came back on Parents' Day. There's this big kid inside me who still likes to have fun. So, when we were at the pool, I had to go off the diving board. One of my son's friends asked him, "Hey, who's that guy?" My boy looked at him and said, "That's my dad!" That may not sound like much to you, but they were three of the most important words I'd ever heard. I still couldn't tell him that I loved him; I wasn't able to express myself with him in that way, yet. But he had acknowledged me.

Through my efforts, and with the grace of God, my relationship with my son has kept growing stronger and better. This past year, I went up to his high school and watched him play football. Since I was an athlete when I was young, I had always dreamed of having a son on the team. I watched him play tight end, and hit a block, and do well. And I was finally able to say, "That's my son!" We have something real, together, now. It's one more lesson in my ongoing education, in learning about love.

Another lesson had to do with my love life. I was still dating my sister's friend, in the first year of my recovery. And here is where the real love story begins. While I was dating her, I was also starting to look around at other girls. I was feeling a little better now, and I was sprucing up a bit. When I had come into the fellowship, I still weighed over two hundred pounds and had those dark circles under my eyes. I also had quite a few teeth missing. And I had many personality defects, in addition to my physical ones. I had started trying to correct my faults, and I had also begun to work out. After a while, I felt good enough about myself to wonder if I had had enough experience with women. Maybe I should be free to date around.

When I asked my sponsor what he thought, he asked me, "Is this so important to you that you need to tell your girl about it? Do you have to make that decision today?" I said that I didn't, so he suggested, "Why don't you just hang in there? You're going through a lot of changes, and she's been going to Al-Anon. Maybe things will get better." I thought that was good advice, so I kept going to meetings, and my girl accepted the fact that she would only get to see me after the meetings on Saturday nights. She kept going to Al-Anon, and I did hang in there, and our relationship grew.

Right after my first anniversary in A.A., I did my Fourth Step. That was a tremendous awakening. I came to realize how self-centered I was and to see a lot of other defects that I hadn't noticed before. I tried to work on them for the next year.

Today, I believe that if something is bothering you, and you're afraid of it, in sobriety, you should run at it, not away from it. That's the challenge and that's where I find my achievement. It's all too easy to do what I want to do. I did that for seventeen years, and it got me in trouble. I had always believed that anything that looked good and felt good was something I should do. And I would do it, constantly, until I had exhausted every bit of pleasure from it. But doing what I sometimes don't want to do has been a big change in my attitude since I have entered the program.

A good example is what happened at my second Sessions by the Sea, early in my recovery. I could not believe the incredible feelings I had there. I was sky-high. I had gotten up early in the morning to see the sunrise, and I was walking along in the sand. I suddenly saw a church. I had told myself that I didn't want to fear anything, in sobriety. I had been brought up a Catholic, and I looked at that church and thought, "I'd like to go in there. Why don't I?" I realized that I was still full of guilt. And I didn't go in.

But also, as I was walking down that beach, I thought about the fact that there were 3,500 recovering alcoholics and addicts at that convention. The recovery rate for people like me is only one out of every ten. I asked myself why I was one of them. What had I done to deserve this gift of sobriety? I knew that I hadn't done anything to deserve it. My only conclusion was that somebody's prayers had been answered, and I had been given a gift from God. I was a child of God. It wasn't too long after that day when I finally did walk into a church.

The feelings I'd had, that day by the sea, were ones I wanted to investigate further. What I learned was that we don't have any exclusive rights to spirituality, here in the program. There are many other people, outside, who have it, too. As time went by, it got easier and easier for me to be comfortable with the idea of spirituality, and I found the God of my own understanding. That completely changed my life. It changed my attitudes. I believe, now, that as long as we keep trying to get closer, and if we open our hearts, whatever God we believe in will see to it that we never have the desire to drink or drug at the same time that we have the opportunity. God will protect us from temptation.

About my third year in A.A., my employment situation improved. I became a very successful salesperson. I also started becoming inquisitive about something that had never interested me before. I went to a meeting and was asked to lead it. I began by asking questions about love. I told the people there that I had been in a relationship for two or three years, but there was something I didn't understand about it. "Where are all the fireworks?" I asked. "When I had relationships, before, there were always fireworks, and even sirens, at times."

And they asked me, "What makes you think you know anything about love? For seventeen years, all you've been doing is grasping, taking everything you can get out of your relationships, because you are a self-centered alcoholic." Those may not be their exact words, but that's what I heard. And they were right. That meeting really opened my eyes, and those people helped me to learn much more about love.

Just about the time I had finally learned my lesson, however, something happened that really jolted me. My girl had come back from an out-of-town Christmas visit with her family to be with me on New Year's Eve. She surprised me by saying that she thought I was becoming too serious about our relationship. She also felt that, after four years, we might be getting a little complacent about being together. She said that we ought to give each other some space for a while.

I was overwhelmed and angry. I couldn't believe it. I said, "Do you realize that this is the only relationship I've ever had where I've been faithful? I've never cheated on you once, and now you tell me you want some time off?" The only thing I felt I had to offer her was my fidelity, even though I had thought about fooling around during our relationship. I had always heard it's not what you think, it's what you do, that counts.

I didn't know what to do about my problem. So I went to meetings every day and talked about it there, and I prayed. I wanted to call my girl, every day, and sell myself to her all over again. Then I'd change my mind and want to call her and say, "Forget it! I don't want anything more to do with you." Those were my old tapes, the old pride, speaking. After ten days, it all worked out, and we did get back together. She had decided, with time to think it over, that she knew what she really wanted. And I had learned another valuable lesson. By giving her the space she'd needed, I had won her back.

My fifth anniversary was a high point in my recovery. When I had first come into the fellowship, there was only one person at the meetings that I knew from our old drug-using days. I had always wondered what I was going to do about all my old friends, once I got straightened out. At the celebration for my fifth anniversary, twenty-two people attended who were friends from the days when we used to drink and get high together. That's amazing growth in just five years' time. I hope that encourages all of you who are new to the program and are wondering about your life in sobriety. God has made it really easy for me. This is a piece of cake, compared to the pain and frustration I went through when I was using drugs.

Right after my fifth anniversary, I went on a C.D.A. camp-out with my girl. I had decided that this might be the right time to pop the question. Two years before, I had not even considered marrying. But one night, as we were walking on the beach, I just looked over at her and said, "I'm making this walk toward God. And I was wondering if you would like to come along with me?" She knew exactly what I meant, and she answered, "I would."

Six months ago, I had the privilege of walking her down the aisle. That was an extremely important step in my life, because I think I finally understand, now, what love is. I know, and I deeply care about, somebody other than myself. I've learned more about life and love from this lady than I would ever have believed possible. I may be a little new at marriage, but my wife and I have known each other for almost seven years. We've grown, together. And we're still growing because we both have programs and because ours is a triangular relationship. It isn't just the two of us, alone, against the world. We have God with us, too.

So that's my love story. If I have one wish for you, it's that you keep coming back to C.D.A. Then maybe, one day, you'll have your own love story to share with us.

APPENDICES

A The Twelve Steps of Alcoholics Anonymous*
B The Twelve Traditions of Alcoholics Anonymous*

APPENDIX A
THE TWELVE STEPS OF ALCOHOLICS ANONYMOUS

1. *We admitted we were powerless over alcohol—that our lives had become unmanageable.*
2. *Came to believe that a Power greater than ourselves could restore us to sanity.*
3. *Made a decision to turn our will and our lives over to the care of God* as we understood Him.
4. *Made a searching and fearless moral inventory of ourselves.*
5. *Admitted to God, to ourselves, and to another human being the exact nature of our wrongs.*
6. *Were entirely ready to have God remove all these defects of character.*
7. *Humbly asked Him to remove our shortcomings.*
8. *Made a list of all persons we had harmed, and became willing to make amends to them all.*

---

*Reprinted with permission of Alcoholics Anonymous World Services, Inc.

9. *Made direct amends to such people wherever possible, except when to do so would injure them or others.*
10. *Continued to take personal inventory and when we were wrong promptly admitted it.*
11. *Sought through prayer and meditation to improve our conscious contact with God as we understood Him, praying only for knowledge of His will for us and the power to carry that out.*
12. *Having had a spiritual awakening as the result of these steps, we tried to carry this message to alcoholics, and to practice these principles in all our affairs.*

APPENDIX B

THE TWELVE TRADITIONS OF ALCOHOLICS ANONYMOUS

One—Our common welfare should come first; personal recovery depends upon A.A. unity.

Two—For our group purpose there is but one ultimate authority—a loving God as He may express Himself in our group conscience. Our leaders are but trusted servants; they do not govern.

Three—The only requirement for A.A. membership is a desire to stop drinking.

Four—Each group should be autonomous except in matters affecting other groups or A.A. as a whole.

Five—Each group has but one primary purpose—to carry its message to the alcoholic who still suffers.

Six—An A.A. group ought never endorse, finance or lend the A.A. name to any related facility or outside enterprise, lest problems of money, property and prestige divert us from our primary purpose.

Seven—Every A.A. group ought to be fully self-supporting, declining outside contributions.

Eight—Alcoholics Anonymous should remain forever nonprofessional, but our service centers may employ special workers.

Nine—A.A., as such, ought never be organized; but we may create service boards or committees directly responsible to those they serve.

Ten—Alcoholics Anonymous has no opinion on outside issues; hence the A.A. name ought never be drawn into public controversy.

Eleven—Our public relations policy is based on attraction rather than promotion; we need always maintain personal anonymity at the level of press, radio and films.

Twelve—Anonymity is the spiritual foundation of all our Traditions, ever reminding us to place principles before personalities.

JUL 2 2001
CONTENT NOTE 9/02